Gender, Religion and Change in the Middle East

KU-380-275

Cross-Cultural Perspectives on Women

General Editors: Shirley Ardener and Jackie Waldren, for The Centre for Cross-Cultural Research on Women, University of Oxford

ISSN: 1068-8536

Recent titles include:

Gender, Religion and Change in the Middle East

Two Hundred Years of History

Edited by

Inger Marie Okkenhaug and Ingvild Flaskerud

Oxford • New York

English edition
First published in 2005 by
Berg
Editorial offices:
First Floor, Angel Court, 81 St Clements Street, Oxford OX4 1AW, UK
175 Fifth Avenue, New York, NY 10010, USA

© Inger Marie Okkenhaug and Ingvild Flaskerud 2005

Paperback edition reprinted 2006

All rights reserved.
No part of this publication may be reproduced in any form
or by any means without the written permission of
Berg.

Berg is the imprint of Oxford International Publishers Ltd.

Library of Congress Cataloging-in-Publication Data

Gender, religion and change in the Middle East : two hundred years of history / edited by
Inger Marie Okkenhaug and Ingvild Flaskerud. — English ed.
     p. cm. — (Cross-cultural perspectives on women,
  ISSN 1068-8536 ; v. [26])
   Includes bibliographical references and index.
   ISBN 1-84520-199-X (pbk.) — ISBN 1-84520-198-1 (cloth)
   1. Women—Middle East. 2. Women—Islamic countries. I. Okkenhaug, Inger Marie. II.
Flaskerud, Ingvild. III. Series.

  HQ1785.G46 2005
  305.3'0956'0904—dc22

                 2004030703

British Library Cataloguing-in-Publication Data

A catalogue record for this book is available from the British Library.

ISBN-13 978 1 84520 198 2 (Cloth)
        978 1 84520 199 9 (Paper)

ISBN-10 1 84520 198 1 (Cloth)
        1 84520 199 X (Paper)

Typeset by JS Typesetting Ltd, Porthcawl, Mid Glamorgan
Printed in the United Kingdom by Biddles Ltd, King's Lynn.

www.bergpublishers.com

Contents

Introduction

Inger Marie Okkenhaug and *Ingvild Flaskerud*

Middle Eastern gender studies have to a large extent been dominated by an approach that focuses on the implications of Islam on women's empowerment. Islam has often been perceived as a timeless tradition, which has resulted in homogeneous descriptions of women under Islam. However, more recent studies reveal that factors like class, time and place can produce diverse courses of actions for Muslim women (Keddie and Baron 1991: 3). An additional fact that brings nuance to the study of gender in the Middle East is the numerous minority communities living in the region, belonging to the other two main religions in the Middle East, Judaism and Christianity. Historically, these three religions have been characterized by a gender hierarchy, where women have been subjugated to social control and isolation from men. These different societies also shared a central code of honor in which family honor depended on proper conduct by female family members. Religions, that is Islam, Judaism and Christianity, have been seen as playing a central role in the creating and cementing of this structure of suppression. However, in spite of formal restrictions, Middle Eastern women have found various strategies to informally exert power to shape their own status. Observers have pointed to women's influence in the family and at home. Also, the juridical system with its religious courts of law has been an official arena where Christian, Jewish and Muslim women have been given an arena of possible influence over their lives (see, for example, Tucker 1998).

Western imperialism, in the form of state colonialism and Christian mission, is another aspect that has had great influence on the relations between religion and gender. Frequently colonial rule reinforced a gendered hierarchy of power (Thompson 2000: 67). Thus women came under a double set of patriarchal structures: Arab and Western (Dahlgren 2004; Okkenhaug 2004). However, in postcolonial society, national liberation did not necessarily change the patriarchal structures. As shown by Elizabeth Thompson, the resolution of conflicts among male citizens, for example Islamists versus secular nationalists, was attained in part through negotiations, which excluded women from formal rights (Thompson 2000: 227). And in present-day Afghanistan, women's position as key symbols of male and family honor creates an ambivalent attitude to acknowledging violence

1

committed against women, despite the overthrow of an Islamist regime (see Chapter 11 in this volume).

Gender in the Middle East is certainly shaped by and works within a patriarchal society. However, as several scholars have argued, the word patriarchy is ideologically loaded and problematic. The differences in the ways that women are subordinated to men have been interpreted merely as the outcome of different expressions or stages of the same system.[1] This has resulted in an overly abstract and monolithic conception of male dominance, which confuses rather than reveals the intimate inner workings of different gender arrangements. In some usage the term conjures up unrealistic static and deterministic structures of oppression, in which men are omnipotent and women are fundamentally and irretrievably subjugated. This description diverts attention from the active agency used by women to advance and protect their own interests (Kandiyoti 1991: 26). In order to develop a more nuanced understanding of patriarchy, several researchers have suggested analyzing women's strategies in the encounter with male dominance (Nyhagen Predelli and Miller 1999: 69–70). Kandiyoti speaks about the "patriarchal bargain" to which both genders accommodate and acquiesce, yet which may nevertheless be contested, redefined and renegotiated (Kandiyoti 1991: 23–41). This approach acknowledges women as subjects, and allows the researcher to study variations within female-gendered spheres of a community, as well as negotiations between gendered spheres. Moreover, it recognizes the transformable character of patriarchy as a social construction. Patriarchal bargains are not timeless or immutable entities, but are susceptible to historical transformations that open up new areas of struggle or renegotiation of the relations between genders. It may also exhibit variations according to class, caste and ethnicity. It should be remembered that the male gender is just as fluctuating as the female gender. Nevertheless, men and masculinity in the Middle East are still almost non-existing research areas. Important exceptions are Ghoussoub and Sinclair-Webb (2002), who present a collection of contributions discussing male identity in the modern Middle East, and Thompson (2000), who integrates both men and women into a historical account of Syria and Lebanon during French colonial rule.

Sensitive to insight developed from recent studies on gender and religion in the Middle East we cast the net wide, to include studies on Judaism, Christianity and Islam. In its own right each chapter describes and discusses aspects of human experience, social reality and institutional development and management in the region, from the early nineteenth century until the present. However, the overall question that concerns us is how gender roles are negotiated in religious communities, and how these negotiations relate to social change. We are aware of the Western tendency to view every issue of the Middle East through the lens of religion, Islam in particular. As several of the chapters show, factors such as social and economic conditions are formative of gender negotiations. Nevertheless, we believe that a closer look at religious behavior or practiced religion, be it through written, oral or performative sources, can be a rewarding approach. We also appreciate the contribution of historical studies that counter a tendency to read into the past, social and cultural patterns that did not exist (Meriwether and Tucker 1999). Thus, the following analyses are anchored in the religious, historical, political and economic circumstances of the human agent. The authors consider how gender roles are defined in time within religious communities, as well as exploring how women and men themselves develop and apply their own strategies. Throughout, the authors challenge our understanding of religious tradition and patriarchy to offer a more nuanced account.

In Chapter 1, Nahda Younis Shehada takes an innovative approach to the study of patriarchy when discussing the management of family law at an Islamic court in Gaza in 2002. The study of Islamic family law underwent fundamental changes in the 1970s, when new sources and methods were added to the field (Moors 1999). Examination of court documents and oral narratives gave a fresh perspective at predominantly textual study of canon law. The new approach revealed a more flexible, pragmatic and dynamic law than previously assumed. Researchers documented that women, not only historically, but also in the present, use the court as an effective way to protect their interests. However, instead of focusing on women's strategies in the encounter with male dominance in the court system, Shehada analyzes how judges, who are men, respond to male dominance over women within a social and legalistic patriarchal structure. Contrary to an often held stereotypical view, Shehada finds that judges play a significant role in protecting women from their male relatives' abuse. However, despite Palestinian women's recent efforts to improve women's rights, the judges' decisions are not related to a change in their notions of gender equality. They are influenced by the same gender discourses that legitimize the gendered divisions of rights and duties within the family. Nevertheless, through their work they have developed sensitivity to the oppression of women by male kin. This social awareness is joined with ethical principles directed to protect members of the community, and to preserve social order. In studies of legalistic Islam this ethical principle is often referred to as an "ethical voice." Ahmad (1992) has claimed that legalistic (orthodox) Islam has been void of an ethical voice. Although Shehada acknowledges the patriarchal structure of the court system, she argues against Ahmad's position.

Male roles are just as much negotiable and susceptible to change as female roles and there are various masculine roles available. In Chapter 2, Yohai Hakak explores the encounter of Orthodox Jewish (Haredi) young men with the secular male ideal of the Israeli army. He has looked at the ways Haredi cadets react to the army discourse and practices, which in many ways are contrary to that of the Haredi. They reshape their Haredi masculinity, but they do not become more secularized as feared by the rabbis. Instead, it is argued that the meeting with secular masculinity strengthens the religiosity of these young men. When they face aspects of military-Zionist masculinity that are not perceived as religiously threatening, they internalize it and incorporate them for their own needs. This is an example of how social conditions force men to challenge and renegotiate the traditional gender system within a religious community. The younger generation seem to succeed in creating a masculine role that includes both tradition and the contemporary nation-state's expectations of what it means to be a man. Even so, there is an interaction between two cultural models. The representatives for the hegemonic male model, that is the Israeli army, accepted the Haredis' demand for more autonomy, especially in regard to religious practices.

Masculinity and modernity in Jerusalem are also the topic of Inger Marie Okkenhaug's Chapter 3. The focus here is on Anglican male education during Ottoman- and British-ruled Palestine. The Anglican Church transmitted the Christian, Protestant male ideal of the imperial power to Palestinian boys and young men through their educational institutions. However, as shown by Okkenhaug, this was a culture of Anglican-Protestantism that did not include proselytizing. The Anglican-Protestant culture ideals seem not to have been offensive to Muslim, Christian or Jewish pupils, but were rather regarded as useful tools for future success. Palestinians had a pick-and-choose, almost consumer attitude in relation to the Anglican schools. They ignored what they did not find useful and British male behavior models seemed to have been accommodated and used to the Palestinians' advantage. Palestinian parents saw an Anglican education for their sons (and daughters) as a means for social improvement and economic gain for the family.

Christian, Western education and middle-class/elite students using the role models as a tool for change is also the topic of Chapter 4, where Aleksandra Majstorac Kobiljski discusses the strategies of integration and socialization of women students in the multi-confessional academic community of the American University of Beirut from the 1920s to the 1960s. The focus is on women students' agency and how they asserted themselves in the social space of a Christian Protestant University. Women students were integrated not only into a multi-religious student body but also into a coeducational context. Kobiljski shows how these first generations of women from Christian, Muslim and Jewish backgrounds strategized and worked their way through the American University in their pursuit of higher education and social participation, both fighting against and benefiting from tradition, class and religion. While this was an elite institution, the female students were important in the formation of a generation of role models who profoundly influenced their communities and societies in the twentieth century.

Female students at the American University of Beirut became deeply involved in welfare activities, which included work with the urban poor and village welfare. In this they were part of a large and international development. Philanthropic work has sanctioned transgressive behavior as religious exceptions to gender rules for Christian, Jewish and Muslim women living within a religious context. Historically, charitable activities were a legitimate way for women to venture out of the home. While this middle-class or elite-based strategy for social action and responsibility has been seen as the beginning of the welfare state in numerous studies of Europe and North America, voluntary social welfare work and women's agency have been an understudied area in a Middle Eastern context. This is the starting point of Beth Baron's Chapter 5 on women's voluntary social welfare organizations in Egypt in the period from 1900 till the 1960s. She argues that while elite women's social welfare organizations that emerged from the late nineteenth century often were organized along religious and communal lines, their leadership challenged traditional religious leaders. Baron refers to Mine Ener's work *Managing Egypt's Poor and the Politics of Benevolence, 1800–1952* (2003), where Ener shows that, prior to the nineteenth century, providing benevolence was a religious obligation which individuals and the community fulfilled through acts of charity and the establishment of trusts. The rulers and elite had a special social obligation to take care of those in need and demonstrated power through the funding of hostels, hospitals and so on. During the nineteenth century, the state increasingly appropriated religious functions and funds, taking over trusts and the care of the poor. As shown by Baron, however, until the 1960s (when the state took over most of these private health ventures) the state's neglect of social welfare gave women's groups an important role in Egypt's health and welfare. While these women activists did not seem to have much impact on the social policies of the state, Baron concludes that they did influence social welfare practices and their work encouraged women to enter the profession of social work.

Women and health-related work was also central to the Christian missionary movement, which had a great impact on women's lives in the Middle East. In a similar manner to the religious- inspired work among the elite women in Egypt, Protestant women in Europe and North America were attracted to missionary work, because it combined a gender-specific, Christian way of life with a degree of freedom denied to women in the West. In Chapter 6, Heleen Murre-van den Berg presents an overview of the variety of work initiated by Protestant missionaries for women and girls in the Middle East between 1820 and 1914. While the initial aim was the conversion of Muslims, Christians and Jews, the numbers of converts were very few. The lasting effect of the work of these female agents was seen in their practical work in promoting an evangelical lifestyle closely connected with the idea of "evangelical motherhood." Education and schools for girls were central in this endeavor (and in some instances the missionary education's aim to modernize became the driving force). The people of the Middle East welcomed mission schools for girls and Murre-van den Berg argues that these schools not only taught girls modern domestic science, but also stimulated women academically.

Arab women were encouraged to take an active role in their society, and were encouraged to write and publish about issues of importance to society. Thus the mission schools were instrumental in producing a new female leadership in the Middle East.

In the post-colonial era of nation building, the modern, educated Middle Eastern woman has to a large extent been indistinguishable from secularism. In Turkey, the secular government of Atatürk invented a new Turkish woman that was seen as the opposite of the traditional Muslim female. By the early 1980s, however, religious women's roles were dramatically redefined in Turkey. This new Islamic woman was educated, and was involved in social and political activities. Nevertheless, as Jenny B. White describes in Chapter 7, not all female members of the Islamist movement could pursue this lifestyle, or the involvement could vary during a woman's life. White ascribes such deviation to inconsistency in the Islamist ideology, which supported both activism and patriarchy. On the one hand, the Islamist movement created opportunities for Muslim women to seek education, to work and to be politically active. This was attractive to many women. Conversely, Islamist ideology also asserted that women's primary duty was to remain at home and dedicate herself to her family. Thus, gender roles became a negotiable issue within Islamist environments. White observes that male Islamists generally reinforced traditional notions of women's duties. Another important factor that affected the outcome of gender–role negotiations was the economic resources available to the involved parties. Thus, marriage and childbirth were situations that typically activated negotiations and the result for women was often a return to the domain of patriarchal values. As a consequence, Islamist ideology seems to have opened doors for women, White remarks, but these tended to be revolving doors for lower-class women.

While discussing Islamist attitudes to gender roles, negotiations over roles, and pointing to configuration of gender roles, White draws attention to the subtle function of women's veil in negotiating and expressing identity, values and roles. The complex connections between gender, religion and change are often played out in religious symbols. Muslims have used the veil as a symbol to express resistance to secularization, as well as a marker of an Islamist ideological stance versus a more general Muslim identity (Lindesfarne-Tapper and Ingham 1997; El Guindi 1999). The veil as a symbol is thus in concordance with symbols in general, for which it is an intrinsic character to be multivocal and multi-interpretable (Leeds-Hurwitz 1993). In Turkey, Islamists have utilized the *tesettür* veil to communicate a collective religious and ideological stance. However, White points out, during the 1990s the *tesettür* veil came to reflect contradictory cultural and political-cultural philosophies. Like elsewhere in the Middle East, women Islamists in Turkey used the veil's traditional symbolic value as a signifier of female honor and modesty to communicate in their local environments their adherence to equivalent values. A recognized status as honorable and modest was utilized by women to strategize in negotiations over changing gender roles. This eventually gave women access to an active life in public space, and the veil became a signifier of Islamic modernity. Within the context of contradictory Islamist ideology, supporting both activism and patriarchy, women became responsible for signaling through their veiling practices which of these two collective ideological stances they pursued at a personal level. To complicate this, additional meaning was attributed to the veil when it was exploited by commercial interests and entered the fashion market during the 1990s. Middle-class Islamist women now manipulated the veil to indicate modern lifestyle and values, in addition to class distinction, thus challenging values traditionally fostered by Islamists. Moreover, as fashion *tesettür* signified ideals of beauty, the veil has been diluted from the political ideology of the Islamist movement and become filled with new meanings which open up alternative lifestyles to yet a new generation of women in Turkey.

Women in Christian communities in the Middle East have also been able to utilize core symbols to create alternatives to dominant conservative and patriarchal female gender notions. One important key symbol in Christianity (as well as in Islam) is the Virgin Mary. From a gender perspective there are numerous contradictions in this symbol. Patriarchal clergy has upheld the symbol Mary as the ultimate model of feminine virtues such as submission and obedience, whereas modern feminist theologians have emphasized her agency. In Chapter 8, Willy Jansen suggests that in order to understand how gender is constituted at the crossroad of structural constraints and individual agency, it is necessary to analyze the meanings attributed to key symbols in specific situations by specific people. Her present focus is on the implications of recurring visions of Mary by a Catholic girl in Jerusalem in 1874, and the apparitions of Mary above a Coptic church in Cairo in 1968, to female empowerment at the time. It is argued that the visions created an atmosphere that inspired a revival of the symbol of Mary (as a symbol of ethnicity, nationalism and religious identity). In this context groups of women were able to reinterpret and give alternative meanings to the symbol of Mary, which empowered them to change their identities and to take on new religious, economic and social roles.

In Jerusalem, the young visionary Mary Alphonsus upheld a supposedly repeated request from the Virgin to found a Congregation of the Rosary. She established allies among the local Catholic Church establishment, and a congregation of all Arab nuns was eventually set up. Their aim was primarily to bring education to girls and to increase devotion to Mary. The project was revolutionary at the time. Until then, there were no women convents among the Arabs of Palestine, and women did not publicly work in education and health care. In order to accomplish these changes, the visionary and her supporters hailed the purity and virginity of Mary, as well as her powerful protective qualities. The apparitions in Cairo took place in a period of social change and political unrest. For members of the Coptic community this involved, among other things, emerging educational facilities for Coptic girls, which generated increased mobility for women, and social and political awareness. As a result many women experienced that they no longer fitted into traditional prescribed gender roles. In this context, the apparitions of Mary promoted the development of a new group of religious active women, called the Daughters of Mariam. Differently from the contemplative nuns in the Coptic Church, the Daughters of Mariam emphasized Mary's active work in the community. They engaged in various social projects, and their work had a wide range of consequences for many girls and women around them. Church work became a way of expressing individuality, independence and capacities (see also Baron, Chapter 5, and Murre-van den Berg, Chapter 6). Thus, as these cases show, reinforcement of religious identity can offer security when gender identity is doubted. Jansen suggests that it also served to restore respect for women who took up new gender roles.

Fawaz has argued that the autobiographical and narrative remains as valuable and as legitimate in modern scholarship as theory (Fawaz 1998: 2). In Chapter 9 Leah Shakdiel tells her personal story about the endeavor of two generations of women towards their empowerment in the Torah world. In her narrative she also includes a reading of Pnina Greitzer's film *BeÉzrat Nashim* (2000) and relates it to feminist research of female identity as well as her own experience as a religious Zionist. Jewish religious parties were the first to force the Israeli government to grant automatic exemption for women from military service. However, in the late 1960s, young religious Zionist women, like the author herself, wanted to do their patriotic duty and live out their generation's ideal of gender equality by serving in the army. Shakdiel was not allowed to do so, but twenty years later, her daughter was breaking new grounds within the Israeli Defense Forces. Shakdiel suggests that after the beginning of the first Intifada (Palestinian uprising in 1987), the religious Zionist movement changed its focus. The messianic need to settle on occupied territories in the 1970s and 1980s decreased with the Intifada. Then the religious community focused on the production of modernized religion, which included a reawakening of women's issues within the religious Zionist community.

In this "feminist revolution," religious women have pushed for new positions of religious leadership. Not only is there Torah learning (formerly a male arena) for adult women, but also written Torah scholarship by women is being published, which is a new phenomenon in the history of Orthodox Judaism. And in order to meet the needs of the growing numbers of religious women who want more than alternative national service, the army has offered new forms of military service. Thus, the young women who take part in this project undertake two male roles simultaneously, that of the Torah scholar and that of the soldier, thus reinventing themselves on several layers: in relation to nation, religion and gender. Even so, there is a discord between the life phases of these young middle/upper-class women and later married life. As wives and mothers they face a traditional gender hierarchy, manifested in the gendered, formal education of their own sons and daughters.

Shakdiel is not blind to the political circumstances that these religious Zionists live within. She hints at the shortcomings of a feminist project that ignores the wider circumstances of its political basis. Even so, she sees herself and other religious feminist activists as agents of change concerning the struggle to decrease militarism's dominating role in Israeli society.

A central focus in these studies of women's lives in the Middle East has been on their capacity to take initiative. While Leah Shakdiel points to the relations between political development, women's religious evolvement and activism, Nefissa Naguib (Chapter 10) argues that in order to understand the multifaceted aspects of gender and change, human agency must be considered within larger national and international frameworks of political decision-making and economic development. Such factors can be just as important to gender relations as religious ideology and practice. Accordingly, she suggests a stronger awareness of the implications of complex emergencies (such as war, occupation, dysfunctional institutions, poverty and water shortage) on women and men's opportunity to initiate action. Applying complex emergencies as an analytical category on "family" rather than "gender relation," Naguib sheds light on the transformation of the institution of patriarchy in a local community. She demonstrates how complex emergencies affect gender roles and the strategies available to individuals. Through the focus on family, she conveys how options may vary between generations, thus surfacing variations within a gender. Naguib's suggestion is developed out of an ethnographic study of a Palestinian village on the West Bank. Given the current social and political unrest in many countries, the approach should have relevance to studies elsewhere in the region, and beyond.

Afghanistan is another region where people have suffered due to what we can call "complex emergencies." The Taliban represented the culmination of a longer trend of fusing traditional gender hierarchy with religious rhetoric to the detrimental effect for women. However, war, exile and life in refugee camps have disrupted the traditional value system which places men as the providers and protectors of women, and partly suspended the structure of *mahram* relationship, that regulates the (honorable) contact between sexes. In Chapter 11 Karin Ask presents us with a careful ethnographical study of how Afghan women have dealt with the complicated and baffling situations created when the re-enforced values of traditional patriarchy are simultaneously undermined (through war and exile) by those who enforced them. She concentrates on women's role in shaping the living Afghan tradition during difficult circumstances in the 1990s. Afghan women have traditionally contributed to the social and cultural reproduction of the household through a complex nexus of gift exchanges (*badal*) and religious ceremonial outlays. The spiritual return for such transactions is religious merit and God's blessing, and in the tribal tradition personal dignity and familial honor. It was important that this social and religious work continued during war and exile. It has proved to be essential to reinforce kinship networks, and build the social capital that binds communities together. Moreover, Ask observes, it stitches together the gap between personal and communal experience of violence and loss, which has roused personal, communal and national traumas. In order to continue their social and religious work, as well as try to restore education and health care for women, Afghans developed strategies in which they combined codes, rules and categories from the local tradition, with knowledge acquired during exile (in Pakistan and Iran). In addition to contributing to the scholarly discussion of gender, religion and social change, this chapter provides valuable information about the influence of women in the non-institutional spheres of Afghan society. It is highly relevant to the current situation of reconciliation and reconstruction on the national level.

The observed separation of gender in many communities in the Middle East have inspired an understanding of gender models that suggested either alternative male and female worldviews, or complementary genders within a single worldview. In Chapter 12, Azam Torab argues against such models, claiming they are based on coexisting, dualistic and mutually exclusive gender models. Instead she supports a model that understands gender as inherently flexible. The empirical setting for her discussion is the ceremonial votive meals (*sofre*), which are dedicated to Shia saints and supernatural spirits, who are believed to act as intercessors with God for requests and favors. *Sofre* is an all-female activity, which religious authorities and many men in Iran criticize as "popular," meaning based on superstition, and thus held to be un-Islamic. However, Torab claims that denigration of women's votive ceremonial meals does not suggest denigration of women, gender antagonism or domination. Indeed, men feel dependent on women's access to the supernatural when problems arise in their daily lives, and they ask women to act on their behalf. Thus, Torab argues, by helping men to resolve their problems women can strengthen their own position. They benefit from this when negotiating their relations with men, thereby transforming "domestic" activity into a political agency. An underlying argument here is that gender is not the cause of ritual, but an effect. Through votive ceremonial meals, women create a collective, unitary identity as "women" by drawing on the powers and capacities that are defined as female. They thereby create a sphere of political agency. This means that women can appear both weak and powerful, and men seem both to dominate women and delude themselves. The implication of this observation is of importance to the study of gender relations; it means that the symbolic and the social do not necessarily correspond. As Torab argues, women and men may be represented as powerful symbolically but discriminated against socially.

The connection between the symbolic and the social, between religious ideal and social practice has been a central theme in this anthology. We have wanted to highlight the heterogeneity in expressions of gender relations, negotiations and religious formation, as well as diversity in geographical and historical articulations. We thus want to contribute to recent scholarship that question research rooted in timeless religious institutions as explanations of Middle Eastern gender inequality. The authors represent a wide range of disciplines: history, anthropology, sociology, theology and the science of religion. We all met in Bergen in the fall of 2003, where we enjoyed lively, interdisciplinary discussions. We believe these conversations from various fields of study have given a fruitful result as seen in these twelve chapters.

Acknowledgments

We would like to thank Ellen Fleischmann, who presented a paper on female education in Lebanese mission schools, and Benedicte Solheim and Janne Bøe, who presented a paper on urban and rural Muslim Palestinian women, for valuable contribution to our discussions in Bergen 2003. Significant insight was also offered by three ethnographic/documentary films: *Eine Blume für die Frauen aus Kabul* by Siba Shakib (1998), *Standardbearers of Hussein: Women commemorating Karbala* by Ingvild Flaskerud (2003) and *Al Karamah – Human Dignity* by Moslih Kanaaneh and Frode Storaas (1997), which introduced us to aspects of women's conditions in Afghanistan, Iran and Israel. The Iranian lawyer and human rights activist Shirin Ebadi had been scheduled to give a paper on "The Status of Women in the Middle East and its Relationship to Culture and Islam: with Specific Focus on the Status of Women in Iran." A more important event only days later, the Nobel Peace Prize Ceremony, prevented her participation. We present our congratulations!

Kjersti Gravelsaeter Berg, Centre for Middle Eastern and Islamic Studies, and Eva Fauske, Department of History at the University of Bergen, offered valuable practical assistance in the organizing of the conference. Funding was raised from the Norwegian Council of Research and Centre for Middle Eastern and Islamic Studies. We would also like to thank Knut Vikør, who read and commented on part of this manuscript.

Note

1. Kandiyoti (1991: 26–7). Patriarchy can be defined as the male's formal control over women and family, exercised by fathers, husbands and brothers. In the so-called

"classical patriarchy," the extended family gives the senior man authority over everyone else, including younger men.

References

Ahmad, L. (1992), *Women and Gender in Islam: Historical Roots of a Modern Debate*, New Haven, CT: Yale University Press.

Dahlgren, S. (2004), "Can a Woman Decide upon her Marriage? The Case of Compulsory Marriage in the Anglo-Muhammadan Court System in Colonial Aden," in I. B. Mæhle and I. M. Okkenhaug (eds), *Gender, Religion and Social Change in the Middle East and Mediterranean*, Oslo: UNIPUB.

El Guindi, F. (1999), *Veil: Modesty, Privacy and Resistance*, Oxford: Berg.

Ener, M. (2003), *Managing Egypt's Poor and the Politics of Benevolence. 1800–1952*, Princeton, NJ: Princeton University Press.

Fawaz, L. (1998), "Swimming against the Tide: Personal Passions and Academic Fashions," *Middle East Studies Bulletin*, 32(1): 2–10.

Ghoussoub, M. and Sinclair-Webb, E. (eds) (2000), *Imagined Masculinities: Male Identity and Culture in the Modern Middle East*, London: Saqi.

Kandiyoti, D. (1991), *Women, Islam and the State*, London: Macmillan.

Keddie, N. and Baron, B. (eds) (1991), *Women in Middle Eastern History: Shifting Boundaries in Sex and Gender*, New Haven, CT London: Yale University Press.

Leeds-Hurwitz, W. (1993), *Semiotics and Communication: Sign, Codes, Cultures*, London: Lawrence Erlbaum.

Lindesfarne-Tapper, N. and Ingham, B. (eds) (1997), *Languages of Dress in the Richmond, Middle East*, Richmond, Surrey: Curzon.

Meriwether, M. L. and Tucker, J. E. (eds) (1999) *A Social History of Women and Gender in the Modern Middle East*, Boulder, CO and Oxford: Westview Press.

Moors, A. (1999), "Debating Islamic Family Law: Legal Texts and Social Practices," in M. L. Meriwether and J. E. Tucker (eds) *A Social History of Women and Gender in the Modern Middle East*, Boulder, CO and Oxford: Westview Press.

Nyhagen Predelli, L. and Miller, J. (1999), "Piety and Patriarchy: Contested Gender Regimes in Nineteenth-Century Evangelical Missions," in M. Taylor Hubert and N. C. Lutkehaus (eds), *Gendered Missions: Women and Men in Missionary Discourse and Practice*, Ann Arbor, MI: University of Michigan Press.

Okkenhaug, I. M. (2004), "Mission and Education as Liberating Strategies: The Case of Mabel Warburton," in I. B. Mæhle and I. M. Okkenhaug (eds), *Gender, Religion and Social Change in the Middle East and Mediterranean*, Oslo: UNIPUB.

Thompson, E. (2000), *Colonial Citizens: Republican Rights*, New York: Columbia University Press.

Tucker, J. (1998), *In the House of the Law: Gender and Islamic Law in Ottoman Syria and Palestine*, Berkeley, CA and London: University of California Press.

1

Justice without Drama: Observations from Gaza City Sharia Court

Nahda Younis Shehada

Introduction

Several authors have argued that the codification of Islamic family law has made the state a main player in the process of interpretation of the Sharia,[1] which leads politicians to decide what to exclude and what to include of people's customary norms (*adat, takhaleed, a'raf* etc).[2] The process of exclusion and inclusion depends upon many elements, primarily the worldview of the legislators, their power and the level of socio-economic development of the society itself. After the fall of the Ottoman Empire, Arab successor states composed personal status codes (*qawaneen al-ahwal asshakhseyya*) to govern family affairs. This implied standardization of sharia and a minimization of the judges' (*qadis'*) subjectivity. The codification of family law entailed a "fixation" of specific gender roles and relations. The main implication is that the application of the Sharia in modern times is no longer flexible, unlike in the pre-modern plural legal system.

On the basis of my fieldwork in the Sharia court of Gaza in 2002, I shall argue that even after the process of codification, the application of sharia is still flexible. *Qadis*, lawyers and people in general, in their search for gaps and room in which to maneuver, prefer either to alternate or to mesh the codified and the uncodified "customs." When the *qadis* find that codified law is deaf, they do not hesitate to apply *'urf* (customs, norms and social traditions) in order to provide "justice." In this sense, *qadis* of Gaza City sharia court are still able to practice their power of discretion.

This chapter aims to give a flavor of the everyday justice of the sharia court of Gaza City. It focuses on the *qadis'* struggle to maintain their notion of justice ('adl) within the limits of sharia. Contrary to a stereotypical view, *qadis* play a significant role in protecting women from their male relatives' abuses. To achieve this, they may not pay as much attention to the text of family law as to the context of the dispute, showing sensitivity towards the weak party and to the wider social ramifications of their judgments. When the family law is not helpful, they may refer to customary practice or may adopt "progressive" attitudes that take into account the complexity of "modern" life.

The key element in the *qadis'* discretion is their self-perception as members of their community rather than as mere implementers of the law. Their decisions are informed by their understanding of the sharia not just as a body of texts, but rather as a set of ethical principles that aim at, on the one hand, protecting the weaker members of the community and, on the other, preserving the social order. *Qadis'* notion of "justice" and "fairness," I argue, is derived from the ethical voice of Islam (Ahmad 1992). I here refer to Ahmad's distinction between two voices in Islam, the technical voice and the ethical voice. Ahmad (1992) argues that throughout Islamic history, the technical (orthodox) voice has dominated the legal and institutional realms, while the ethical voice of Islam was widespread among the laypeople. In this sense, *qadis* who exercise authority in the sharia courts (as representing the Islamic legal institutions) are supposed to be orthodox and androcentric. However, my observations show that the same *qadis* considered by Ahmad as androcentric and orthodox act as "protectors" of the female litigants, shielding them from the harm their male kin might inflict upon them. They often draw on the ethical message of Islam to scold men and remind them of the framework within which they have to work out their relationships with their female kin. In this context, they frequently refer to fairness, love, compassion, care, peace and human treatment (*adl, mahabba, ta'atuf, rifq, salam, muamala insanyya*) to enforce the ethical message of Islam. The application of family law in the sharia court is an undetermined, flexible and blurry "process" as any other social process in real life. Constructing dichotomies between two distinct groups in the Islamic history does not stand up to the empirical evidence. I found that the boundaries between the two voices and the two holders are rather blurred. In my view, it is only at the ideological level that these two voices become distinct.

It is worth noting, however, that *qadis'* protective behavior is not informed by notions related to gender equality. As with the rest of society, *qadis* are influenced by the same gender discourse that legitimizes the gendered division of rights and duties within the family. Yet their daily encounter with the unfairness, oppression and injustices inflicted on women by their kinsmen enhance their sensitivity towards women's cases. *Qadis'* sympathy with the female litigants, their efforts to find "just" solutions and their explicit rejection of men's abuses trigger frequent accusations by male litigants that they are favoring women. For example, a husband who was ordered to pay *nafaqa* (maintenance) to his wife told the *qadi*: "You are rewarding my wife for her rebellious action, your attitude is not Islamic."[3] Another man, whose custody case was rejected by the *qadi*, shouted at him: "No wonder Israel is achieving victory over us. Our *qadis* are as corrupt as our leaders. The moment they smell a woman's fragrance, their hearts are softened and they forget Allah."

The Application of Family Law in Contemporary Sharia Courts

The sharia system is based upon *fiqh* (Islamic jurisprudence), which is defined as "scientific" reflection upon Koran and its interpretation. The sharia is applied by (the sharia) courts, which have jurisdiction in matters of personal status and familial relations. This law is primarily based on the Hanafi doctrine, one of the four major Sunni schools of law. It also incorporates rules from other Sunni schools.

The Family Law (also referred to as the "Personal Status Law") in Palestine is derived from Jordanian and Egyptian laws, which in turn are of Ottoman origin and rely on the Islamic sharia. The Jordanian law is implemented in the West Bank, while Egyptian law is implemented in the Gaza Strip.[4] The Ottoman Law of Family Rights 1917 includes a provision referring to the Hanafi School, to be used when judges are confronted with particular cases overlooked by the specific text in the law.[5] The Ottomans, Welchman (1999) argues, set an example by introducing rules from non-Hanafi sources into the codified law on the basis of public interest (*maslaha*). This model was the basis upon which Arab states codified sharia in the form of national family law by drawing from different Islamic schools.

It is often argued that the socio-economic changes in the Muslim societies during the twentieth century, which triggered a shift in the roles of the nation-state, sharia and religious establishment, eradicated the use of *'urf* in the application of codified Islamic family law.[6] These arguments can be seen in Samadjian (1996), Sonbol (1996) and Tucker (1998). I will first outline the ideas presented by these authors and then take them up point by point for discussion.

Sonbol (1996) uses the marriage and divorce cases of minors to illustrate the flexibility of the Islamic courts during the Ottoman period. Different *madhahibs* (schools of Islamic jurisprudence) prevailed in different parts of Egypt, a diversity which provided people with a flexible application of sharia. Sonbol (1996) argues that, with the establishment of the nation-state and the accelerated hegemony of modernity, the state's codified law (*qanun*) has moved society from dependence on different and flexible interpretations of the sharia (from different *madhahibs*) and *'urf* into the state's construction of social relations. At the heart of the state's codification of the law was the fixing of gender relations through legislation. In Sonbol's view, the state's codified law adopted only a partial interpretation of the sharia, ignoring that in the past there had been space for different *madhahibs* to be applied. Sonbol believes that the sharia was never fixed; it was constantly changed and modified as part of historical process. The difference between the past and present is that, in the past, the state played a minor role while in the twentieth century, "the state has become a conscious and intentional moulder of gender laws" (Sonbol 1996: 256).

Sanadjian (1996) is also negative about the process of codification. She argues that the codification of people's norms into rigid articles of law, whether these laws were codified by the nation-state or by the colonizers, has brought about a process of exclusion and inclusion of people's practices. The issue of what to exclude or include depends upon many elements, including the worldview of the legislators, their power and the level of the socio-economic development of the community or society. In general, people observe Islamic norms, but when these norms are codified, they become rigid due to the tendency of Islamic scholars to draw definite lines between what is allowed and forbidden (*halal* and *haram*), a practice that contradicts the Koranic verses defining all practices as allowed (*halal*) unless they are specifically prohibited by God, through his Prophet. This process made the application of the sharia less flexible (flexibility in the sense of interaction between the community and its environment). Therefore, codification was a means of excluding many "positive" practices that had been permitted earlier.

In her work on the *fatwas* and *qadis'* decisions in Syria and Palestine during the seventeenth and eighteenth centuries, Tucker (1998) emphasizes that the application of sharia was flexible and incorporated '*urf*. She argues that the fluidity of sharia application in fact originated from the *qadis'* ability to employ the appropriate solution for social problems as advocated by different *madhahibs*. She adds that this flexibility is nowhere to be seen now due to the codification of family law, among other things. Tucker believes that Islamic sharia (defined as a set flexible rules and fluid regulations) and the nature of Islamic law (as uncodified and subject to the *qadis'* discretion and *muftis'* subjectivity) were more beneficial to women than the codified law after the establishment of the nation-state following the eradication of colonialism. *Qadis* and *muftis* were more attentive to the customs and norms of their communities; thus, gender rights and duties were subject to modifications within certain limits to suit the worldviews of the *qadis* and *muftis* as to what constitutes justice. Tucker concludes that the codification undertaken after the establishment of the nation-state was meant to "fix" a definite interpretation of sharia,[7] thus standardizing it and minimizing the effects of *qadis'* subjectivity.[8] Codification, therefore, was a way to fix gender roles and relations.[9] Moreover, in Tucker's view, codification no longer allowed *qadis* to exercise discretion and *muftis* to interpret the sharia,[10] which, in the context of gender analysis, causes the relegation of women's rights.[11] Tucker views the codification of family law as preserving gender relations, while reducing the flexibility characteristic of pre-modern times.[12] Tucker expresses regret that the flexibility of the pre-modern legal system is nowhere to be seen today.[13]

Discussion

I agree with Sanadjian (1996), Sonbol (1996) and Tucker (1998) that codification has made the state a main player in the process of interpretation of the sharia. I also agree with them that most of the sharia regulations – past and present – refer to *'urf* in their application. What is more appealing to me is the fact that even after the process of codification, *qadi*, lawyers and people in general are still relying on *'urf* as a way to solve contemporary social problems. Hence, in the context of the Gaza sharia court, *qadis* and lawyers (as representatives of the legal and religious institutions) and people (as active social agents who seek to protect their interests), in their search for gaps and room in which to maneuver, prefer either to alternate or mesh the codified and the uncodified customs. In the course of this chapter, I shall demonstrate how this process is taking place.

What can we learn from this? Is this flexibility found only in Palestine? This question can be answered only by conducting a comparative study of sharia courts in different Islamic countries. I admit that the specificity of the Gaza court may influence the application of family law. Palestine is still an embryonic state and is not yet capable of imposing its rules over the sharia court; thus, the court may acquire some sense of independence in using different systems of justice. However, these specificities may bear out my analysis rather than weaken it, in that they reveal the diversity of sharia courts' modes of operation not only across time but also in different contexts.[14]

My ethnographic fieldwork suggests that abstract analysis (mainly ideological, influenced by the political economy approach) of the hegemonic role of state and the shifting functions of *qadis* and the sharia court does not satisfactorily explain why the sharia court in Gaza applies codified law differently from the presumed method. In my view, sharia is not applied in a vacuum; it is bound by the context in which the *qadis'* worldview, state structure and people's agency all affect the perception and implementation of Islamic family law. Highlighting one element (in this case, the role of the state) and downplaying others (the *qadi* and people's agency) does not provide an understanding of what is really going on in the contemporary sharia courts. We need to look at how these factors and actors interact and when and how, in the process of their interaction, they come to construct a particular social reality. What sorts of knowledge/power/discourse exist and under what circumstances do actors (including the *qadis*) downplay the codified law and bring '*urf* to the fore? What are the enabling factors that allow the *qadi* to shift smoothly between codified law and *'urf* and yet claim that they do not exceed the limits of sharia? And what are the wider social ramifications of such processes?

Understanding the application of laws that concern disputes requires adopting a suitable methodology that allows the researcher to observe the process personally through an ethnographic approach, which involves understanding how the family law is actually applied; what is included, what is excluded, and how the actors interact. This may give us some insight into this complex process and enable us to identify and characterize the often-conflicting interests, practices, values and strategies, without prejudging the roles of the state or the harm caused by codification.

The studies quoted earlier are based on extensive review of historical material and the methodology adopted has produced sophisticated and valuable analyses. However, when they compare historical observation with present-day practices, the three authors base their conclusions on political abstractions; they do not produce empirical material, case studies, observations or even statistics to prove that current practices differ from those of the Ottoman period. In other words, while their historical material is well analyzed, they resort to judgmental abstraction when considering the present. Furthermore, one cannot escape the impression that the three scholars demonstrate a tendency to draw a dichotomy between the pre-modern application of Islamic law and the postcolonial/modern nation-state application. This logic causes them to resort to further dichotomies such as: codified versus uncodified; fluidity versus fixity; flexibility versus standardization; modern versus pre-modern and, in the case of Tucker, *qadis'* subjectivity versus binding-law objectivity. These dichotomies lead them to formulate a depressing and hasty conclusion typified by Tucker: "The legal system that permitted such flexibility is nowhere to be seen today, nor is it really conceivable in the context of contemporary society" (Tucker 1998: 186).

Tucker, Sonbol and Sanadjian portray contemporary Muslim societies and individuals in the Muslim nation-state as if they were mere objects in the application of law by the state. This portrayal does not take into account the capabilities and knowledge of people (Long 2001) and depicts them as passive victims of the state's law. It does not acknowledge processes of interaction between people's agency and societal structure(s), leaving the state's laws and its coercive power to dictate people's destiny.

The Daily Practice of Present-day Gaza City Sharia Court

The sharia court is a socio-legal space constructed and used to solve familial problems, but it is also an arena where worldviews of *qadis*, litigants, lawyers and clerks interact. In the course of interaction, the nature of the dispute is clarified; shared/divided expectations emerge; interests are justified and rationalized; and boundaries are elucidated. The people who are involved in familial conflicts have access to various and unequal sources of power. By using the sharia court as a space for negotiating rights and obligations, they make the court an arena for contesting meanings that underlie the essence of social relations, i.e. the struggle for power and legitimacy. The sharia court is thus not neutral space; it is a social organization constructed to reproduce the existing distribution of power along the lines of gender, class, social status and locality.[15]

This understanding should not prevent us from discerning the overarching approach of the members of this organization. Conceptually, the court's clerks, lawyers and *qadis* perceive the female litigants as weak individuals who need protection. They play their protective role in the context of wise, strong, masculine men protecting weak and powerless women from the abusive behavior of their male relatives. I often heard the *qadis* telling husbands: "You should take care of your *hurma, walyya* [which means weak and helpless]." In this sense, the *qadis* and other court members become protective once men step beyond what is considered to be proper Islamic behavior. Thus, their protection is not transformative nor is it revolutionary; rather, its impact is bound by the *qadis'* understanding of Islamic justice that appreciates maintaining the social order on the one hand, and protecting the weak members of society, on the other.

Qadis' Decisive Roles

The power structure of the marriage institution is established on the fundamental balance of rights and duties, which is based on the responsibility of the husband to maintain his wife (paying her *nafaqa*) and she – in exchange – is obliged to be obedient to him. This requires the husband to provide clothing, food and dwelling, which vary according to time, place and local customs (Welchman 1999).[16] When a case of *nafaqa* is brought before the *qadi*, he does not question the absolute right of women to get it because it is an inviolable right. However, the mechanisms, tools, amount of *nafaqa* and time limits are all subject to negotiation. *Nafaqa* is the main pillar of marriage: "Whether the man works or not, whether he is absent or present, the wife's right to *nafaqa* is preserved. She does not need to claim to be poor. *Nafaqa* is her right, whether she is poor or rich."[17]

During my daily visits to the court, I found that in some cases, the *qadis* and lawyers seem to have the same objective. For example, in some *nafaqa* cases, I got the impression that there was a consensus between the *qadis* and lawyers about the amount of *nafaqa* to be paid to the wife. Samir Hassaneyyah told me:

Yes, in *nafaqa* cases, we (the *qadis*, the *katebs*) play our favorite game.[18] The objective behind the game is to get as much monthly *nafaqa* as possible from the husband. The game begins as follows: the *qadi* starts by telling the man: "You have to pay 100 JD as *nafaqa* to your wife. What is your response?"[19] The man would – usually – say, "I cannot pay this much, I can commit myself to paying 20 JD," for example. Husbands always complain of their economic hardship and tell the *qadi* about their inability to provide their wives with the specified *nafaqa*. In this scenario, I would play my role as the lawyer of the woman to dismiss the husband's claim that he could not pay the 100 JD. The *qadi* would start negotiating with me (as agreed before the session), telling me: "The man cannot pay what we propose to him. Can you make a concession?" The husband would take advantage of the *qadi*'s stance and start bargaining with me. I (for my part as a lawyer) would appear to be angry and tell the man: "We are not in a market, selling and buying tomatoes, this is the right of the wife, as the Islamic sharia declares. Do you want me to work against God's will? Against the sharia?" After arguing for a while, I would give the impression of making a great concession. The *qadi* would settle the amount between 40 and 60 JD, which is the range in all *nafaqa* cases. The game does not end here. To forestall the hassles of the court of appeal, the *qadi* would then tell the husband: "Now you have committed yourself to paying the agreed amount." This sentence, when it is written in the *sijil* (record), identifies the husband as the one who committed himself to paying the amount; thus, the amount does not appear to have been set by the *qadi*. The consequence is that the man would not be able to appeal the *qadi*'s decree because he was the one who committed himself to paying that amount of money and had signed the *sijil* stating that.

I also witnessed another strategy to convince a husband to accept the court's estimate of *nafaqa*. When a woman sues for *nafaqa*, the normal procedure (as we have seen) is for the court to estimate the amount due and to convince the husband to accept it. If either party does not accept the sum offered, the *qadi* calls on each party to provide a representative (from his/her family) who, together with a court representative, will estimate how much alimony should be paid. If this proposal is also rejected by one of the parties, the *qadi* tells them that there is only one alternative: he will nominate a three-member committee from within the court (a court committee) to go to the husband's house and his place of employment to check his income. This would entail transport costs, which would have to be paid by the husband in addition to the *nafaqa*. It is also possible for the court's committee to set a higher amount than that initially suggested. Faced with this threat, the husband may either accept the amount first suggested or try to reconcile himself with his wife (with the full encouragement of the *qadi*), thus minimizing his losses. In this way, the *qadi* uses negotiation, threat and force to arrive at a solution that enables him to feel that he is complying with religion, family law, customs and norms, while preserving the institution of the family as best he can.

What is significant in the *qadis*' conduct in Gaza is that although they apply family law as such in their judgments, they are highly sensitive to the social context. Therefore, when they find that the family law does not help to solve a problem, they turn to the principles of sharia such as *istislah* and *istihsan* in their wider significance; they turn to customary practices or adopt "progressive" attitudes that take the complexity of "modern" life into consideration.[20] For example, when couples go before a *qadi* to sign their marriage contract, he asks them if they have married before even though he knows that the text of the family law does not oblige him to do so because it allows a man to marry more than one woman without his wives' knowledge or acceptance. The *qadi* asks this question to both the man and the woman, but of course the purpose is to get the man to say whether he has another wife or not in the presence of the bride. When I asked Qadi Mohammed Faris about this, he answered: "Yes, our intention is to make sure that the bride knows whether she is marrying a married man or not, because the contract necessitates honesty and fidelity from both sides." It is interesting that this "progressive interpretation" of the marriage contract is different from the public discourse of the *qadi* during the 1997–8 Model Parliament campaign to reform the family law.[21] At that time, the *qadi* opposed the proposal made by feminists that a husband should be obliged to disclose his marital situation to the new bride as well as inform his current wife about his intention to marry again. They interpreted the proposal as being against the rights assigned by Islam to men.[22]

Qadis also help the women who come before them by advising them on how to handle their cases. I attended a case involving a woman who had married a Palestinian living in Bahrain. She lived with him for two months and then returned to Gaza because of his ill-treatment of her. She filed a case for *nafaqa*, knowing that it would be very difficult to reach him and oblige him to pay, but in the hope that she would then be able to get a divorce on the basis of his not paying the *nafaqa*. When she came before the *qadi*, he asked her, "What do you want? If you want *nafaqa*, you know that there is little possibility of obtaining it. But if you have a different intention, let me know because in that case I can help you." So she told him that she wanted to be divorced as soon as possible. He then advised her to file for divorce on the grounds of the husband's absence. When I asked Qadi Muhammad Naji why he had given her that advice, he said: "If a woman wants a divorce because she does not receive *nafaqa*, that takes time, much longer than a divorce on the grounds of absence. I wanted to make the case easier and quicker for her."[23]

Judgments going beyond the codified text are also given in cases that involve women working outside the home. The family law makes women's work outside the home conditional on the husband's permission, but the *qadis* deem that when a man marries a working woman, he effectively accepts that situation and cannot expect the court to support his refusal to let the wife continue working. In one case, a husband filed for divorce because his wife refused to obey his demand that she stop working outside the home. The man was a manager at one of the top hotels in Gaza and did not need his wife's salary. When I talked to the wife, she said the real reason for her husband's demand was that he wanted to divorce her without accepting the financial consequences of his decision. Her deferred dower and *tawabi'* were 6,000 JD each.[24] Qadi Al-Juju dismissed the husband's case in front of his wife, telling him that he had not provided sufficient reason for divorce due to *nushooze* (divorce due to disobedience).[25] Later, the *qadi* told me that he suspected the man had wanted to have his wife declared *nashis* (disobedient) by the court so that he could divorce her without meeting his financial obligations to her. It was clear that the *qadi* was conversant with contemporary gender relations and had taken them into account when ruling on the case. Thus, he had used *istislah* and *istihsan* as a means to contextualize the sharia and arrived at a judgment that would be fair to the victim.

Qadis in Gaza are thus, to some extent, open to developments in society. This is demonstrated by a discussion I heard between Qadi Al-Juju and a lawyer representing a non-governmental organization (NGO) that provides a physical space for divorced parents to see their children. (The only alternative for divorced parents to see their children is at a police station.) The *qadi* made several suggestions to the lawyer on how to improve the space provided by the NGO. He pointed out that if facilities were made available where children could play and have fun, it would be much friendlier. Families could eat together. A TV and a video player could be installed to show parents films about other cases like theirs, which might influence them to get together again. Al-Juju also suggested that the NGO could set up a hotline to provide advice on raising children and on marital problems.

My observation of the court proceedings showed that *qadis* are genuinely sensitive to the emotional aspects of the disputes brought before them. In one case, Qadi Al-Juju was asked to declare a couple divorced before they had consummated their marriage, which made it a revocable divorce (*baynuna sughra*). The woman had brought to court her prompt dower in addition to the gifts she had received. The *qadi* checked to make sure that they were all there and then handed them over to the husband. During the divorce proceedings, a male friend of the husband started crying and the *qadi* told him: "Don't worry, don't cry, he can have her back within a few minutes if somebody intervenes and brings them back onto the right track."

Qadis further try to ensure that litigants are not exploited by their lawyers. I have often been told by lawyers that *qadis* like them to be honest and professional, and to serve the public (particularly women) well. Once, I heard a *qadi* scolding a lawyer for what he regarded as unprofessional behavior: "I want you to take this case without charging the woman, because she is poor. You have been selfish and have taken high fees from other women in the past."

Implicit strategies are also used by the *qadi* to help the weak party to get a better deal. I witnessed a case in which a woman had filed for *nafaqa* but did not appear in court for the hearing. The *qadi* asked the doorman whether he knew her address or telephone number. When the doorman said he did, the *qadi* asked him to phone her and remind her of the hearing. The husband, who was present in the court, asked the *qadi* to postpone the case because of his wife's absence, but the *qadi* gently told him: "Your wife must be busy preparing your children for school." The *qadi* waited until the woman arrived about an hour later, and then started hearing the case after reminding her to respect the court's timetable.

In another case, when a man who was petitioning for custody over his children appeared in court only five minutes late, the *qadi* postponed the hearing, telling him that he should respect the court's timetable. These cases demonstrate the *qadis'* attitudes towards the litigants. A woman might lose her case and a man might win his, but what is important is how the *qadis* behave with different litigants.

Qadis are not the only court members who play their protective roles in the sharia courts. The scribe who sits at the door of the court and is assigned the duty of writing down the claims of the litigants, translates the women's anger over their problems into a passionate, loaded discourse framing their cases in a way that it portrays them as victims of their spouses. Some litigants were so pleased with his description that they exclaimed they would not have been able to write their cases so well themselves. He frequently answers women's questions about the best legal approach and he offers such advice free of charge.

The doorman who calls the women to the courtroom does not shout out their names, to save them from public embarrassment. He does not allow male litigants to enter the women's waiting room, another expression of his protective behavior. His knowledge of the court system enables him to offer advice to any woman who asks him for counsel. He frequently volunteers to persuade lawyers to represent poor women free. I even witnessed him consoling a woman who had lost her case, telling her that he would "speak" about her case to a member of the court of appeal and advising her to approach that specific member.

Clerks working in different departments of the court behave in the same way. Their familiarity with the problems of female litigants makes them sympathetic when approached by women. For example, the archive staff do not turn away or look down on women who need a copy of a divorce document, while in the social milieu of Gaza, divorced women are regarded negatively. Abu Wael, who is responsible for the divorce documents, demonstrated the stance of the court clerks in the following incident. Once, I asked him about the case of a specific women and he answered: "She is *hurma, waleya* [connotes a weak woman needing protection] from Hebron [in the West Bank]. She has nobody in Gaza... If he [her husband] insists on divorcing her, I will make him pay all her rights."

Conclusion

As we have seen, *qadis* do not stick rigidly to family law when ruling on cases. They exercise a degree of discretion to ensure that litigants receive justice. The family law sets out guidelines for *qadis* to follow, but how they interpret and apply these guidelines is dependent not only on the text of the law, but also on the specific case, the power resources of the litigants, their identities, their economic conditions, and most importantly, the *qadi*'s philosophy of what constitutes justice. The family law acts as a medium through which the *qadi* exercises his "reasonable" autonomy. The *qadi*'s discretion is not necessarily based on gender equality. My observation showed that the *qadis* perceive themselves as having been given the responsibility to preserve the social order and to protect the victim. Respecting the social order also means taking into account the weight and relations between the parties' respective kin groups.

The most important question to ask now is: were the developments after the establishment of the nation-state really a break with the traditional flexibility and fluidity of Islamic jurisprudence?[26] More specifically, has the codification of law really, as claimed, had a drastic impact on women's rights? If women's rights have suffered in the twentieth century, are the reasons really related to the state's codification of law? Should we try to find an explanation for the weakening of women's rights in the legal sphere or should we look for it in other areas? Unfortunately, this question is not the focus of my study. However, I would like to mention again that my ethnographic research in the sharia court suggests that Islamic law as codified does not in itself provide a satisfactory reason for the weakening of women's rights in modern Palestinian society.

I believe that women's rights have not suffered in the modern era because of the codification of law but rather for reasons that lie in areas less related to Islamic law, Islamic family law, and the codification of law. Reading the history of Islamic law is needed to answer contemporary questions, as suggested by Tucker (1998), with whom I agree fully, but it is also necessary to adopt a suitable and more people-centered methodology that helps to answer such questions. In other words, to understand the women's position in the modern era, it is not enough to point to the codification of the law as the sole reason for their oppression. Instead, we need to see how *qadis* and lawyers struggle to maintain the concept of fairness on the one hand and answer the difficult questions of the contemporary world on the other. The present-day *qadis* of Gaza City court not only have studied their own heritage, but also incorporate the necessities of modern life into their judgments and treatment of litigants. Contrary to Tucker's assumption that *qadis* have now lost their subjectivity, Gaza *qadis* are still loyal to the heritage of Islamic law, which asserts the concepts of fairness, of considering the context, and of protecting the weak. However, they are also still loyal to the heritage of Islamic law which draws a sharp division in gender roles and responsibilities.

Notes

1. For the definition of sharia, Vikør (1998) rightly argues that there is no clear idea about what constitutes the "Sharia." It has never been defined or collected in a systematic

manner or in a single written body of work. The Sharia is best understood as shared ideas of Islamic society, based on a literature that is broad but not necessarily consistent or approved by any single authority. He points out that this situation contrasts with the legal systems in the contemporary world, where the law is defined as a systematic set of sections written into a code and authorized by a specific elected body. However, the Sharia does not have such a specific form; therefore, it is known as an uncodified set of laws. For Muslims in Palestine, the legal relations inside the institution of family is regulated by family law and implemented by sharia court. Sharia courts deal with personal status issues, such as marriage, divorce, inheritance, custody, etc. Family law is regulated according to sharia and codified in the form of The Ottoman Islamic Law of Family Rights 1917 and the Gaza Law of Family Rights 1954. The public perceive the court as a religious institution because of two reasons: first, the family law is derived from Islamic sharia, and second, because the judges are graduated from Islamic religious studies.

2. For example, Sanadjian (1996), Sonbol (1996) and Tucker (1998).

3. Later, I will explain this term.

4. For the West Bank, the Jordanian Law of Personal Status, gazetted in 1976. For the Gaza Strip, the Gaza Law of Family Rights, issued by the Egyptian governor-general in 1954.

5. Until now, the Sharia courts have utilized Islamic law on personal status on the basis of the writings of four classical Sunni schools of law (Hanafi, Hanbali, Malki, Shafi'i). The Ottomans gave formal precedence to the Hanafi school, and hence it was the basis of the first codification of Islamic family law to be issued and implemented as state legislation in the Ottoman law of family rights (Welchman 1999)

6. As defined by the *Encyclopaedia of Arabic Civilisation* (Stephan and Ronart 1959: 389).

7. "Codified law cannot, by definition, be flexible and fluid law" (Tucker 1998: 184).

8. "Legal codes no longer offer a variety of possible interpretations; rather they work to standardise cases and minimise the judicial subjectivity" (Tucker 1998: 184).

9. "[A]s soon as the law is codified, gendered rights and gendered duty become incontrovertible points of law, brooking no adjustments or modifications except from on high" (Tucker 1998:185).

10. "The prior history of Islamic legal practice ... in which the interpretative powers of the muftis, the discretion of the *qadis* ... comes to resemble, indeed, an artefact without much relevance to the new legal systems in the various states in which codified Islamic law governs family matters" (Tucker 1998: 185).

11. "[T]he ability of any individual woman to seek a legal judgement tailored to the specifics of her case is greatly reduced in the context, on the one hand, of impersonal codes and courts that are charged with strict and accurate application of the law, and, on the other hand, the obsolescence of the institution of the community based mufti" (Tucker 1998: 185).

12. "[T]he process of codifying Islamic law must entail the enshrinement of a gendered right and privilege without the accompanying flexibility and judicial activism that had been the hallmarks of Islamic justice" (Tucker 1998: 186).

13. "The legal system that permitted *such flexibility is nowhere to be seen today,* nor it is really conceivable in the context of contemporary society." (Tucker 1998: 186, italics added).

14. Another social element that requires the *qadis* to depend on customary practice is the relative isolation of the Gaza Strip from the outer world and the higher degree of conservatism among the population. Unlike the West Bankers, who have "comparatively" easier mobility between the West Bank and Jordan and consequently to the outer world, Gazans are used to facing enormous difficulties to get out of their tiny strip. The West Bankers also had the "privilege" of being treated as Jordanians for a long time, having access to a Jordanian passport even when they were under occupation, while Gazans were able to move out of Gaza only when they had the ambiguous travel document provided by the Egyptian state. Gazans, moreover, tend to move to the Gulf countries, "especially Saudi Arabia," and are exposed to their conservative culture, while the West Bankers have been exposed to relatively liberal societies such as Iraq, Syria, Lebanon and Jordan. I have often heard Gazan "intellectuals" complaining that Gazans live in a big prison where the only interaction with the outer world is through their relatives, who come every summer from the Gulf countries carrying with them, in addition to their gifts, more conservative and conservatively interpreted religious beliefs about society and social norms.

15. I am borrowing the term *organization* from Long (1992) and intentionally using it to emphasize that the court is a field for power struggle between different actors with different interests. Viewing the court as a social organization means observing a set of social arrangements being worked out between the parties involved. The court in this sense is "made up of a complex of social practices and normative and conceptual models, both formal and informal" (Long 1992: 36).

16. For more information regarding the *kafa'a* principle, see for instance Welchman (1999: 97–102), who summarizes the *hanfi* rules in this regard, which has been incorporated in the Ottoman Islamic Law of Family Rights 1917, Jordanian Law of Personal Status 1976 and the Law of Family Rights 1954 (applied in Gaza).

17. Qadi Hasan Al-Juju in an interview with him during my fieldwork in 2002; Al-Juju is a practicing *qadi* in the Gaza City Sharia court.

18. The *kateb* is the scribe who is responsible for writing up the cases in the court record. Most of the *katebs* are graduates of sharia colleges, who start their professions as *qadis* by acting initially as *katebs* in order to bridge the gap between their theoretical knowledge of Islamic law and its actual practice in the sharia court. The *katebs* often go beyond their specific duty of writing up the cases; they may intervene in the case proceedings, clarifying issues to the litigants, reminding the *qadis* of missing information, proposing some practical alternatives, or advising the parties to take specific actions. The *qadis* pay considerable attention to the *katebs'* views; however, the specific wording of the cases is dictated (word by word) by the *qadi*.

19. Each 1 JD (Jordanian dinar) equals 1.6 dollars.

20. The principle of *istihsan* (seeking the most equitable solution) and the principle of *istislah* (seeking the solution that will best serve the public interest) are both considered

to be among the bases of Islamic *ijtihad* (interpretation of Koran and Sunna) (Dwyer 1990: 2). The space limits of this chapter prevent me from expanding my argument to discuss the controversial debate around the issue of *ijtihad*.

21. The Model Parliament project was the culmination of four years of work by a number of women's organizations and human rights centers which reviewed gender-based discriminatory laws and proposed and lobbied for amendments to them, in addition to raising the consciousness of women about their legal rights. It was established in 1997 with the aim of proposing Palestinian laws and legislation based on equality and human rights. The specific objective of the Model Parliament's campaign in Gaza focused on family law reform.

22. This dual discourse concerning family law constitutes a core part of my PhD study.

23. Before codification, divorce was a territory of men. The first attempt to interfere was in 1917 with the Ottoman Law of Family Rights, when Ottomans delineated the situations where women could also request the *qadi* to dissolve the marriage bond (*tatleeq qad'i*). My research in the archives of the sharia court of Gaza City suggests that most of the situations upon which women request judicial divorce are related to non-payment of *nafaqa*. I explore this issue in detail in my dissertation. As for the process of codification it was in fact a historical process involving complex interaction, in theory history and local practice, between legal norms and systems. These were known by some authors and activists as *takhayyur* (selection) and by others as *talfiq* (fabrication). Codification is further explored in my dissertation.

24. The dower is the financial right of women. Once the marriage contract is signed, women are expected to receive their dowers. The dower is divided into two parts: first, the prompt dower is received by the bride either shortly before signing the contract or immediately after it. In contemporary Palestine, families tend to divide the prompt dower into two parts: the cash dower, which is used to buy clothes and gold for the bride, and *tawabi'*, which is used to buy furniture. The second financial right of women is her defer dower, which should be received after divorce or after the death of the husband (deducted from overall inherited wealth). When a man decides to divorce his wife unilaterally, he should pay the *tawabi'* (as part of the prompt dower) and the defer dower.

25. The institution of house of obedience is established on the equation by which maintenance is the husband's responsibility and obedience the wife's duty. Article 40 of the Family Law of Gaza Strip specifies that "The wife is obliged to live in her Shar'ee [legal] husband's house after she receives her dower, she is obliged to travel with him if there is no reason for not doing so. The husband has to treat his wife well and she has to obey him." Article 66 states that "if the wife becomes *nashiz* and left her husband's house, she has no right to *nafaqa* during the period of her disobedience."

26. I am referring to the establishment of the nation-state as shorthand to refer to the codification of sharia in the form of family law. Palestine, despite its status as being under occupation, does not differ from other Muslim and Arab states in that sense; the sharia is applied in the form of codified law, the Law of Family Rights 1954 in Gaza and the Personal Status Law 1976 in the West Bank.

References

Ahmad, L. (1992), *Women and Gender in Islam: Historical Roots of a Modern Debate*, New Haven, CT: Yale University Press.

Dwyer, D. H. (1990), "Law and Islam in the Middle East: An Introduction," in D. H. Dwyer (ed.), *Law and Islam in the Middle East*, New York: Bergin and Garvey.

Long, N. (1992), "From Paradigm Lost to Paradigm Regained," in N. Long and A. Long (eds), *Battlefields of Knowledge: The Interlocking of Theory and Practice in Social Research and Development*, London and New York: Routledge.

Sanadjian, M. (1996), "A Public Flogging in South-western Iran: Juridical Rule, Abolition of Legality and Local Resistance," in O. Harris (ed.), *Inside and Outside the Law: Anthropological Studies of Authority and Ambiguity*, London: Routledge.

Sonbol, A. (1996), "Adults and Minors in Ottoman Sharia Courts and Modern Law," in A. Sonbol (ed.), *Women, the Family and Divorce Laws in Islamic History*, Syracuse, NY: Syracuse University Press.

Stephan, S. and Ronart, N. (1959), *The Encyclopaedia of Arabic Civilisation*, Amsterdam: Djambatan.

Tucker, J. (1998), *In the House of Law: Gender and Islamic Law in Ottoman Syria and Palestine*, Berkeley, CA: University of California Press.

Vikør, K. (1998), *The Sharia and the Nation State: Who Can Codify the Divine Law?*, http://www.hf-fak.uib.no/institutte4r/smi/pao/vikor.html.

Welchman, L. (1999), *Islamic Family Law: Text and Practice in Palestine*, Jerusalem: Women's Centre for Legal Aid and Counselling (WCLAC).

2

From the Army of G-d to the Israeli Armed Forces: An Interaction between Two Cultural Models

Yohai Hakak

Introduction

This chapter explores the interaction between Haredi cadets and the Israeli army system, during a basic army-training course for Haredi young men.[1] The Haredi cadets arrive with a masculine model which in many aspects is totally different and even contrary to that of the army. I will show the ways the Haredi cadets react to the army discourse and practices and the occasions in which they choose to internalize it, or resist, subvert and reshape it. As a whole it will be shown that during the basic training course the Haredi cadets reshape Haredi masculinity. In contrast to the fears of the Haredi rabbis, it seems that the basic training course does not enhance secularization, and for many of them it even encourages the re-enactment of Jewish heroism, and encourages them to strengthen their religiosity and observance.

Under the circumstances of the prolonged Israeli–Palestinian conflict, army service is still considered as the main civil duty of Israeli citizens. The fact that Haredi youth only rarely serve in the army – in contrast to the majority of other Jewish Israeli youth – is one of the major friction points within Israeli society.[2] In the eyes of the Haredi religious leaders there are two main reasons for not serving in the army: first, army bases, which bring together secular and religious men and women, are considered as enhancing secularization; second, as the State of Israel's army, the Israeli Defense Force (IDF) is identified with Zionist ideology, which like many other modern national movements aims to exchange the attachment to G-d and religion with an attachment to a nation, rendering G-d and spiritual aspects redundant (Liebman and Don-Yehiya 1983). Instead, rationalistic views prevail by which other earthly issues – such as the quality, sophistication and readiness of the weaponry and soldiers – are more relevant. Man and not G-d plays the central role. Haredi rabbis claim that this set of beliefs and assumptions creates a cultural male model whose internal experience is described by them through a quote from the book Deuteronomy (8:17) in the Bible: "My power, and the might of my hand has brought me this wealth." Haredi rabbis fear that these perceptions and values will influence young Haredi men. Many of the cadets I met shared these fears.

On the other hand, due to many years of religious education, the cadets have well internalized the Haredi cultural ideal male model, which holds to values, beliefs and assumptions that in many cases are very different and even contrary to those of the army. This model requires the Haredi man to surrender to G-d's commandments and thus achieve ultimate freedom and protection (Baron 1999). One of the most important commandments is the study of the Torah, which is believed to be the only real guarantee to the protection and well-being of the Jewish people. As a rule, spiritual matters, of which Torah study is their culmination, are considered to be of much higher value than the more earthly ones.

In Chapter 2 I will explore several aspects of the complex interaction between the two cultural models. I show how when the Haredi cadets face aspects of the military Zionist masculinity, which threatens their ability to practice their religiosity or contradict one of its fundamentals, they unite, resist and reject these aspects, while paradoxically strengthening their Jewish masculinity through re-enacting Jewish religious heroism. On the other hand, when they face aspects of the military-Zionist masculinity, which are not perceived as religiously threatening, they internalize and incorporate them for their own needs. Finally, I show how at the end of training, when the cadets are more self-assured with their ability to cope with the army, the shared Haredi identity that helped them unite is less needed and the friction between the different religious and ethnic subgroups become more apparent.

The Haredi Community, Masculinity and Soldierhood

The Haredi community is estimated to be 6–10 percent of the 6 million people living in Israel, but their percentage in the total number of new recruits every year is much lower – about a quarter of 1 percent – several hundreds every year. The arrangements enabling the Haredi community to avoid the recruitment to the IDF were set shortly after the establishment of the state of Israel. Apparently they were established out of a belief that the Jewish state had a duty to rebuild the world of Torah and the Haredi community that was almost wiped out in the Holocaust, and out of the attempts to include the religious parties in parliamentary coalitions. At first about 400 deferrals were approved to yeshiva students but this tendency later gained momentum as the population of the community grew significantly and as this growth was translated into the electoral strength of the Haredi parties.[3] These days, the yearly number of deferrals for Haredi men is about 30,000.

The main importance of this non-enlistment is not the way it influences the army, but is symbolic. By choosing not to participate in what is still looked upon as the most significant of all national obligations, members of the Haredi community have reinforced their marginality and have created resentment in those social sectors that do serve in the military (Cohen 1999). The widespread Haredi avoidance of the army service has its price, and many state and other jobs are denied to the Haredi men who do not serve in the army. Due to this fact, a small minority of Haredi men who decide to leave the yeshivas and go to work do opt to be drafted – usually at a much older age and for shorter periods of time – as a way of improving their job opportunities.[4] This was the main motivation for the cadets I will mention here. Mainly due to the growing economic crisis the Haredi community has been going through in recent years (Horowitz 2002: 19), the number of young Haredi men who leave the yeshivas and go to work is growing, as is the number of Haredi recruits to the army. This is done much to the dismay of the rabbis, who wish to maintain the Israeli reality of the last few decades in which the religious scholar was the only normative male model for Haredi men, at least until several years after their marriage.

In many cultures there are strong ties between soldierhood and manhood or masculinity (Arkin and Dobrofsky 1978; Morgan 1994; Mosse 1996). This connection is especially strong within the Israeli society and shapes its hegemonic male model. The roots of this model are in the Zionist movement (Almog 2000) which wanted to end the persecution of Jews by making them a nation like all other nations. As part of this endeavor, Zionism attempted to get rid of the characteristics of exiled Jewish masculinity and create "Judaism of muscles" (Nordau 1902; see also Gluzman 1997). The new Zionist man is portrayed as closely resembling the warrior and soldier. He is physically strong, tough, assertive, capable of enduring pain, connected to his land and can protect it and his people in battle when needed, even if that involves a high personal price (Gal 1986; Ben-Ari 1998). This model maintains its hegemony also in present-day Israel (Sasson-Levi 2000).

Researchers who attempted to explore the way army training and service influence the cadets and soldiers used theories and ideas from the field of gender studies concerning the construction of masculine identity (Gilmore 1990; Badinter 1995). According to these ideas, in order to become a man, the boy needs to cross a critical edge and abandon his childhood. He also needs to go through a series of trials and tests. These tests require carriage, physical ability and self-control, and could include the possible struggle with other men, with nature or with one's self-limitations. In accordance with these ideas, researchers have examined the challenges, tests and internal dynamics, which compose the army service.[5]

Other researchers have stressed the cadets' and soldiers' ability to resist the demands of the army, and maintain a relative sense of agency (Feige and Ben-Ari 1991; Sasson-Levi 2000). As Connell (1987 1995) claims, every society offers one hegemonic masculine model and several competing alternative models, which all strive for the hegemony. This notion guided Lomski-Feder and Rapoport (2003), who explored the way the masculine model with which new immigrants from the former Soviet Union arrive to the Israeli army shapes their interaction with the Israeli hegemonic masculinity. They showed how the new immigrants resist the dictates of the army hegemonic masculinity, infantilize it and preserve their own original masculinity. Other researchers have also shown how one group of soldiers constructs their identity in relation to other groups of soldiers (Sasson-Levi 2000).

The interaction between two male cultural models will also be central to this chapter. The young Haredi cadets arrive in the army with an alternative male model to that of the army masculine model. Haredi masculinity has been shaped during the long Jewish history. The connection between the changing historical circumstances and Jewish masculinity has been explored in several studies (Gilman 1991; Eilberg-Schwartz 1992; Cantor 1995; Boyarin 1997; Jacob 1997). Here I will only mention some of the main conclusions arising from these studies. It seems that a major change in Judaism's relations to masculinity occurred after the destruction of the Second Temple and the exile that followed it. In exile, while Jewish men could not carry weapons, the definitions of masculinity changed. Real manhood was expressed in the ability to subdue and conquer ones own urges and drives, instead of subduing and conquering other men, through the use of physical force and fighting abilities. Jewish men were called to avoid conflicts – especially with other non-Jewish men – in order not to enrage the gentile authorities (Satlow 1996; Boyarin 1997). They are commonly described as effeminate, passive, bodily weak, hunched, with pale skin, and with no roots in a specific land.

The control and discipline of the body were perceived as necessary in order that the spiritual aspects could flourish. These tendencies became stronger during the Middle Ages due to Hellenist influences, which identified femininity with the body (Boyarin 1993). They became stronger with the appearance of Hassidism and the Moral Movement in the eighteenth and nineteenth centuries. The body was identified as the place of the evil urge and a possible host for profanity (Atkes 1982; Catz 1998 [1970]). With the import of the institutional model of the Volozin Yeshiva to Israel, and the making of it into the main barrier between the young Haredi youth and the secular world around them – these tendencies and perceptions were strengthened. These characteristics make Haredi masculinity different – and on many occasions even opposite – to the army masculinity.

In spite of these sharp tensions, the Haredi community's relationship to the army has been the subject of very little research. Friedman (1991) describes the Haredi relationship to the state as a threat, and the army as a secularizing agent. Stadler and Ben-Ari (2003) made a first attempt to explore yeshiva students' attitudes toward the possibility of serving in the army. They show that while the rabbis reject the idea, the young men have more ambivalent thoughts on the issue. This research is another step toward gaining the missing knowledge.

My fieldwork was carried out during one month of basic training for Haredi cadets in Israel in 1999. I joined a platoon of fifty Haredi cadets, all in their early twenties, and followed them during their training. At the end of training I interviewed fifteen of them. This research is part of my doctoral research, which deals with masculine identities in four different settings within this community. These settings are a Lithuanian yeshiva, which is the social site that constructs the ideal male model of the religious scholar, and three other newly emerged sites – an occupational training program in hi-tech professions, the Haredi headquarters at the right-wing Likud party, and the army basic training program I write about here. In my research as a whole I attempt to observe how the newly and growing appearance of Haredi men in these setting influences Haredi masculinity and society. The finding presentation will start with the cadet's reactions when they fear their religiosity or basic religious beliefs are being threatened. Then I will move to instances when they are less threatened religiously.

Discipline, De-individualization and Creating Unity

In order to discipline the cadets and imprint on them its demands, the army system strips them of their every day identity as part of a process of de-individualization. On the first day they are separated from their former surroundings and brought into a transitional army base were they change into army clothes and get their ID number. Then they are taken to the boot camp, which is a "total institution" (Goffman 1961) and where all of their needs are to be taken care of. They cannot leave the base and family visits are very limited.

In the boot camp the cadets are exposed to strict discipline, which involves a lot of pressure, threats and harassment. The power relations between the cadets and their commanders are very clear. The cadets are referred to and treated like infants, and in stark contrast, their commanders are presented as superhumans. During everyday interaction with the commanders, the cadets are barely allowed to ask questions. They should answer only when spoken to. All of this is true especially during the first few days when the commanders are setting the rules. Thus, despite my many requests, I was allowed to enter the base for the first time only on the third day. "We want to get a hold on them first," explained Motti, the lieutenant, implying the possible use of force he and his colleagues would not like me to witness.

Later on that third day, when a group of cadets who had a shift in the base kitchen refuse to wash the dishes of another non-Haredi platoon, the major is very angry. He assembles the whole platoon right away and scolds them harshly. He stresses that, "there will be no difference between one platoon to another. You will do what you are told." The major shouts at them and frightens many. The army's attempts to erase the special distinctions between the different cadet groups, which are also stressed in the major's words, repeat themselves on several other occasions in the first few days. After the major's harsh reprimand, the cadets are very anxious and angry. "I'm surprised the guys did not stand up to him," protests Avi. "If it wasn't only the third day, the guys would have left the place. Later on [the major] claimed that he did not know what sort of people he was dealing with. It gave us a blow – this is how you all treat us? So we will treat you all accordingly."

In a more typical pool of new recruits the separation of the cadets from their former environment, the continued de-individualization attempts, and the fact that the cadets don't know each other in advance leaves them unable to resist the disciplinary pressures. But in the case of the Haredi cadets, these efforts seem less successful. From Avi's words it is clear that he and his friends perceive themselves as a unique group of people, totally different from a regular cadet group. Their appearance with beards, big black skullcaps and side-locks distinguishes them visually, and their daily religious practices distinguish them further, both from other cadets, and from their commanders and staff. This fact enhances their ability to unite against the pressures they are exposed to and to respond to them. Just as Avi explained to me later on: "We have unity. We don't know each other from before, we came from different places in the country, but on certain issues we get together, and the commanders can't have it against us all." As expressed by Avi, this unity helps the cadets defend themselves and react. The use of unity as a strategy is characteristic of many minorities under threat, and has been highly developed by Jews in exile. Haredi rabbis still often emphasize this characteristic. As an example could serve the words of rabbi Baruch Mordechai Ezrahi, a leading Haredi yeshiva head, who wrote:

> This ability to unite is unique and preserved to the people of Israel... It is possible to be a part of Israel only while functioning as part of the community, the public. The other nations of the world have millions of individuals, but as for the people of Israel – even if it is only one person – he is considered as if he is a public, a group. This is why the people of Israel will always win over the other nations.[6]

In rabbi Ezrahi's words is implied the difference between the Western liberal tradition, which has as its basic cornerstone the Individual, and Judaism, which sees the Jewish community (Clal Yisrael) as the basic entity. Signs of unity among the cadets appeared very quickly.

On the morning of the fourth day the Haredi cadets make their way to one of the remote study rooms. Since the early hours of the morning they have been involved in an intense series of activities, and the hot weather is having its effect on them. Shahar the sergeant is giving them clear orders: "You have one minute to get organized under the shade in front of us, and to give me the attention call so that the whole base can hear you! Is it clear?!" "Yes sir," the cadets reply. "One minute!" shouts the sergeant again, "Go!" The cadets storm forward, get in line and give the attention call. "And you think that this is an attention call?!" asks the sergeant. "I said the whole base should hear it!" After two more attempts the sergeant is satisfied. He then orders them to raise their water canteens: "Drink half. I don't want you to get dehydrated on me." The cadets raise their water canteens but instead of drinking, they shout in unison the blessing for water as loudly as they possibly can: "Blessed be the Lord, our G-d, king of the Universe, through whose word everything came to be, amen," and then hastily drink the water. The sergeant, stunned by the unexpected text looks half angry, half bemused. He is a young sergeant and has never witnessed such a response, but he does not say a word and orders them to go to the study room.

The sergeant's demands to shout the attention call louder are part of the disciplinary process that every group of cadets goes through and which aims to adjust them to the expectations of the army. As part of the attempt to reduce uncertainty in every possible future battlefield, there is an attempt to transform body and behavior – which are considered as unexpected factors – into more controlled and expected ones. The cadet's decision to shout their blessing indicates their search for sources of power and autonomy within the limiting and demanding army setting. Here, the blessing before drinking water is part of their routine religious ritual life – which is formally acknowledged by the army. As they are aware of their rights they bring the religious text into the public sphere, while using the sergeant's previous demands to shout to express and present their unique Haredi voice. While doing so they enhance their autonomy in a situation in which their sergeant limits their freedom. The cadet's ability to unite was especially high around the religious practices and routines, as became much clearer only few hours later that day.

Zionist versus Jewish Heroism

In the evening of the fourth day the cadets learn that they are meant to stay at the base during the coming Sabbath and be on guard duty. This information troubles and enrages many of them. This would be for most of them the first time in their life not to observe the Sabbath. As a sacred time, one of the Sabbath's most important commandments is the avoidance of any work and secular activities. Indeed, they all knew well before that they would be required to stay one Sabbath at the base, but they thought it would be later on during the training period. Others have heard that a previous Haredi platoon protested and the Sabbath guard duty was canceled.

They all gather under one of the tents to find ways to cancel their impending stay at the base.

Yariv approaches the group with his cell-phone. "I called rabbi Moshe Grilack," he announces, "but he is abroad. I also called rabbi Joshua Pollack. He will look into it, but he thinks it's too late." Rabbi Grilack is an influential Haredi journalist and rabbi Pollack is an Haredi politician. Other names of influential Haredi people are mentioned.

As was shown by Bial (1980), pulling connections and creating political pressure were important sources of power in the difficult conditions of the Jewish existence during 2,000 years of exile. While in exile, Jews usually could not carry weapons for their protection. They had to find ways to gain protection from local authorities, often through using political means. As many Haredi rabbis still perceive life in Israel as exile among Jews, the Haredi community still preserves many similar practices and characteristics, at least in so far as its relationship with the state agencies and the non-Haredi parts of the population.

On the night of the fifth day the cadets are getting ready for a Jewish religious fast (the 17th of Tamuz) that will start at 3:00 a.m. The commanders, in an attempt to show consideration, wake up in the middle of the night and make sure that the food for the meal before the fast is brought straight to the cadets' tents 40 minutes before the beginning of the fast. The commanders perceive this as an act of generosity on their part, but the Haredi cadets have different views. They declare that because of their impending Sabbath guard duty they will not eat the food, and will not get up the following day for practice. In simple words they declare a non-violent and passive mutiny. The commanders in response wake up the lieutenant and together with him they explain to the cadets that if they do not stay, the base will be left unguarded. Only after a half of an hour of persuasion do the cadets give up and start eating.

The preservation of the Sabbath as a holy day has been central to many other disputes between Haredi and secular Jews in Israel. In the army context it unites the Haredi cadets against their non-Haredi commanders and helps them to increase their autonomy. Friedman (1991) have shown how after the Holocaust, as part of recovering from the destruction of the Jewish world, the different traditional Jewish sects have emphasized their shared Haredi identity on the account of the particular sect or subgroup identity. He also shows how as the Haredi community became stronger it gradually allowed for these particular groups to emphasize more fully their unique characteristics. Still, the shared history, the shared emphasis on the study of the Torah and the shared need to defend the Haredi social structure continues to unite the Haredi community, at least in its relations with the other parts of Israeli society.

Other religious practices, such as the Jewish dietary rules, and the time and place for prayer became also issues for negotiation and of which the cadets were the experts, and the ones who knew the rules better than their commanders. Several times they left the base dining room because one of them claimed there was some religious flaw with the food. As they knew very well all the complicated dietary rules, they had fierce arguments with the base rabbi, who was called for by their commanders. Since the army rabbis are orthodox – not Haredi (meaning not Ultra Orthodox) – the cadets claimed they were also less observant, and therefore not trustworthy. By the army laws, religious soldiers are entitled to receive time for prayer three times a day. But since the length of each prayer is different and also changes through the year, this opens another area for negotiation. As part of this, it happened that soldiers got an extra prayer time to say the blessing for the new moon five times in one month. Their commander was not aware of the fact that this prayer is said only when the moon is full.

I would like to claim here that the nature of the army base as a "total institution" and especially the demand to serve during the Sabbath made the cadets feel that their religiosity was in danger and forced them into acts of Jewish heroism – in contrast with army Zionist heroism. As I mentioned earlier, according to the literature that deals with Jewish masculinity from a historical perspective, it seems that Jewish religion did not give much acknowledgment to muscular prowess in and out of the battlefield. And if it did in certain streams, this acknowledgment diminished even further after the second destruction of the Temple and the exile that followed it, about 2,000 years ago (Boyarin 1997). Real manhood was expressed by the ability to conquer ones inner urges and drives and subdue them for a higher spiritual cause, mainly the work of G-d. Real heroism was the willingness to suffer and even sacrifice life for the sake of a religious belief. These values and perceptions are still central in the present-day Haredi community.

Zionist ideology on the other hand produced an ethos of martyrdom, in which the secular mourning for fallen soldiers was interwoven with a consciousness of historic continuity, whereby the entity above the individual became the nation, instead of G-d (Sivan 1991). Hence, death by *kidush ha-moledet* (sanctifying the homeland) replaced the long-standing tradition of *kidush ha-shem* – sanctifying and sacrificing one's life in the name of G-d (Fishbane 1994: 60). Since in present-day Israel the Haredi way of life is not threatened in any way there are very few opportunities for young Haredi men to experience Jewish heroism. This makes the army circumstances a unique opportunity where young Haredi men can re-enact Jewish heroism precisely through its positioning within the home territory of Zionist heroism – yet in contrast to it. I've shown here how the cadets reacted in response to the de-individualization attempts of the army setting, which made them feel their religiosity was in danger. Their religious practices and rituals helped them resist the disciplinary measures, and create autonomy within the limiting army setting, while re-enacting Jewish heroism.

Pride, Self-confidence and Heresy

In many instances the cadets' religiosity and ability to practice it were not threatened, but they met with situations they interpreted as dominated by heretical assumptions. Next I will show how they responded to these situations. On this ground they rejected different aspects of their commander's behavior and many aspects of the lessons they had. These problematic perspectives could be expressed through a body posture and movement of a commander who was too proud and self-assured and stood with his hands on his waist and his head lifted as if in pride. "It's like a pimp who goes with his chest wide open or a prostitute that jiggles her butt," explained Elad, "this is why we don't like it." In this case the commander's posture was experienced by the cadets as too demonstrative. The body in Haredi perspective, with all its importance, is considered as a destination for discipline and control in order to allow the spiritual aspects to flourish. The Haredi man is expected to

> always practice modesty... Even when he is alone in a darkened room, he should not say: "I am alone, who can see me"; for he is always in the presence of the Divine whose Glory fills the whole universe, and unto whom darkness is like light... He should not walk haughtily – with an outstretched neck – a sign of pride... By the manner of their walk you can distinguish between the wise and the foolish. (Gantzfried 1988)

In other cases, the heretical perspective was imbued in the commander's perceptions and explanations of reality and its determining powers. In one such case the commander was asked why when there are intelligence alerts about terrorists' plans to kidnap soldiers, soldiers who go home for a holiday don't take off their uniforms, and thus avoid the risk. The commander, being a product of the Zionist proud army education was appalled by the suggestion. He argued that he was carrying a gun, a pistol, and a hidden knife. In addition he mastered several fighting techniques. "No one can touch me," he concluded and was also deemed a heretic. The commander's over-confidence in his human power, while neglecting any attribution of the consequences to G-d was unacceptable in the eyes of the cadets and they expressed their feelings unfalteringly.

The Shooting Range

The cadets' interaction with the army system, and their responses to it, were more varied than one might think until now, and not always did they resist it. I will deal next with one of these instances. In addition to the army's attempts to discipline the cadets it also tries to give them different kinds of knowledge and skills. A few days further along their training I accompany the cadets to their first shooting drill. They are very excited and nervous. One of them, Yuval, starts singing quotes from a love song of one of the famous Israeli female singers, expressing his excitement: "I don't know what's happening to me. I'm shivering, I'm hot, I'm cold." His friend, Natan, steps aside from the group, opens up the book of Psalms, a prayer book, and reads: "I will lift up my eyes to the hills/Where does my help come from? / My help comes from Yahweh, / who made heaven and earth" (Psalms 121, A Song of Ascents.)

When they get to the shooting range, the commanders, fearful of shooting accidents, are very strict. Their lieutenant is giving orders about what they must do. Then he instructs them to lie on the floor and he shows them how to hold their weapon in this position. Finally the order to pull the trigger is given and the place is filled with a great noise. When they finish and unload their weapons, they head to the targets to check their achievements. Shahar, the sergeant, accompanies them and writes their scores in a little notebook. Elad, approaches me with glowing eyes. "My brother," he says while reaching out his hand to slap mine, "I scored five out of five, you can write that yeshiva students can shoot." The ones who scored less well are disappointed. "My weapon was stuck," explained Moshe, "so the sergeant came to help me. He fired one bullet so I was left with only four. Then I managed to hit with three of them, but I consider that as hitting four out of five." Elad, another cadet, was among the satisfied ones. "This is the first time I ever shot," he said with an excited look. "At the beginning I was nervous and did not do well, but sergeant David saw it and approached me. He put his hand on my shoulder and said, 'Cheer up brother,' and that's what did it. He gave me the courage and reassurance to shoot them all right in. I'll remember him for the rest of my life."

In accordance with the literature that describes masculinity as an achievement that is never guaranteed and always needs to be proved and reaffirmed (Badinter 1995), the shooting drill is one of these moments of desired reaffirmation. The cadets' ability to control their bodies and their weapon is also a test of their masculinity. The intensity of the feelings that were brought up by the drill indicates that the cadets ascribed real importance to this ability. This intensity of feeling is interesting due to the fact that according to the Haredi masculine model using a weapon has no importance and is even considered to be an undesired earthly capability, which the rabbis reject adamantly. The importance the cadets do ascribe to the shooting drill could be explained as the result of the fact that using a weapon in itself is only a technical capability, which they perceive as easily separated from heretical values. This tendency to use the instruments, and resources of the modern surrounding, while rejecting its values, is shared by many other fundamentalist groups. The excitement aroused by the shouting drill is also the result of a continuous import of new masculine characteristics from the wider

Israeli society into the Haredi community, and the revival of alternative and more assertive masculine voices from within the Jewish tradition.

As they leave after their basic training, the cadets take with them several aspects of this new masculine model to which they were exposed. As the cadet Jacob explained to me after the end of the training: "I believe that when you know how to hold a weapon and can respond to an attack – it's different. You don't feel that helpless … and it's important for your life later on. Even without a weapon you feel different." Like Jacob, many other cadets described the shooting drill and the basic training itself, as a series of difficult tests and their ability to cope with them successfully made them feel stronger in their lives outside the army base.

Lithuanians, Hassidim and Sephardim[7]

If at the beginning some of the cadets were frightened of the unknown military system, close to the end of the training they became much more self-assured as a group. At the beginning, and in order to protect themselves, the cadets emphasized their shared Haredi identity. As time passed the differences between the different religious and ethnic subgroups among them became more obvious. At the swearing in ceremony, the base commander called two of the Hassidic cadets to approach and receive the mark of excellence. Their friends cheered them and they were very excited.

Motti, the lieutenant, explained the reasons for choosing them to me: "Moshe went with a garbage bag in his hand throughout the whole month. He collected every piece of garbage he saw. He is very quiet, always on time, and doesn't make any problems. Shlomo is also very disciplined. He always did what he was told, was always on time and it was easy to work with him." From Motti's explanations it is clear that both of the Hassidic cadets were very disciplined and fulfilled all the orders they were given, in contrast to many of the other cadets, who were more resistant. This tendency required explanation. A possible one comes from Elimelech, one of the Hassidic cadets:

> I always felt that the staff were observing me more carefully and quickly than the others. The lieutenant told me at the beginning that he got my name quicker than the others… My appearance was more unique… 'The tall one with side locks and the beard – this is Elimelech'. They were looking at me as a Haredi and because of that I felt I must be very careful and set an example. I became more observant, I prayed with more intention.

I will not deal here with the complex theological, historical and social differences between the three main subgroups composing the Haredi community in present-day Israel. This has been done in many other studies. For the current discussion what is important is to mention the different appearance of each one of these subgroups and its relation with the outer world. Whereas the Lithuanians emphasize more adamantly the importance of the study of the Torah until a much older age, the Hassidim settle with shorter periods of study. The Lithuanians consider the study of the Torah as the main protector against the outer world temptations. The Hassidim "compensate" for their shorter period of study with more unique appearance that is meant specifically to differentiate them from their surrounding thus not enabling them to blend within it. All three groups have unique appearance, but the Hassidim also maintain the long side-locks and wild beards. These characteristics remain very visually obvious in army uniforms, distinguish them from the other Haredi cadets and expose them more to the inspecting eye of the commanders. The Hassidim maintain higher segregation in their own communities and their knowledge about the Israeli society is more limited. They are also much less fluent in Hebrew and many prefer Yiddish in everyday life. For these reasons their knowledge about the army, before conscription, is lesser even than the other cadets, and many still look at it as very alien territory. In these circumstances it is clearer why the Hassidim were more obedient as to the army's regulations and rules, than the other cadets.

While the Hassidim were receiving the mark of excellence, the Sephardim cadets were creating the opposite responses. One day before the end of the basic training the commanders gathered the cadets to a concluding talk with the base commander. The base commander gave the cadets an opportunity to express themselves and Yuval, one of the Sephardic cadets, took the opportunity and criticized the other commanders fiercely, thus embarrassing them in front of their own commander – the base commander. Later on I understand that his words enraged many of the other cadets who did not share his view and did not want to shame their commanders in such a way. A group of thirty of them – most of them Hassidic and Lithuanians – wrote an apologetic letter to their commanders and the base commander expressing their appreciation. This incident brought about the release of a lot of suppressed anger and dislike among the cadets themselves. The Hassidic and Lithuanian cadets – both from "Ashkenazi" Eastern European origin – criticized the Sephardim cadets. "They lived next to Arabs for many generations and they caught their habits," Elimelech explained to me, "The Ashkenazis lived in more civilized countries like Germany, Poland, Russia. Yuval, the guy who criticized the commanders, is a Sephardi and like many of them he has an inferiority complex. He always felt that they enslaved him. He and his friends never volunteered to do anything." Other Ashkenazi – Hassidic and Lithuanian – cadets added to the criticism. "To put us with the Sephardim is like to put us together with Bedouin cadets. These are two different mentalities. Our group (the Ashkenazi Lithuanian and Hassidim) was much better … better educated from home… Some of them were very unpleasant. It was difficult to be with them."

As the training was coming to an end and the cadets felt secure enough in their relations with their commanders, there was no need to keep the close unity as at the beginning stages. Other divisions within the group also became clear, such as a division between the married and unmarried cadets, and those who were born in Israel and those who immigrated to it. But these differences will be dealt with elsewhere.

Conclusion

To conclude, I have shown several aspects of the complicated interaction between the Haredi cadets with their cultural male model, and the army setting and its own cultural male model. I have shown how the cadets reacted in response to the de-individualization attempts of the army setting, which made them feel their religiosity was in danger. Their religious practices and rituals helped them unite and resist the disciplinary measures, creating autonomy within the limiting army setting, while re-enacting Jewish heroism. For that, they had to emphasize their shared Haredi identity on the account of their particular ethnic and sub-religious identities. Next I have shown how the cadets also rejected the hidden modern and heretical and unG-dly assumptions and values they observed in the army setting. Their responses were very different in relation to technical knowledge and skills – such as using weapons – since it was not perceived as loaded with heretical values. As I have shown, the whole experience was perceived as enhancing their self-assurance as men, while also allowing them to re-enact Jewish heroism, making them more assured of their religiosity. Towards the end the need for unity decreased and this allowed for the differences and controversies between the subgroups to be expressed. In contrast to the fears of the rabbis, it is clear that the cadets were not secularized through this basic training course, and in many aspects their religiosity was even strengthened. At the same time they are changing the army setting itself too. Indeed, through the whole experience Haredi men do reshape the characteristics of Jewish Haredi masculinity, making it resemble Israeli Masculinity more, yet still separated from it. The growing number of Haredi young men who are drafted to the army and then go to work, instead of continuing their religious studies, will gradually strengthen the legitimacy of this alternative male model in the Haredi community. These changes are part of a whole series of changes this community is going through in the current Israeli context.

Acknowledgment

Notes

1. Haredi is the singular for Haredim – the Haredi Jews. The word "hared" means tremble and comes from the book of Isaiah (66:5): "Hear the word of the LORD, you who tremble at his word." I use the Hebrew term "Haredi" (and not Ultra Orthodox Jews) because members of the community use it to characterize themselves, and because it is a broader classification which encompasses not only the Eastern European groups but also mainstream orthodoxy in Israel. See for example in M. Friedman (1993), "The Haredim and the Israeli Society," in J. Peters and K. Kyle (eds) *Whither Israel: The Domestic Challenges* (London: Royal Institute of International Affairs and Tauris), p. 177. S. C. Heilman and M. Friedman (1991), *The Haredim in Israel* (New York: American Jewish Committee). H. Soloveitchik (1994), "Rupture and Reconstruction: The Transformation of Contemporary Orthodoxy," *Tradition*, 28(4): 105. For the historical perspective see M. K. Silber (1992), "The Emergence of Ultra-Orthodoxy: The Invention of a Tradition," in J. Wertheimer (ed.), *The Uses of Tradition: Jewish Continuity in the Modern Era* (New York: Jewish Theological Seminary of America) p. 23, footnote 4. And also, M. Samet (1987), "Orthodoxy," *Kivunim*, pp. 99–115 (Hebrew).
2. For a review of the history of this conflict and the attempts to solve it see Ilan (1999).
3. For more information about the numbers of deferrals see Ilan (1999).
4. Usually the term yeshiva relates to religious seminaries for unmarried young men. After marriage, men go to Kolel, but here I will use the term yeshiva for both institutions.
5. For research on those issues in the Israeli context see Sion (1997) and Ben-Ari and Dardashti (2001). These researchers related to the army service and training as a series of tests ad trials that after the soldier pass them he wins the desired masculinity.
6. Ezrahi, B. M. (1998) *Mordechai's Blessing*, Jerusalem: Yad-Meir Institute.
7. The name "Lithuanians" comes from the name of the place of origin of this religious subgroup – Lita in eastern Europe. Hassidism originated also in eighteenth-century Eastern Europe by the Baal-Shem-Tov. The term "Sephardim" relates to Jews who originated from Arab countries.

References

Almog, O. (2000), *The Sabra: The Creation of the New Jew*, Berkeley, CA: University of California Press.

Arkin, W. and Dobrofsky, L. R. (1978), "Military Socialization and Masculinity," *Journal of Social Issues*, 34(1): 151–68.

Atkes, E. (1982), *Rabbi Yisrael Meir Salanter and the Beginning of the Musar Movement*, Jerusalem: Magnes Press (Hebrew).

Badinter, E. (1995), *X Y, on Masculine Identity*, New York: Columbia University Press.

Baron, M. (1999), "Real Willpower or an Evil Urge: The Perception of Freedom of Two Haredi Rabbis," *Hagut Behinuh Yehudi*, (a): 98–125 (Hebrew).

Ben-Ari, A. (1998), *Mastering Soldiers: Conflict, Emotions and the Enemy in an Israeli Military Unit*, Oxford: Berghahn.

—— and Dardashti, G. (2001), "Tests of Soldierhood, Trials of Manhood: Military Service and Male Ideals in Israel," in D. Maman, Z. Rosenhak and E. Ben-Ari (eds), *Military, State and Society in Israel: Theoretical and Comparative Perspectives*, New Brunswick, NJ: Transaction.

Bial, D. (1980), *Power and Powerlessness in Jewish History*, Urbana, IL: University of Illinois Press.

Boyarin, D. (1993), *Carnal Israel: Reading Sex in Talmudic Culture*, Berkeley, CA: University of California Press.

—— (1997), *Unheroic Conduct: The Rise of Heterosexuality and the Invention of the Jewish Man*, Berkeley, CA: University of California Press.

Cantor, A. (1995), *Jewish Woman/Jewish Man: The Legacy of Jewish Patriarchy*, San Francisco, CA: HarperCollins.

Catz, D. (1998 [1970]), *The Musar Movement: Its History, Sages and Methods*, Jerusalem: Weise Press (Hebrew).

Cohen, S. (1999), "From Integration to Segregation: The Role of Religion in the IDF," *Armed Forces and Society*, 35(3): 387–405.

Connell, R. W (1987), *Gender and Power*, Cambridge: Polity Press.

—— (1995), *Masculinities*, Cambridge: Polity Press.

Eilberg-Schwartz, H. (1992), *People of the Body: Jews and Judaism from an Embodied Perspective*, New York: State University of New York Press.

Feige, M. and Ben-Ari, E. (1991), "Card Games and an Israeli Army Unit: An Interpretive Case Study," *Armed Forces and Society*, 17(3): 429–48.

Fishbane, M. (1994), *The Kiss of G-d: Spiritual and Mystical Death in Judaism*, Seattle, WA: University of Washington Press.

Friedman, M. (1991), *The Haredi Society: Sources, Trends and Processes*, Jerusalem: Jerusalem Institute for the Research of Israel (Hebrew).

Gal, R. (1986), *A Portrait of the Israeli Soldier*, New York: Greenwood Press.

Gantzfried, S. (1988), *The Shortened Shulhan Aruch*, Jerusalem: Orot Haim.

Gilman, S. (1991), *The Jew's Body*, New York: Routledge.

Gilmore, D. D. (1990), *Manhood in the Making: Cultural Concepts of Masculinity*, New Haven, CT: Yale University Press.

Gluzman, M. (1997), "The Yearning for Heterosexuality: Zionism and Sexuality in Altnoylend," *Theory and Criticism*, 11: 145–63.

Goffman, E. (1961), *Asylums*, Garden City, NY: Doubleday.

Horowitz, N. (2002), *Our Town is Burning: Haredi Politics between the Elections of 1999 and 2000*, Jerusalem: Floersheimer Institute for Policy Studies.

Ilan, S. (1999), *Deferment of Recruitment of Yeshiva Students: A Proposal for Policy*, Jerusalem: Floersheimer Institute for Policy Studies.

Jacob, L. (1997), "The Body in Jewish Worship: Three Rituals Examined," in S. Coakly (ed.), *Religion and the Body*, Cambridge: Cambridge University Press.

Liebman, C. S and Don-Yehiya, E. (1983), *Civil Religion in Israel: Traditional Judaism and Political Culture in the Jewish State*, Berkeley, CA: University of California Press.

Lomsky-Feder, E. and Rapoport, T. (2003), "Juggling Models of Masculinity: Russian-Jewish Immigrants in the Israeli Army," *Sociological Inquiry*, 73(1): 114–37.

Morgan, D. H. J. (1994), "Theater of War: Combat, the Military, and Masculinities," in H. Brod and M. Kaufman (eds), *Theorizing Masculinities*, London: Sage.

Mosse, G. L. (1996), *The Image of Men: The Creation of Modern Masculinity*, New York and Oxford: Oxford University Press.

Nordau, M. (1902), "What's the Meaning of Physical Exercise for us, Jews?" in B. Netanyahu (ed.), *Zionist Writings*, Jerusalem: Zionist Library (Hebrew).

Sasson-Levi, O. (2000), "Constructing Gender Identities in the Israeli Army," a doctoral research paper, The Hebrew University of Jerusalem (Hebrew).

Satlow, L. M. (1996), "Try to be a Man," *Harvard Theological Review*, 89(1): 19–41.

Sion, L. (1997), "Images of Manhood among Combat Soldiers," Shaine Working Papers no. 3, Jerusalem.

Sivan, E. (1991), *The 1948 Generation: Myth, Profile and Memory*, Tel Aviv: Maarachot, Ministry of Security (Hebrew).

Stadler, N. and Ben-Ari, E. (2003) "Other-Worldly Soldiers? Ultra-Orthodox Views of Military Service in Contemporary Israel," *Israel Affairs*, 9(4): 17–48.

3

To Give the Boys Energy, Manliness, and Self-command in Temper: The Anglican Male Ideal and St. George's School in Jerusalem, *c.*1900–40

Inger Marie Okkenhaug

Introduction

In 1887 the new Anglican Bishop in Jerusalem, George Francis Popham Blyth (1887–1914), arrived in Palestine. Blyth was to adhere to a new policy that was to change missionary efforts among the Anglicans. There would be no attempt at proselytizing among the Eastern Christian, Jewish or Muslim communities, since years of proselytizing had failed to produce converts. This led to a strategy not of conversion, but of influence, based on the assumption that "if the Muslim cannot be converted into a Christian, he might, through education, be made more aware of the Christian way of life" (Okkenhaug 2003: 171; see also Tibawi 1961; Hummel 2003).

Education was to be a central feature of Anglican tasks in the next fifty years. However, as was not uncommon in Protestant missions, the main aim was education for girls. Women were seen as the key to religious change and social improvement – two interlinked factors in the missionary project. Mission schools often gave priority to educational institutions for girls; accordingly, the bishop's first educational venture was the girls' school and training institution, St. Mary's.[1]

The number of girls attending the school increased rapidly and soon members from influential Arab families in Jerusalem also wanted their boys educated in a British school. Thus the Anglican Church was encouraged to establish a day primary school for boys on English public school lines.[2] In the years before World War I, St. George's School was one of the leading secondary schools in Palestine, a position it continued to hold during the Mandate period (Okkenhaug 2002). The local population's wish for an English school was not atypical in areas that had come under Western influence. Similar to upper-class parents in India and

Africa, Palestinian Arabs of the elite were interested in reinforcing their traditional dominance by acquiring "manifestations of modernity," for example a
Western education (Mangan 1986: 108). The Ottoman authorities were not
providing adequate modern schools in Palestine at the time. European institutions
(usually established by various churches) offering various forms of education
had thus markedly interested parents. In Palestine it was not uncommon for one
family to send their children to various European schools. And they would go to
considerable lengths to secure an education for their sons. Said K. Aburish (1988)
describes how children from the village of Bethany would walk for one hour each
way to Jerusalem, where one brother went to St. George's, one to a French church
school and a third to the Italian school.

What were the dominating values or ideas of the Anglican public school in
Jerusalem, Christian morality or preparations for the real world? Victorian
manliness has been described as a philosophy, which, through prestigious and
proliferating educational institutions, developed a swift and ubiquitous influence
throughout the English-speaking world. This "manliness" was middle class in
orientation and was committed to physical activity. However, manliness was
not a simple and coherent concept. As J. A. Mangan and James Walvin point
out, "manliness" was a portmanteau term that embraced a variety of overlapping
ideologies that were regionally interpreted and changed over time (Mangan and
Walvin 1987: 3). What did the "English manliness" ideal mean when transferred
to a Palestinian context? How did Arab and Jewish male students relate to the
gender system of the colonial culture? Did they accept the British male ideal
uncritically or did they selectively adopt certain aspects of it and reject others?
During the interwar period, nationalism became an increasingly dominating factor
in Palestinian life. How were gender identities negotiated in a time of growing
opposition to British rule?

St. George's School before World War I: The "Christian Gentleman" and "Muscular Christianity"

When St. George's School was opened in October 1899 there were fifteen boys. The
pupils were recruited from the "better" families in Jerusalem, mainly Christians,
but also Muslims and some Jews, from the age of 8 to 20. The Muslim boys were not
admitted to the boarding school, only to the day school. The bishop wanted to set
up a dormitory for Muslim boys only, run by a Muslim head, since it was difficult
for Muslim boys to live in a Christian house.[3] This was apparently encouraged by
Muslim families, but did not materialize because of state intervention.

In 1900 there were forty-three boys and two years later the number had increased
to seventy-three. The Anglican establishment saw this as a positive development,

as St. George's was not a free day school, unlike all other day schools in Jerusalem at the time. As in England where public schools catered for the upper and growing middle classes, St. George's had a distinct class profile. The school was developed as a fee-paying school for children from well-to-do homes. This class aspect was explicitly voiced in the school profile, and made a clear elitist distinction in relation to already existing mission schools.[4] Since conversion was impossible in a Muslim-dominated society, and unpopular with the Greek Orthodox, proselytizing was not part of the school's ideology. Instead the Anglican mission opted for "Christian influence through education." St. George's School, built on a public school model, was given a central role in this work.

In England the public schools were presented as Christian communities that instilled godliness and morality in their pupils. Boys who went through this school system became moulded in the Christian gentleman ideal of the Victorian period. This ideal of Christian manliness, which in the late nineteenth century stood for neo-Spartan virility as exemplified by stoicism, hardiness and endurance, was the pre-eminent quality of the English public school system (Mangan and Walvin 1987: 1). Mangan, however, argues that the insistence that public schools moulded their boys into Christian gentleman was merely a figment in the minds of naive or calculating headmasters. In reality school life was secular and "beliefs were often materialistic not idealistic, custom was often callous not Christian" (Mangan 1987: 136, 152–3). He concludes that this masculine ideal type, based on public school athleticism, could also be seen as a form of social Darwinism. As James Walvin has pointed out, in games, only the fittest survived or triumphed (Walvin 1987: 249). John Tosh, in his study of masculinity and the middle class in Victorian England, does not emphasize the Christian aspect of these institutions, but rather the creation of a manliness that could succeed in the social realities facing young men from the middle class during that period. He argues that they offered a "crash course in manliness" (Tosh 1999: 118).

In the school journal, *St. George's Chronicle* (later *St. George's Journal*), the religious aspect of the Anglican institution was very much downplayed, while "courses in manliness" dominated the pages. In the first edition of the journal in 1907, Blyth compared his own school, St. Paul's of London, "one of the oldest of English grammar schools," to St. George's. By choosing St. Paul's school motto *Doce, disce, aut discede* (teach, learn or depart!) as St. George's, the bishop made a direct connection between the establishment in Jerusalem and English public school traditions.[5] Blyth, educated at Lincoln College, Oxford, was part of a male elite that brought schools based on their own educational background to various places of the world in the name of the British Empire (Tibawi 1961: 222). Like Frederic Lugard in Hong Kong and Nigeria and Lord Curzon in India, Blyth was a product of "an educational system which had total confidence in itself and its values in the self-appointed task of insuring a moral backbone into the native races of the British Empire" (Mangan 1986: 109). Thus the bishop's manifesto was not different from that of an ambitious headmaster in England:

> May it [St. George's] grow up to be one of the Great Public Schools of the East, and be its name guarded by the good and pure lives of its Scholars. May it give clean and manly evidence of satisfactory growth of the "mens sana in corpo sano"; both in class-room and play-ground.[6]

A healthy body was necessary for a healthy mind; this was the backbone of the Christian gentleman. The fact that this maxim would be taught equally "both in classroom and playground" shows how important games were in the school's educational program. As will be discussed later, pupils were taught morals through games. At St. George's, the headmaster of twenty-five years, K. L. Reynolds, transferred this physical, athletic ideal to the school curriculum. Reynolds' love of sports was clearly well known and a former student stated that "we were taught to take sports seriously."[7] The same student gave Reynolds credit for being the man who created real interest in sports in Jerusalem. This focus on physical training for young men was central to the ideal of Christian manliness. This ideal, which became increasingly dominant in both the United Kingdom and the United States during the nineteenth century, stressed love, goodness and compassion. However, by the end of the nineteenth century, manly virtues had changed from the model of the Christian gentleman of liberal sentiments to that of a more conservative imperial pioneer and hunter. This new masculinity was closely linked to the new imperialism of the time, and it was characterized by racial superiority and physical force, which was seen as necessary in order for the British to compete successfully on the international arena (Kent 1999: 203, 248).

In England, sports and physical games had become part of the public school's curriculum, and strengthening and developing the body became an increasingly important part of the education of young men. By the 1880s the importance of physical education had also been adopted in state-owned schools. The aim was to promote discipline and intelligence among the pupils. The military aspect of this scheme was not a coincidence, since the teaching program was largely based on army training methods (Horn 1989: 56–7). At St. George's the connection to the military model was represented quite directly by the bishop's son, an army officer, who taught drill to the older boys when he was on leave from his regiment.[8]

The Anglican stress on physical education for men was typical for Christian organizations that towards the end of the century had included physical culture in their program. One of the champions of "muscular Christianity," the Young Men's Christian Association leader Luther H. Gulick, argued that the purpose of all physical exercise was to develop altruism, cooperation and self-control, that is, to achieve spiritual aims by physical means. The physically trained body was seen as an instrument that would strengthen the masculine character and will. Organized team sports within the English educational system acted as a collective strengthening of the British Empire's moral and physical world rule. The English Board of Education recommended games like cricket and football as a way of creating "an esprit de corps, and a readiness to endure fatigue, to submit to discipline and to subordinate one's own powers and wishes to a common end" (Horn 1989: 60). At St. George's these ideas were taught to the Palestinian boys; cricket and football were played every afternoon, "and did much to give the boys energy, manliness, and self-command in temper."[9]

Success on the football pitch and cricket field in public schools was equivalent to training for the conquest of the real world. These were also manly virtues that, as Lori M. Miller reminds us, represented important culturally sanctioned attributes of Victorian masculinity such as "decisiveness, stoicism and pugnacity" (Miller 2000: 39). However, this Victorian male was being challenged in the years around the beginning of the twentieth century. In the United Kingdom at that time there was an intensification of anxiety about gender and sexuality. The ideas of masculinity were called into question by the educated and assertive "new women" who entered the job market in large numbers. Feminists attacked marriage, which also involved a critique of masculinity. A new awareness of homosexuality among men raised questions about how one might truly recognize manliness and what role the British public schools played in fashioning masculinity and promoting homosexuality (Kent 1999: 248). In an all-male environment like St. George's, the emphasis on self-control and morality that characterised this particular concept of manhood implicitly seems to articulate an underlying uneasiness about its supposed effeminate opposite (comment by Ellen Fleischmann). The British tendency to see the colonized as "feminine" and "emotional" was an additional aspect to the Anglican stress on manliness, self-command and decisiveness (Cooper and Stoler 1997; Kent 1999; Stoler 2002).

In the mission discourse physical education did succeed in creating new men out of what were seen as unfit Arab boys. Spiritual proselytizing was exchanged for bodily transfiguration. The mission supporters at home were given vivid images:

> it is an essential part of our education to play them [games], for we see, under our very eyes, the happy results: boys who were at first corpulent, clumsy and dull, have become thoroughly regenerated. One can hardly believe ones eyes; the change is so great. ... we have no field of our own to play in ... Here is a grand opportunity for an old public school lover of cricket and football to become a benefactor.[10]

"Muscular Christianity" was clearly the ideal, with the emphasis on "muscular" and "masculine." However, not all of the imperial representatives in Jerusalem shared Reynold's conviction "that the healthy mind could only exist in the healthy body."[11] This educational profile was strongly criticized by representatives within the Anglican mission community. A clergyman visiting Palestine in the 1920s lamented that the Anglican secondary schools there were modeled on English public schools to such a degree that they were teaching more about cricket than the Cross (Pittman 1995). It has been argued that by the end of the nineteenth century, the ideal of manliness had evolved into "muscular Christianity" which tended to exaggerate commitment to muscle at the expense of Christianity (Mangan and Walvin 1987: 3). It might seem as though this development also applied to St. George's. Even so, the Anglican community itself was not a homogeneous or monolithic entity with regard to what constituted the masculine ideal.

However, the physical, masculine sportsman ideal was not accepted uncritically by the Arab population. In the early days, boys would walk off the football field in the middle of a game if they were bored. How much local opposition there actually was to the muscular male ideal and school sports is difficult to assess. It does seem as though Palestinian boys more or less willingly accepted it as a part of the English educational package: "to Syrians, and especially to those of the past generation, [sports] it is next to foolishness. But our school is doing good work in the country by popularising English games. Already our boys play football, cricket, and hockey; and they play these games very well, too."[12]

As well as developing the masculine body, these games had an additional value that was highly prized by the Anglican school. It taught the boys "team spirit." This was important in male character training: "by working together, follow the rules, sink their own interest for the common success, they learn fairness and self-control."[13] According to the school reports, in the years before 1918 boys in the Anglican schools were taught team spirit to a much larger extent than the girls were. While Anglican female education aimed at creating a new Christian, Western-influenced Middle Eastern woman who would change society from within the home, the part imagined for the Anglican-educated male was located outside the home sphere. This was in accordance with the separation of spheres that was the ideal of relations between men and women in England during this period (Davidoff and Hall 1987). The Anglican educators saw this as a gender pattern that could also easily conform to Middle Eastern life. Girls were educated for a life within the domestic sphere, while boys should prepare for a public role. Football and cricket would prepare the Palestinian man for mastering a public role where the ideals of unselfishness and cooperation were important social assets. However, this "public role" was built on very Western notions of what constituted a "public" space and how a man was supposed to behave in it. Elizabeth Thompson has shown how the traditionally western distinction between a "private" civil society and the "public" state fits poorly with conditions in the Levant (Thompson 2000: 173). Here the public sphere is not necessarily defined in opposition to a private sphere, which seems to be contrary to the Anglican representatives' understanding of Palestinian society.

A "Man of Character"

It has been argued that Victorian England was preoccupied with the issue of health. By the last part of the nineteenth century, many of the concerns that formed part of the more general agitation about health were given expression through the games-playing "cult" (Haley 1978: 7). This link between a healthy body, morals and a useful role in society were part of the message contained in *St. George's Journal.* The focus on a healthy body seems even to have taken on a spiritual and political dimension, as seen in the Palestinian teacher lecturing boys on "Right Living." Here physical training is portrayed as a way of taking control over one's life, both socially and in a broader, political sense in relation to Ottoman rule:

> Although ... people living in this country are not entirely masters of themselves still, there were departments of activity in which they have a free hand. The chief of these activities were those centred in the human body. Our body is our own – the managing, upbringing and developing of it lie completely within our command ... it is man's duty to develop his body, and bring it up to the highest pitch of usefulness and activity.[14]

This complies with R. J. Park's observation that by the end of the nineteenth century "the dominant cultural value defined a man of 'character' as the man who made his mark on the world" (Park 1987: 17). In a multi-religious society like Palestine, this "man of character" ideal also included tolerance of one's neighbour's religion. The Anglican vision of a future Palestine began to express peaceful coexistence in an increasingly multi-religious and cultural society. This ideal was to be given prominence and new value in British-ruled Palestine after World War I. However, already in 1905 it was seen as a vital characteristic of St. George's:

> [A] prominent feature of our school is that it contains boys of all religions. Christians, Greeks, Latins, Anglicans, Mohammedans and converted Jews ... we have not had one single fight for religion's sake. So nobly do the boys answer to the summons of this liberal public school appeal to a higher life, and strenuously and pluckily they do strive after the Christian gentleman ideal.[15]

This ideal was seen as transcending religious and national conflicts and represented a view that might have been possible within Anglican schools in Ottoman Palestine. However, the Christian gentleman ideal was to be increasingly challenged during the political realities of the interwar years.

In Palestine, the period before World War I was a time of change. Arab nationalists, many of whom were educated at Western mission schools in the area, were becoming more visible. The new times demanded a new Arab man. For the Anglican Church it was especially the Christian Arabs who were of interest. After the Young Turk revolution in 1908 and the promises of social and political reforms that followed, Blyth proclaimed that the "'Unchanging East' ... is a misnomer. The East is moving ... at present we can direct them." Here a political side of the Jerusalem and East Mission (J&EM) educational project becomes apparent. The J&EM was confident that British prestige in Palestine created a "great desire for English education." However, it was a question not only of education, but also of British rule. The Anglican bishopric felt that in Palestine "people had for many years been wishing that the British would go in and possess the land." When Turkey entered the war on the side of Germany, the prospects of a new Palestine with the "final expulsion of the Turks from the Holy Land" seemed to come closer.[16]

The Christian Arabs were seen as partners of cooperation in a future British-controlled Palestine. A substantial number of Greek Orthodox and Protestants educated in these institutions joined the professional class of lawyers, doctors and pharmacists and can be seen as the dominant part of the Arab middle class in Ottoman Syria at the time of World War I. From the 1870s on, the idea of an independent "Syria" had spread especially among those who had attended American schools and the Protestant College in Beirut, that is, mainly Orthodox and Protestant Christians (Hopwood 1969: 176). Some of these were active in various cultural societies and committees, which were the only channels for social and political expression before 1914. At this time, some Arabs expressed definite political aspirations for a democratic system with equal representation, whether pan-Ottoman or pan-Arab (Seikaly 1995: 32).

This concurrence of interests between the British mission and their Palestinian students does not, however, mean that Christian Palestinians preferred British rule to Arab independence. Not only the British, but also other European educational institutions had a strong influence on the local population. Seikaly argues that

> the tendencies to ally with the Western powers whose cultural and financial influence had been imbibed by the local inhabitants did not, however, contradict the tendency towards identification with the general trend of Arab nationalism and some form of independence of Ottoman control. (Seikaly 1995: 37)

Even so, this helps explain why the local population wanted a modern, secularly oriented education in the fifteen-year period before World War I.

The Mandate Period

When Palestine came under British rule (occupied in 1917, a formal mandate in 1922), the Anglican Church had to redefine its role in a country that had in practical terms become a British colony. There was a great demand for British education among the Arab population, Muslim as well as Christian. While the Jewish/

Zionist community catered for most of its own pupils, the British government in Jerusalem was supposed to be in charge of educating the Arab population. However, the demand for education among the Arab community was much greater than the government schools could absorb all through the Mandate period. The government established two secondary institutions for Arabs, the Men's Training College (later Government Arab College) and the Women's Training College, both in Jerusalem. While private Arab schools were opened during the Mandate period, offering primary and higher education for boys and girls, for example at Bir Zeit, Arab youth, and especially women, had to rely to a great extent on foreign missionary schools for secondary and higher education. Government priorities, and a growing sense of competition with a highly educated Jewish population, led Muslim Arabs to make use of the secondary education provided by foreign mission schools (Okkenhaug 2002: 60–80).

The new Anglican bishop, R. MacInnes (1914–32), interpreted these Palestinian demands for education as acceptance of Anglican education.[17] For the Palestinian population, education was the means of achieving social mobility (Moors 1995, Fleischmann 2003). In addition, the mission schools represented continuity from pre-war times. Moreover, the fact that Britain now had a high status as one of the victors should not be underestimated.

This development meant that St. George's, which had been closed during the war, reopened again in 1919, now under the name St. George's College. Ten years later there were 218 students, with a majority of Christian students.[18] By 1935 the number had grown to 255, with 156 Christians, 33 Jews and 66 Muslim students. [19] St. George's was one of the most expensive schools in the country and the government schools, which were cheaper, were first choice for most Muslim students. However, leading Muslim families, like the Husseinis and Nashashibis, sent their boys to St. George's.[20] Often prominent Arab families had attended St. George's for several generations. This was true for both Muslim and Christian Arabs. One example of the latter is Edward Said, who was third generation to attend the Anglican College in the 1940s, both his father and grandfather having been old St. George's boys (Said 1999: 108).

The fact that the Anglican Colleges (the girls' institution, the Jerusalem Girls' College, was the female equivalent of St. George's) were educating the Palestinian elite was a prominent point in Anglican self-representation (Okkenhaug 2002, 2003). As seen in Bishop Francis Graham Brown's address to a British audience:

Old pupils are found in every walk of life in Palestine, as clergy, teachers, doctors, professional and businessmen, civil servants, helping in their different spheres to build up the country. Old pupils of the Girls' College are teaching in mission and government schools, working as nurses in hospitals and welfare centres, and as secretaries and clerks in responsible positions in government offices, training women teachers for elementary schools in the Government Training College.[21]

The bishop characterized the Anglican education as "of a Christian standard and quality." What did this mean in practical terms? An old-fashioned public school with more emphasis on cricket than Christ, or a modern educational institution?

In the 1930s St. George's was presented to the British public as a missionary school, conducted on public school lines, which aimed at having the best public school traditions "with a very definite Christian atmosphere." When the Anglican work in Palestine was presented in *The Church Times* in 1935, the Bishop of Jerusalem (George Francis Brown, 1932–42) strongly emphasized the educational institutions and the Christian influence these had on Palestinian youth.[22] However, this was meant for mission supporters at home. When looking at the debates and topics in *St. George's Magazine,* edited by a staff member, Christian influence is not a topic. To the British public it was important to insist on the missionary aspect of the Anglican schools, as a way of legitimizing their work. However, in reality, the teachers in the (mission) field knew that conversion was impossible. There were two boarding houses with about 100 boys and the day boys were also divided into two houses. There was great keenness in connection with house matches of all kinds. Of the staff, there was one English headmaster with two or three English assistants and some Palestinian teachers. The boys sat for the Oxford and Cambridge School Certificate, which they took in English. As to religious instruction, the pupils had to attend religious classes, regardless of religious background. I have not been able to find material that discusses what the term "religious instruction" implied, but there was no attempt at proselytizing. While no non-Christian was compelled to attend chapel, the boarders all had to attend school chapel in the cathedral every morning. Muslim students had to participate and could compete and sometimes win the scripture prize.[23]

Academically, St. George's was probably one of the best Christian schools in Jerusalem in the period before and right after World War I (Tibawi 1961; Okkenhaug 2002). However, by the 1930s, the school had "fallen behind on the more purely academic side." On the sports side the situation was different: "its prestige in games is still as high as it ever was."[24] The focus on games is also reflected in the school magazine, where it is seen as a typical trait of the English public school. In 1925 the editor was trying to make the "magazine more like an English school magazine. Therefore games take up very much more space."[25] Was this emphasis on physical education the reason for the fall in academic standards? Reynolds' successor as headmaster, C. R. N. Blakiston, stated that in his ideal school he would place 90 percent of the emphasis on character and 10 percent on learning.[26] The activities that could promote "character-training," like cricket and football, were certainly in the foreground of school life. So was boy scouting, a movement that has been called the most successful reassertion of manly values at this time (Tosh 1999: 196). In 1926 the second rally of the Baden-Powell Palestine Boy Scouts Association was held at St. George's, with over a thousand spectators.

The high commissioner, who was Chief Scout for Palestine, attended the rally "and gave a most encouraging address to the boys."[27] In addition, there was a troop of some thirty Armenian scouts who had walked nearly all the way from Beirut with their priest scout masters! However, some years later the Arab scout movement was to become more and more nationalistic and eventually developed into paramilitary youth groups that used their skills to fight against their British masters. This was a phenomenon that was widespread throughout the Middle East, especially in Iraq, Syria and Lebanon during the 1930s (Thompson 2000; Fleischmann 2003).

Student Life: The Story of a Young St. George's Boy

How did the students themselves experience life at St. George's? There is very little written material on this in the Anglican sources; however, one or two glimpses do give some indication that student life in Jerusalem might not have been so different from public school life in the United Kingdom or for that matter in India .

In the United Kingdom the issue of Christian morality is seldom mentioned in former students' description of their life in their public schools. Mangan argues that these schools generated sensible realism and stoicism, and not Christianity, but a hard, secular morality (Mangan 1987: 139). In these institutions religion was not a spiritual commitment but a social habit. These observations coincide with autobiographical stories told by former students from one of the better class of schools: Marlborough College. A former student wrote that when he was there around 1900, his "sharpest and most immediate reaction in recalling those desolate years" was the cold. "We were always cold... After the cold the accent was on cruelty." Another pupil, who was there in the 1930s, described it as "even then still a pretty harsh, arid place" (Mangan 1987: 151). If St. George's as it repeatedly presented itself also in the 1930s was building on the best of public school traditions, one might assume that these traits could also be found here. And it seems as though Mangan's description of public school life in general as "frequently a physical and psychological struggle for survival against hunger, cold and callousness" (Mangan 1987: 151) could also be a fitting description of life at the Anglican institution in Jerusalem, even in the interwar period.

The following autobiographical story was published in the St. George's magazine and gives an entirely different picture of the school. It is quite extraordinary in being an account by one of the younger boys whose schooldays seemed to be almost beyond endurance. The staff censored all articles that were published in the school magazine, and there is no mention of negative issues such as not receiving enough food. However, the same brutality and bullying by older boys in the role as prefects seems to be part of the daily routine, as well as the cold (in every aspect) environment:

The most interesting thing I can think of, is how I spend a cold day at school; how when the bell rings in the morning to wake me up from my warm bed to go out through the whistling wind to the washing room for a cold wash, which I hate so much. I remain in bed, pretending to be still asleep; when suddenly as I have been expecting, I feel the arms of the prefect holding me and throwing me out of bed, with a scolding, if not an order remark.

After having washed I have only about twenty minutes to get ready before the breakfast bell, which I think, are not nearly enough for me in such cold weather.

After breakfast, I have to go to the Choir practice. I like to go to the Choir on such a day because I get a bit warmer when I put on my choir things.

After the morning service the school begins; and from that time till 12 o'clock at noon is a time of pleasure to every boarder, because he rests from the prefects, who are continually putting order marks.

After lunch, I somehow spend my time by warming myself or playing some sort of game just to pass my time. At last the bell rings and then, I unwillingly enter into the classroom, and occupy myself by listening to the wind blowing against the windows till the bell rings again.

At 4 o'clock, I have about two hours in which I can enjoy myself, so I quickly run upstairs and take the best place near the stove where I sit till it is time for me to go to the Choir again; so I carefully wrap myself with my overcoat, but not with a muffler because they are forbidden but I don't know why. (Because they make your chest weak. – Ed.) Then I go to the Choir room again.

After the service we go to supper where I have my nice warm tea so as to enable me to study my next day's lessons, and then I once more, retire to bed.[28]

The school clearly expected the boys to obey rules blindly without having any idea of why they existed and to submit to authorities like the prefects. However, this brutal quality of the school was criticized by contemporary educators. There were those in the Anglican establishment who criticized St. George's for being out of touch with the more liberal educational ideal of the interwar period. In the 1930s Anglican educationalists evaluated all the Anglican mission schools in Palestine. Even if "the children were well instructed and they learn well," St. George was not seen as a child-friendly environment.[29] Quite the contrary, it was described as "a trifle inhuman":

> The school seemed to have been stuck in the nineteenth century mould: Many of the rooms are gloomy, including the Kindergarten's; the dormitories are chilly in winter and forbidding, and Mr. Postgate's suggestion that they harden the boys belongs surely to a past era.[30]

The fact that the school was also criticized for being understaffed and that the classes were too large indicates that the financial situation was worse than it had been. The difficult financial situation might partly explain the old fashioned and harsh quality of the school's physical environment. There simply was not funding to create a school according to contemporary standards.

Christian Character Building or Academic Learning?

What ethical themes and educational advice dominate the magazine? Did they also belong to the past? While there was generally little of Christianity as a universal religion, Anglo-Protestant cultural ideals dominated school life. The Protestant themes of duty and hard work are found repeatedly in the school magazine articles, where popular topics are "do your duty" and "how to succeed," "how to be efficient and don't waste time." In the article "Hunt a job," the boys are advised to:

> clean yourself of those notions and feelings that interfere with your success. Watch your personal appearance. Look clean. Have your coat brushed and shoes polished, also you [sic] hair combed, and no mourning on your fingernails [dirty fingernails]. Never go into the office of an employer with your mouth smelling of tobacco. Many people object to this smell but there are no people who object to its absence.[31]

Such a course in self-improvement was clearly intended to help young Palestinian men to succeed in the modern, i.e. Western world.

In 1929 C. R. N. Blakiston became the new principal of St. George's. His predecessor, Reynolds, who had molded the school to his ideas since the very beginning, was described by a student writing in the school magazine as the students' real friend.[32] Even if this was the official version, the school seemed to have had a human headmaster who was respected in all religious communities in Jerusalem. Blakiston had been headmaster at St. George for a year in 1904–5. However, former students from that period did not seem to have been in touch with him when he came back (as he complained in the school journal), a fact that indicates how unpopular he was in Jerusalem. Blakiston's second stay at St. George's lasted for three and a half years.

While Blakiston modernized the school buildings and introduced a more elite selection of pupils, the new headmaster seems to have had traditional, even old-fashioned ideas of what constituted a public school. He was fond of using the school journal to vent his frustrations and he was not a person to beat about the bush: He opened his farewell speech with the following: "One would like to say all nice things, were it not for a natural repugnance to sham and humbug. There is one thing my worst enemy will not accuse me of, and that is to say polite things that I do not mean."[33]

Blakiston wanted the Anglican institution in Jerusalem to produce good public school boys. But the Arab (and some Jewish) boys did not live up to his expectations. What did they do wrong?

The first grievance was that Palestinian boys were not favorably inclined to a system that placed 10 percent of its emphasis on academic learning and 90 percent on character in order to create the foundations for "becoming a man of purpose and achievement."[34] Blakiston was shocked by the fact that some boys did not want to become prefects because it would take time from their studies. Palestinian boys seemed to have placed more emphasis on academic learning than the English teachers did at St. George's! The latter were themselves products of public schools, with the Weltanschaung of the public school, where education centred on character building rather than on academic merits, as Blakiston repeatedly explained to his students.

The second serious accusation against the St. George's boy was his failure to grasp the true meaning of Christian "character building," instead confusing it with "politeness." In the words of Blakiston:

> In an excellent speech which was delivered by one of our leaving boys ... allusion was made to the fact that the distinguishing feature of a St. George's boy's character was politeness. I also noticed that this word 'polite' appeared with a frequency which almost bewildered me in the [end of term] Reports.[35]

Blakiston's "bewilderment" shows that there existed a cross-cultural, mutual misunderstanding between teacher and students. The St. George's boy interpreted the main part of the Anglican character building, that is the stoic ideal of never showing your feelings and "stiff upper lip" as mere outward appearances. Edward Said, who went to an English public school in Cairo, expressed the same feelings for the British "playing the game" ideal:

> I did learn something about "fair play" and "sportsmanship" ... I understood that both were about appearances; "fair play" meant complaining loudly to an adult that something your opponent did was "not fair," and sportsmanship meant never revealing your real feelings of anger and hatred. (Said 1999: 48)

The third problem with the St. George's boy in relation to the public school mould was "loyalty." Referring to St. George the saint, who represented "Courage, firm Determination and unswerving Loyalty," Blakiston firmly asked for the quintessence of what constituted the Victorian male ideal, the Christian knight. Again we see an example of misunderstanding or cultural insensitivity considering that Christian knights played a major negative role from the Palestinian point of view. The history of the crusades would be well known to the Palestinians attending the Anglican schools.

The lack of loyalty also included former students, who according to the public school tradition were supposed actively to create an "old boys' network" that would be useful in business etc. However, the St. George's Old Boys' Association was content with being "a casual football club." Blakiston was "disappointed with the coldness and indifference shown by the Old Boys... In all the best English schools there is an 'old boy' tradition ... it was something of this kind which I hoped to find awaiting me here. But ... I hoped in vain."[36]

However, it was not only a question of moral obligation. The issue was also about funding. The school was poor and an active old boys association could have been a good source for financial help. Even so, the concept of loyalty had a wider, political dimension. The aim was loyal citizens: "A generation of young men who will put the Country before the Faction, the Community before the Individual: men of wide sympathies and useful ideals: men who are out to serve their fellow-men, and in all things to 'play the game'."[37] To underline his point, the headmaster suggested a new school motto: *Deo, Patriae, Amicis* (For my God, my Country, and my Friends!).

This was written in August 1930, only a year after the "Wailing Wall" riots had taken place in Jerusalem. Ironically, Blakiston had no consideration for the political reality in which the boys at his school lived. After the riots in 1929 the national conflict between Arabs and Jews increased. The Arab and Jewish boys placed their families first and that led to loyalty toward their country, which, to an increasing degree, they learned to interpret as Arab or Jewish Palestine. Certainly none of the groups saw a British Palestine as the final solution to what their future nation was to be like. This was a development that was strengthened by political developments in the neighbouring countries at the time, with growing opposition to French rule in Syria and Lebanon during the 1930s (Khalidi 1997; Shepherd 1999).

While Palestine experienced the serious riots between Arabs and Jews at the same time as Blakiston started as headmaster, this is not a topic discussed in the St. George's magazine. The Anglican Church saw itself as negotiator between the different national and religious communities in the country and their schools with pupils from Muslim, Christian and Jewish backgrounds were their main instruments in this policy (Okkenhaug 2002: 141–72). In a period where Palestinian national identity was growing and Britain was seen as the main obstacle to independence, relations with the British educational institution might not be of the best. However, as Aburish has shown, attending a foreign school was not seen as incompatible with identifying with Arab nationalism (Aburish 1988). Being active in an old boys' organization was another matter. This would have demanded a different loyalty and commitment to the British institution that did not exist between Arab and Jewish "Old Boys."

Blakiston's accusation that the Palestinian boy treated the school as a shop, and "takes what he wants and pays for it," underscores the notion that Palestinians had a pick-and-choose, almost consumerist attitude to the Anglican schools (Ellen

Fleischmann's phrase). They ignored what they did not find useful–for example, the public school ideal. Palestinian parents were not different from other people who came under British rule and were exposed to Christian missions. They saw an Anglican education for their sons (and daughters) as a means for social improvement and economic gain for the family. On the Indian subcontinent, the upper classes sent their boys to English public schools, wishing to reinforce their traditional dominance by acquiring powerful "manifestations of modernity." For people under British imperial subjection, an English education was the vehicle "to help their sons become traders profitable to the family, or salary-earning Government servants." In African areas the chiefs did not necessarily seek a new culture but rather a new weapon in order to share the white man's power (Mangan 1986: 187). In Uganda, Anglican missions established schools based on the public school model for the children of the local elite. Parents who wanted their children to play a part in British-ruled Uganda sent their children there (Pirouet 1978). In Southern Rhodesia during the same period, mission-educated men used patronage ties to government and missions as a way of fighting for scarce resources. These men, like men educated at the Anglican school in Jerusalem, used their educational status to demand respect as professionals, as Carole Summers argues (Summers 2002: 180).

Conclusion

It is difficult to carry out an assessment of Anglican education as represented by St. George's. In the case of Palestine, wars and displacement make a historian's task more difficult. What is known is that during the disturbances in the years of the Arab revolt (1936–9), the Anglican men's schools had to close down for some time because of conflicts between Arab and Jewish pupils.[38] However, even in the 1940s when the headmaster at St. George's insisted that the aim of the school was the education of Christians in a Christian atmosphere, one-third of the 300 students were Muslims. Prominent Christian and Muslim families sent their boys to St. George's for generation upon generation.[39] Here their sons would be exposed to education appropriate for a middle-class life of the outward-looking, wealthy urban elite in Palestine, regardless of religious background.

Through their educational profile, the Anglican school implied a profound assumption of cultural superiority, including the male ideal of the English middle class. Even so, while St. George's was promoted as an English public school, with the physical training of athletic gentlemen as its main activity, this might not correspond with what actually went on in the school. Blakiston's repeated use of the Christian athlete and public school rhetoric in the school journal implies that Arab and Jewish students did not easily adopt these ideals. The fact that these boys were in an environment with males on the same social level may have made them comfortable with being part of the school. The ideals of Anglican-Protestant culture ideals seem not to have been offensive to either Arab or Jewish pupils, but rather regarded as a useful tool in the struggle for male success in a time of great social and political change.

Acknowledgments

I would like to thank Ellen Fleischmann and Yohai Hakak for their valuable comments on this chapter.

Notes

1. Jerusalem and East Mission Archive, St. Antony's College, Oxford (J&EM, IV/4). Report written between 1915 and 1918.
2. J&EM, L/I, *St. George's Journal*, Christmas 1928.
3. *Bible Lands* III, 1909: 119.
4. J&EM, IV/4.
5. J&EM, IV/4, *St George's Chronicle,* July 1907 no. 1.
6. Ibid.
7. J&EM, L/I, *St. George's Journal*, 1929, by Izzat Tannous.
8. J&EM, L/I, *St George's Journal*, Christmas 1928.
9. *Bible Lands* III, 1908: 56.
10. *Bible Lands* II, 1905: 96.
11. *Bible Lands* II, 1905: 96.
12. Ibid.
13. Ibid.
14. J&EM, L/I, *St. George's Journal*, 1907.
15. *Bible Lands* II, 1905: 96.
16. *Bible Lands* III, 1909: 120.
17. *Bible Lands* VI, 1921: 100.
18. J&EM, L/I, *St. George's Magazine,* Easter 1928. There were seventy-two Greek Orthodox, twenty-seven Protestants, ten Roman Catholics, thirteen Armenian Gregorians, three Assyrians, two Maronites, one Abyssinian, sixty-nine Moslems and twenty-one Jews.
19. J&EM, XXXVII/2.
20. J&EM, XXXVII/4.
21. J&EM, XXXVII/2 *The Church Times,* February 8, 1935.
22. J&EM, XXXVII/2 *The Church Times,* February 8, 1935.

23. J&EM, L/I.
24. J&EM, L/I, Rapport by K. L. Reynolds.
25. J&EM, L/I, *St. George's Journal*, Christmas term, vol. 2, no. 1, 1925.
26. J&EM, L/I, *St. George's Journal*, December 1932.
27. J&EM, L/I, *St. George's Magazine*, summer term 1926.
28. J&EM, L/I, *St. George's School Magazine*, summer term, vol.1, 1925, by G. Kawar.
29. J&EM, XXXVII/5.
30. J&EM, XXXVII/5.
31. J&EM, L/I, *St. George's Journal*, summer term 1926.
32. J&EM, L/I, *St. George's Journal*, summer term 1929.
33. J&EM, L/I, *St. George's Journal*, July 1933.
34. J&EM, L/I, *St. George's Journal*, December 1932.
35. J&EM, L/I, *St. George's Journal*, Christmas 1930.
36. J&EM, L/I, *St. George's Journal*, April 1931.
37. J&EM, L/I, *St. George's Journal*, August 1930.
38. J&EM, XXXVII/3, Report by Mabel Warburton, December 1936, Emery 1/4, October 8, 1938.
39. J&EM, XXXVII/4 1940. Letter to Bishop Francis Graham-Brown, dated May 18, 1940.

References

Aburish, S. K. (1988), *Children of Bethany: The Story of a Palestinian Family*, London: Tauris.
Cooper, F. and Stoler, A. L. (eds) (1997), *Tensions of Empire: Colonial Cultures in a Bourgeois World*, Berkeley, CA: University of California Press.
Davidoff, L. and Hall, C. (1987), *Family Fortunes: Men and Women of the English Middle Class*, London: Hutchinson.
Fleischmann, E. (2003), *The Nation and its "New" Women*, Berkeley, CA: University of California Press.
Haley, B. (1978), *The Healthy Body and Victorian Culture*, Cambridge, MA: Harvard University Press.
Hopwood, D. (1969), *The Russian Presence in Syria and Palestine 1843–1914*, Oxford: Oxford University Press.
Horn, P. (1989), *The Victorian and Edwardian Schoolchild*, Gloucester: Alan Sutton.
Hummel, T. (2003), "Between Eastern and Western Christendom: The Anglican Presence in Jerusalem," in A. O'Mahony (ed.), *The Christian Communities of Jerusalem and the Holy Land*, Cardiff: University of Wales Press.
Kent, S. K. (1999), *Gender and Power in Britain, 1640–1990*, London: Routledge.
Khalidi, R. (1997), *Palestinian Identity: The Construction of Modern National Consciousness*, New York: Columbia University Press.
Mangan, J. A. (1986), *The Games Ethic and Imperialism: Aspects of the Diffusion of an Ideal*, London: Frank Cass.

—— (1987), "Social Darwinism and Upper Class Education in Late Victorian and Edwardian England," in J. A. Mangan and J. Walvin (eds), *Manliness and Morality: Middle-class Masculinity in Britain and America*, Manchester: Manchester University Press.

—— and Walvin, J. (eds) (1987), *Manliness and Morality: Middle-class Masculinity in Britain and America*, Manchester: Manchester University Press.

Miller, L. M. (2000), "The (Re)Gendering of High Anglicanism," in A. Bradstock, S. Gill, A. Hogan and S. Morgan (eds), *Masculinity and Spirituality in Victorian Culture*, London: Macmillan.

Moors, A. (1995), *Women, Property and Islam: Palestinian Experiences 1920–1990*, Cambridge: Cambridge University Press.

Okkenhaug, I. M. (2002), *"The Quality of Heroic Living, of High Endeavour and Adventure": Anglican Mission, Women and Education in Palestine, 1888–1948*, Leiden: Brill.

—— (2003) "Education, Culture and Civilization: Anglican Missionary Women in Palestine," in A. O'Mahony (ed.), *The Christian Communities of Jerusalem and the Holy Land: Studies in History, Religion and Politics*, Cardiff: University of Wales Press.

Park, R. J. (1987), "Biological Thought, Athletics and the Formation of a 'man of character': 1830–1900," in J. A. Mangan and J. Walvain (eds), *Manliness and Morality: Middle-class Masculinity in Britain and America*, Manchester: Manchester University Press.

Pirouet, M. L. (1978), *Black Evangelists: The Spread of Christianity in Uganda, 1891–1914*, London: Rex Collings.

Pittman, L. G. (1995), "More than Missionaries: The Anglican Church in Palestine 1918–1948," unpublished paper, MESA.

Said, E. (1999), *Out of Place*, New York: Knopf.

Seikaly, M. (1995), *Haifa: Transformation of an Arab Society 1918–39*, London and New York: I. B. Tauris.

Shepherd, N. (1999), *Ploughing Sand: British Rule in Palestine 1917–1948*, London: John Murray.

Stoler, A. L. (2002), *Carnal Knowledge and Imperial Power: Race and the Intimate in Colonial Rule*, Berkeley, CA: University of California Press.

Summers, C. (2002), *Colonial Lessons: Africans' Education in Southern Rhodesia, 1918–1940*, Portsmouth, NH: Heinemann.

Thompson E. (2000), *Colonial Citizens: Republican Rights*, New York: Columbia University Press.

Tibawi, A. L. (1961), *British Interests in Palestine 1800–1901: A Study of Religious and Educational Enterprise*, Oxford: Oxford University Press.

Tosh, J. (1999), *A Man's Place: Masculinity and the Middle-Class Home in Victorian England*, New Haven, CT and London: Yale University Press.

Walvin, J. (1987), "Symbols of Moral Superiority: Slavery, Sports and Changing World Order, 1800–1940," in J. A. Mangan and J. Walvin (eds), *Manliness and Morality: Middle-class Masculinity in Britain and America*, Manchester: Manchester University Press.

4

Women Students at the American University of Beirut from the 1920s to the 1940s

Aleksandra Majstorac Kobiljski

Introduction

Feminist studies of women in the Middle East have long followed a path of deconstructing and uncovering patterns of patriarchal oppression. In attempting to examine these patterns, feminist scholars have inadvertently rendered subjects of their studies powerless victims of patriarchy and also religions and ideologies. This resulted in calls for a different approach to the study of women's status and their roles in society. Treating women as active agents of their own lives has been mirrored by a change in research strategies. Greater effort is being made to give women of the Middle East a voice and relevance in discussing their own past and present. A number of scholars have incorporated women's social experiences in histories of their communities. Thus, experience of women has been acknowledged as a valuable asset to analysis, with the cautionary remark that it "does not automatically give agency to women" (Müge Göçek and Balaghi, 1994: 4). While acknowledging the existence of detrimental patriarchal constructions hindering women's active and equal participation in the community, it is important to consider the ways women use agency to counter those constructions. In that regard, another concept of great importance is that of women's strategies when faced with obstacles posed by patriarchies, religious orthodoxies and ideologies.

The aim of this chapter is to utilize these two concepts – experience and strategies – to give insight into the lives of a very small group of elite women who studied at the American University of Beirut from the 1920s to the 1940s. The chapter is structured around three main spheres of women's experiences: enrollment strategies, access to campus space and extracurricular activities on campus. These aspects are followed separately (strategies, space and activities) and chronologically throughout three decades. Principal sources for this study are the official publication of the university: *Al Kulliyah* (*Al Kulliyah Review*) and oral histories. *Al Kulliyah* was published from 1920 until 1933. In 1933 it changed format and content to *Al Kulliyah Review*, a student-produced bi-weekly paper which was an important source of students' writing. While being a source, *Al Kulliyah* is also an object of this study because it represents a virtual campus space where women asserted their presence and made themselves heard. Another source for this study are oral histories of women students conducted some fifty to sixty years after their graduation. The strategies they used to widen their choice and increase their participation in campus life are derived from the sources they produced themselves. These sources offer a perspective on issues women students faced daily. If we read these sources against the backdrop of the official documents of the university we realize that women students' discussions focused on a different set of issues than those considered by the university authorities.

While this is a limited, elite-focused investigation, I believe it offers important insight into the formation of a generation of role models who profoundly influenced their communities and societies in the twentieth century. The principal innovation of this approach is that it takes writing and oral histories of women students as the principal source and inspiration for the study of the university as the missionary institution of higher education. Both fighting against and benefiting from tradition, class and religion in a colonial setting of the Mandate period, these women strategized and worked their way through the ivory tower – the elite American University of Beirut. Their struggle, as documented in various sources, can refine our understanding of their pursuit of higher education and participation in society. As such, this contributes to the efforts of including women's experiences and role in the university's history and contributes to the larger field of social history of the region in the Mandate period. Finally, I believe that *historia est mater studiorum* and without overly romanticizing women's history, the study of women's fight for participation and recognition in academic institutions offers important insight for academic women today.[1]

Historical and Institutional Context

The American University of Beirut was founded in 1866 by the Syrian Protestant Mission as a Christian American institution of higher learning for male students. Originally, it was called Syrian Protestant College and operated under that name until 1920, when it was given its present name. Education did not figure among major goals and aims of the American Protestant Mission in Arab countries. Nevertheless, educational efforts, especially the education of girls, were identified early as the pride and joy of the Mission. In view of the unsuccessful evangelization project, by the early twentieth century women became an important target group of missionary efforts through educational projects oriented to their perceived future as mothers and homemakers.

World War I traumatized all strata of society in the region and the capital – Beirut. Massive numbers died on the fronts while women and children starved at home. Three-fourths of adult male population was mobilized (2.85 million troops), and nearly 1 million died on the battlefields (Thompson 2000: 22). The elites did not suffer the horrors of famine but struggled with other kinds of challenges. Their attitudes towards female education – which became a norm – changed greatly in the years following World War I, together with the changing attitudes toward female mobility in public space. Due to the profound distress caused by World War I, many women had to fend on their own and participated in paid labor outside the home. It became obvious that education was a means of providing security and stability for the family. This was especially true for the greatly impoverished middle class, who saw it as an investment. A strong base of girls with solid high school educations, graduating from missionary girls' schools of Tripoli, Beirut and Sidon further fueled local demand for higher education (Fleischmann 2002: 414). This made college education for women seem the next step on the Mission's educational agenda, potentially a profitable one. However, it is important to note that education for women was largely not envisioned by the university administration as coeducation and at most times during the first half of the twentieth century it was treated quite separately – in quality and content – from education for men.

On September 1 1920, the French high commissioner, Henri Gouraud, announced the establishment of the State of Greater Lebanon, a state under French Mandate. In November 1920, the American University of Beirut voted to admit women students to the university's professional schools under the condition that there were at least three women who would be enrolled together. At the same time, the university made an effort to convince the Presbyterian Board of Foreign Missions and other organizations active in the region to establish a Junior College for Girls, or devise another way of offering liberal college education for women. In April 1922, Lebanon witnessed its first elections with universal male suffrage. In the same year, in response to women's demand for education, the university began allowing auditors – of both sexes – to attend classes at the School of Arts and Sciences for a fee, without a claim to a degree. Although it was apparently not directed at women students alone, I argue that this policy was a way of containing the inflow of women candidates with valid qualifications until institutions other than the university developed a single-sex educational option. Eventually, the demand of qualified women for higher education outpaced the ability of missionaries to establish a single-sex liberal college for women. However, efforts towards establishing of such single-sex institution continued and resulted in the introduction of a college freshmen curriculum in the American School for Girls in 1924/25. But again, in 1924 the university yielded to the pressures of demand and allowed women to enter the sophomore year of the School of Arts and Sciences. This decision was passed reluctantly only after the Syrian Mission clearly stated that it could not foresee an immediate way to develop an institution of higher learning for women alone (Faculty Minutes 1927). Passed reluctantly, it was a short-lived provision that lasted only until 1927, when the American Junior College for Girls was founded and offered academic work equivalent to freshman and sophomore years. Women students who wanted to pursue higher education were obliged to graduate from the American Junior College for Girls before enrolling in the American University of Beirut.

The gradual opening of the American University of Beirut in 1920s to women students was part of a larger context of social change at the beginning of the Mandate period. The city of Beirut itself experienced a significant physical and demographic change, with extension of the physical public space and doubling of the population of the city between 1920 and 1932. Mandate authorities viewed education as a tool of exercising French influence over the population. However, the difference in attention and budgets allocated to boys' and girls' public schools was to the disadvantage of the latter. Protestant missionary schools for girls catered to that gap and produced an important base of competent girls who wanted to continue their education. By reluctantly trying to fill in the gap between demand and supply of professional and liberal education for women, the university never intended to, nor did it in fact, encourage coeducation. It was a concession made to satisfy three demands: of women eager to pursue professional training at the university and/or liberal education, of market demand for female medical, and educational personnel, and of a generation of alumni or faculty members who wanted higher education for their daughters. Changed attitudes towards female professional engagement encouraged some women from the upper-middle class to follow in the footsteps of their fathers and pursue medicine, pharmacy and education. On the other hand, the habits of middle-class women changed in the decades following World War I. Consulting a doctor, reading the newspapers and doing shopping became part of the routine for many middle-class women as well as for the elites (Thompson 2000: 85, 175–83). This meant that the demand for and of women professionals became a pertinent and increasingly difficult to ignore.

The resulting acceptance of women to the university and consequent introduction of coeducation was an experiment and not a deliberate act aimed at advancing coeducation. The university's struggle to keep women out of the regular student body was a conscious process which was intensive in the 1920s but continuing throughout the first half of the twentieth century. Within the closed doors of faculty meetings women in the university system were perceived as an unwelcome challenge, but for the general public acceptance of women students was presented as an event marking an active effort by the university to promote regional educational development ("American University of Beirut Notes" 1921). The ambiguous treatment that women student faced and the reasons behind it are difficult to document in entirety. However, the writing of a woman student from 1930s illustrates that this ambiguity of the university authorities was felt and well articulated by women students.

> There was a time, and not so long ago, when the doors of the A.U.B. were obstinately shut to the women of the Near East – and elsewhere. There was a time when some of us ambitious women … had to knock repeatedly at those closed doors, pleading our cause in the most eloquent way we could to be granted the privileges of a college education. (Cohen 1936: 1–2)

The reasons behind this stance of the university merit further study. For the purpose of this work the ambiguity of the university regarding women students is important inasmuch as it sheds light on a sophisticated glass web of opportunities and constraints inherent in an environment which is apparently welcoming but intrinsically confused and uncertain about the presence of women in the regular student body.

Strategies of Enrollment to the University

During the turbulent social and political conditions of 1920s Lebanon, several generations of women students entered the Main Gate of the American University of Beirut as regular students and earned their degrees. The first women enrolled in the professional schools in 1921/22 were Fortune Azriel and Sara Levy from Palestine and Aida Goldenberg from Russia alongside two Americans, Katheryn Hulber and Winfred Rouse, teachers at the American Community School who intended to pursue graduate work at the university (Cohen 1936: 1–2). While Levy enrolled in the School of Pharmacy, Goldenberg and Azriel entered the School of Dentistry. These five women were part of the 524-member student body at the university proper. In general, records are scarce regarding this first generation of students and it is not clear from the records what strategy they employed for entering the university. What is known is that Aida Goldenberg dropped out after the junior year, leaving Fortune Azriel alone in the School of Dentistry. The latter, together with Levy, maintained occasional contact with the Auxiliary Alumni branch and participated in the annual women's luncheons. On the occasion of her graduation from the School of Pharmacy in 1925, Sara Levy addressed the audience of the luncheon as the first woman graduate from the university's professional schools. The following year, Azriel became the university's first woman graduate from the School of Dentistry. Alumni records indicate that by 1930 she married Dr. Samuel Appelrot, professor of physiology at the American University of Beirut and continued to live in Beirut. Little is known about the specific housing arrangements or the use of campus space by these early women students. University sources reveal that in 1920, faculty suggested allowing women students to perform anatomical dissection and microscope work separately from male students; as well as to be assigned a lounge and toilet on the lower floor of the Medical Building (Minutes of General Faculty 1920).

Records are more informative about the second generation of women students in the 1920s. These were the generation of women to whom, in 1924/25, the university gave permission to enroll to the sophomore class of the School of Arts and Sciences. Although it was a short-lived opportunity, several women took advantage of it and enrolled as the first regular students of the School. Adma Abou-Shedid, Munira Saffuri, Gladis Chanklin, Henriette Hakim and Beatrice May Yoly joined women students in the professional schools and those enrolled as auditors. Local middle-class communities' and missionaries' changing attitudes towards female employment marking the decade after World War I (Fleischmann: 2002: 425). Among the first generation of students in the School of Arts and Sciences, there was a marked presence of women educational migrants indicating that the change might have had a regional character. Two of the women students enrolled in 1924/25 were from Egypt. Only a year later, two teen sisters from Damascus and Olga Wahbe from Palestine joined the women's student body along with Beiruti women. This was only the beginning of a steady and ever increasing flow of women students from the different parts of the region parallel to well-established tradition of male educational migration to the university.

Studies of missionary educational institutions often assume the influence that missionaries had on their students and the power they had in arranging further education for their protégées (Okkenhaug 2002). However, it is also important to consider women's own strategies for accessing university education as regular students. Some women students enrolled without prior relations to the university or missionary education, like Adma Abou Shedid (BA in medicine 1926, MD 1931) and some were daughters of faculty members, like Salma Khouri Makdisi (BA 1929) and Wadad Khouri Makdisi (BA 1930). Others had relatives graduating from the university and/or were accompanied by their husband like Ihsan Shakir (BA 1929), or more conventionally by their brothers (Anisa Rawda, BA 1936). The following brief examples give insight into a wide variety of means women employed in order to gain access to the university.

Adma Abou Shedid was the first woman doctor to graduate from the School of Medicine of the American University of Beirut. She did not have any immediate relatives or siblings at the university prior to or at the time of her enrollment. In the summer of 1924, after petitioning for admission, she was required to pass an exam equal to the content of the sophomore year, as a prerequisite for enrolling in the School of Medicine. In the autumn of the same year, she was informed that even though she passed the exam she would only be allowed to study at the School of Arts and Sciences, as there were no other women candidates for the School of Medicine. While waiting for a woman companion – at least one – for the study of medicine, she graduated from the School of Arts and Sciences with a BA in medicine in 1926. In 1926/27 she was finally permitted to enroll in the School of Medicine as its only woman student. Further research is needed to determine what influenced the faculty to change their initial position.

Ihsan Shakir (later know as Ihsan el-Kousy) came from Cario, Egypt. She got to know about the university through her male cousin who was enrolled in the School of Pharmacy at the time. Ihsan was the first Muslim women to enroll (1924/25), the first Muslim to graduate (BA 1929) and the one who needed her husband's approval for the project. Mr. Shakir was persuaded to follow his wife from Cairo to Beirut in pursuit of education. Both of them lacked adequate English language skills and so were not eligible for direct admission to the university. Thus, they initially enrolled as special students for two years before enrolling as sophomores in 1926/27.

When remembering Adma and Ihsan, Wadad Khouri Makdisi-Cortas (BA 1930) writes:

> I still remember the vehemence against the past, the conviction in the present, and the idealism in the future which animated her [Ihsan Shakir] personality... She was in this sense our spiritual leader. The memory of one other person stands clear in my mind and that is of the first Lebanese lady to take up medicine. I mean Dr. Abouchedid... Our fears of not being able to cope with the intricate subjects, and to brave the challenge of a male atmosphere of study, dwindled when we compared our simple studies with hers. In this sense she was our academic leader. (Cortas 1947: 4–5)

During the 1930s, the trend of the enrollment of daughters of the faculty remained stable. In addition, there was an increased enrollment of daughters of the alumni and a steady stream of women students enrolled from neighboring Syria, Jordan and Palestine. The trend of women's educational migration from countries other than neighboring emerged and women students started coming from Iraqi and Iranian and from as far as Mecca – like Princess Msubach Al-Haydar, daughter of the Sharif of Mecca, who graduated from the university's Institute of Music in 1931 and taught at the institute until 1935.

The war-scarred decade of the 1940s in Beirut was marked by apprehension brought about by the memories of the suffering of World War I. On campus, the decade was marked by the presence of Polish refugees. They formed a separate and poorly integrated group on campus. "The Poles ... act slavishly among themselves and japonically with the A.U.B. people" (Druby 1946: 19–20). The first refugee students came to the university in 1941 but the largest waves were in 1943/44 and 1945/46 and in 1947 they numbered 83. In 1945, a special sophomore class was formed for Polish women students. Later, some of these students entered

Schools of Pharmacy and Medicine as well as other fields of study. But by virtue of their refugees' status, some of them did not stay long enough to graduate or they dropped out for other reasons. For example, although sixty-one Polish student registered in October 1947, thirteen had dropped out by February 1948 and a number of others were expected to leave in the course of the academic year ("Around the Campus" 1948: 8). With the increasing influx of Polish students, the women student body witnessed a market diversification from both social and class point of view. Polish girls practiced European values and on campus there was a sense that they "brought in an element, because they were more available to go out with boys than the local girls ... and a lot of young men that I know, dated Polish girls" (Da Cruz 2004). However, the cross-influence of various migrant groups and local women student population merits a further separate study beyond the scope of this discussion.

Women Students' Spaces

Women students' use of traditionally and dominantly male campus space was closely related to their extracurricular activities. The way in which women students strategized to obtain access to both space and activities changed during the three decades. The patterns of space usage and activities can be considered twofold and are not at all times absolutely separate issue. Activities in the virtual campus space, such as journalism and, on the other hand, activities in real space such as parties and athletics form the twofold fabric of space usage. The extracurricular activities of the early women students during the 1920s were largely restricted to the departmental activities such as speech contests and visiting faculty members and their wives in their homes. The relationship between women students and faculty wives was strengthened by the fact that the president's wife was considered to be in charge of young women's guidance. Other senior faculty's wives were deemed responsible for socially supporting and guiding the students. When in 1925/26, the Women Students' Organization (WSO) was initiated by Ihsan Shakir and with the subsequent inauguration of the women's lounge in January 1926, inviting wives of the faculty members for tea became a well-established social event on campus. Being "at home" for the faculty wives occurred frequently and it took place in the women's lounge.[2]

The claiming of the campus space in extracurricular activities was part of an ongoing assertion in the public space by women outside of the university walls but it was mediated by the relative fragility of the ideas of coeducation and higher education for women. On the one hand, in order to reach the university, women needed to walk the streets or ride the trams, thus challenging the notions of female presence in the public space at the beginning of the Mandate period. On the other hand, once attending the university, women students, at first, downscaled their participation in campus public space. In the second half of 1920s and throughout the 1930s, the women's lounge remained the base from which they occasionally ventured into activities outside classrooms and library: "The first thing we did was either go to our class directly or go to the lounge ... It was relaxing" (Abu-Izzedine 2003). During the 1930s, the lounge largely remained an exclusively female space.[3] By the end of the academic year 1937/38, the Women Students' Organization petitioned and obtained permission to hold two tea parties to which men students could be invited. However, women students did not use this permission but instead organized a flower ball in West Hall, asserting their presence in another dominantly male communal space.

West Hall, unlike the women's lounge, was built as student activities space at the time when women were not part of the student body. Beginning in the second half of 1920s, the university community witnessed a rise of interest in drama. West Hall became the epicenter of this wave, since most performances were given by Dramatics Club and performances took place in its auditorium. Women students were not allowed to perform in plays with male students (co-act) but by the mid-1930s they were occasionally allowed to perform for the university community (faculty and alumni) audience or have their act as a section of the University Night variety show, several times a year. In 1937/38, the English Department offered a course in the history and development of drama. In the first year, six male and six female students took the course, though the rules of the university still did not permit them to co-act. Nevertheless, women students attended the performances of the Dramatics Club and constituted the audience for performances and entertainment events of other clubs. Thus, they acquired social experiences such as attending social functions in mixed setting other than the immediate kin group, and not readily available to them outside of the university. In addition, the 1930s were a decade of great interest in music. The Institute of Music was located in the West Hall itself and its students were mainly women. Thus, some female students did join male students on the stage of the West Hall since early 1930s by providing musical accompaniment for various clubs events and during the performances given by the institute.

West Hall was not only the venue of performances and other social events but also part of the everyday routine of many male and female students. It housed a cafeteria where students of both sexes went for sandwiches, muffins, juices, coffee, tea and fruit. It was a place where "everybody knew everybody else, especially girls" (Abu Izzedine 2003). But to go to the cafeteria was an adventure and not an easy one for the novice to the campus. It usually took women students some time to muster the courage and start going to the cafeteria. However, as in all other activities they carefully watched each step. Often they would buy a snack in the cafeteria and eat in the women's lounge. In sum, in the 1930s, the West Hall gradually became the principal place for association between male and female students and according to the university authorities there was "no indication of a lack of propriety, respect or responsibility demanded from all concerned in these activities" ("Co-acting" 1937: 1).

The chapel was also part of the everyday routine for a great majority of students from 8:30 to 9:00 a.m. Monday through Friday. The attendance was considered mandatory and was a common practice among students of different religious backgrounds. Initially, women were seated at the back of the chapel's middle section, where two rows were designated for women students. At the same time male students were seated alphabetically with their schools and departments. In the university's male jargon the women's section used to be called "the harem" (Abu Izzedine 2003). The wife of the president – Mrs. Dodge, whose presence in the chapel was perceived as very supporting – would sit together with women students in the special section. In 1938/39 the seating arrangement of women students was changed and they were seated alphabetically with their classes. It is difficult to establish the cause and the way this change took place as well as to answer the question whether it was partly due to Mrs. Dodge's influence.

In the fall of 1939, the university inaugurated its first formal arrangement for women students' lodging by establishing a hostel. The hostel housed eighteen students out of a total of fifty-two enrolled that year. This housing arrangement put an end to migrant women students having only two housing options, either boarding with the students of the American Junior College for Girls or staying with relatives in Beirut. The hostel had a sitting room on the first floor where women students were allowed to receive visitors, including men students. At the same time the women's lounge remained an exclusively female space. Although some commandos among the student residents of College Hall claimed to have traversed the " unknown," the lounge was a peaceful campus retreat for women and was off limits to male students.

Women Students' Activities

Mainly because of the efforts of the Women Students' Organization the use of campus space by women students expanded during the 1930s. The organization continued to host tea parties in the lounge but they greatly widened the scope and physical perimeter of their activities. By 1933/34, the organization started offering orientation tours of campus for women students. Although some of the women students were familiar with the campus prior to the enrollment, they had little familiarity with the inner campus space, with the possible exception of the library.[4] Organized at the beginning of each academic year, orientation tours were of great importance because they facilitated familiarity of the campus for women students who were excluded (by virtue of not entering the university in the freshman year) from the week of activities – organized and sponsored by the university for male students. Aimed at acquainting them with professors and the campus, women students had no such opportunity. Using WSO, women students found a way to transmit knowledge of physical campus space from seniors who were familiar with it to a new groups of women students.

During the second half of the 1920s, outside the lounge and departmental functions women student's activities were devoted to the organization to fight against illiteracy, the Boy Service Club, which was organized within the Brotherhood.[5] In the beginning of the 1930s, WSO increased the intensity of its cooperating with the Brotherhood. In addition to the fight against illiteracy, women students started helping with organizing receptions and other social activities of the Brotherhood. By becoming more closely involved with the Brotherhood, women students and the WSO slowly gained access to its welfare activities, which in the 1930 included work with poor urban youth and summer village welfare projects. By 1934 welfare activities of the Brotherhood branched out and formed the Civil Welfare Society (CWS) with two branches: city and village welfare. Women students largely turned towards CWS with occasional direct involvement in the Brotherhood activities. Although this seems to follow the general pattern by which earlier generations of women of the middle classes and elites would engage in welfare work in the late nineteenth and throughout the twentieth centuries, in order to get out of the domestic realm young female university students in interwar Lebanon do not fit that pattern.

Women students were already venturing out of home every day to attend classes; some of them migrated to Beirut for the purpose of their studies and thus did not need to engage into welfare to get out of their homes. What seems as a more pertinent need was a socially appropriate framework to gain access to social events on campus. Although the activities of the Brotherhood had an important welfare component, women students largely chose to venture into CWS thus gaining participation and access to a great number of campus events that were undertaken in the name and for the benefit of the CWS causes. Engaging in campus events within the framework of welfare efforts offered an appropriate way of engaging with the mixed social and public space of the campus. Thus, gaining experience and social skill for participating in the male-dominated social environment of the university. This experience was later capitalized on in the way women engaged in non-welfare activities on campus. I argue that by choosing CWS activities over the Brotherhood, women students made the choice of prominence – engaging in social functions and activities within the broad framework of the welfare as a means to gain wider experience range and larger exposure on campus.

By the second half of the 1930s, women students were deeply involved in all CWS activities, on and off the campus. During the first half of 1940s the efforts in the field of civil welfare increasingly took on a form of relief work. Although women students were, more then ever before, expected and needed in the CWS, they turned towards other clubs to which they gained access using CWS experience. Clubs like Debating and International Relations prospered in the period and became the agoras of the University. Women students increasingly took an important part in the debates around these two clubs. Some of them became members of the clubs' administrative structure becoming secretaries or vice-presidents in these organizations. By the mid-1940s female secretaries on club cabinets (including sports) were not uncommon. The International Relations Club was the first to elect a female president in 1943/44, Polish senior political science student Felicia Fedorowich. Debates and lectures on topics such as the new alumna, the future of Near Eastern woman, and their political rights supplemented those on the League of Nations, the postwar reconstruction. Two large-scale Arab women's conferences in Cairo in 1944 and in Beirut in 1949 which were known to the university community, and many other smaller conferences held in Beirut, provided additional staple of controversial topics for campus debates. In addition the end of the 1940s was marked by informal debates of the question of Palestine which became crux of social and political events in the following decades.

With the introduction of the course on journalism in 1933/34, the American University of Beirut opened a new chapter in documenting its history. Starting from December 1933, the magazine *Al Kulliyah Review* became a bi-weekly publication produced by all the members of the class. Although it was not the first student publication, it became one of the most important sources of information about campus life.[6] From its inception, the journal was a venue where women students' participation in campus life became visible and traceable. In the very first issue of *Al Kulliyah Review* there were two women students among sixteen members of the staff, Aviva Lerner and Rose Ghurayib. Due to the nature of the writing assignments and events they had to cover, journalist – including women students – had a unique pretext and a secured doorway for participation in campus-wide events. In addition, women journalists retained exclusive access to reporting on the WSO and the American Junior College for Girls which made them an indispensable asset on the editorial team.

In the realm of virtual or intellectual space of campus, *Al Kulliyah Review* was important for expressing views on various issues, including those specific to women students. They used the space of the *Review* to address and actively attempt to change their condition. In 1934, Aviva Lerner (BA 1934) wrote in an article on the attitude of male students towards women playing tennis:

> As soon as a girl is seen playing on the tennis court, be she student or a visitor, several students instantly appear, form groups and begin mocking, criticizing and jeering. The remarks are made loud enough to be heard by the players, and the impression of it is not

at all very pleasant. They interfere with the game and make the player, already somewhat self-conscious, more so. The girl begins to feel uneasy and timid. Her movements become awkward and her balls go wrong. The game is simply spoiled for her, and the next time she has the opportunity of playing on the AUB courts she will think twice before she places herself once more in a similar unpleasant situation. (Lerner 1934: 4)

The pages of the *Review* also served for the criticism of the faculty by women students. In 1938, one women student wrote a lengthy article in which she not only articulated the awareness of the problem of the way some faculty members addressed their classes but also revealed women students' reactions and actions to counter it:

It was hard for the old professor to adopt himself to the new rules of coeducation! He, a professor of one of the old European universities, did not recognize nor consider the women students who attended his classes. He daily came to the class, greeted his students saying "Good morning, gentlemen!" and began his lecture addressing the gentlemen only! ... Irritated as they were, they [the women students] asked their class-mates not to attend classes on a certain day... The professors made a good step. All of them addressed their classes "gentlemen and ladies." Now the ladies were acknowledged as a real part of mankind! (Shukair 1938: 12)

The *Al Kulliyah Review* also served as an important and potentially anonymous space for women students outside of the class of journalism to express their opinions. One example is an anonymous woman student's article asking why women students were expected to cheer for the football team. Importantly, the article demonstrates how aware women students were of their numbers in proportion to the student body and how they used this argument well to defend themselves from criticism:

It has come to our ears that the women students are being criticized for not attending the athletic matches and cheering on the Varsity to victory... Why don't critics stir up a little normal enthusiasm among the men students? Foot ball [*sic*] is your game not ours! ... As a group we are a very very small percent of the student body. The percent of on-lookers at the matches from our group is high. When the same percent is duplicated among the men students we will make an extra effort to raise ours. Until then. ("Who Cheers for Veracity" 1936: 1)

From 1939 to 1943, *Al Kulliyah Review* was forced to change drastically its format. From a bi-weekly it became a monthly magazine and included the Arabic and French sections. The early 1940s saw only a few shortened issues of the *Review* published, with blanks during 1942 and part of 1943. In 1943 the class of journalism was suspended and students edited subsequent issues from 1944 trough 1946 with assistance of the Alumni Association and the student committee of the School of Arts and Sciences.

The irregularity of the *Review* does not allow a continuous view of campus life in the first half of the 1940s. Therefore more research is needed using oral histories in order to fill in the gaps and add new perspectives. Nevertheless, *Al Kulliyah Review* remained an important avenue for promoting women students' writing. In 1946 the *Review* kept the same format but became a more regular publication with a noticeable rise in student participation. Women students not only were regularly on the editorial board but also very often had the privilege of interviewing senior faculty members for the *Review*. A regular section on women students was featured in the *Review* from 1944 to 1946. One student even writes sarcastically about the rising voice of women and suggests the distortions and limitations of their participation in campus life.

> Besides filling the liberary [*sic*], as someone commented, the women students are participating in all the University activities. Four of the most important committees, namely West Hall Clubs Cabinet, Debating Club, Scientific Society and – this Review, have ladies as secretaries. Dramatics and Badminton – have lady chairmen Also permit me to suggest the assignment of a male secretary for the Women Students' Committee as a compensatory measure. (Zaphiriadis 1946: 10–11)

Although *Al Kulliyah* was the dominant example of women's involvement in student journals it was no the only one. In 1934/35 a woman student, Anisa Rawda, was elected the editor of the magazine of one of the largest student clubs of the time – the Arabic society Urwat' ul Wuthka. During the 1930s, journalism in general and *Al Kulliyah* in particular were activities in which women students participated disproportionately to their total number. They used the virtual space of the *Review* and means of journalism as much for the practice of the writing skills as for the acting upon their own drives and issues. The virtual space of the *Review* was a particularly important means of expression when the physical campus space was sending ambiguous signals. In the 1940s, despite its shrinking in size, the pages of the *Review* remained a place where women kept expressing their opinions and acting on the issues they faced.

Sport was another arena in which women students gradually started participating. Although tennis, ping-pong and bowling were not unknown to some women students in 1930s, in the beginning of the 1940s, the interest in "ladies' athletics" increased. This marked a considerable change and enlargement of campus space accessible to women students. Athletics were mandatory for freshmen and sophomores. It was also popular among the upper classes. The Field Day was the major sporting event of the season when university-wide competitions in athletic disciplines and team sports took place. Women students were not enrolled as freshmen and sophomores and thus did not participate in the Field Day, but could participate in other tournaments and sporting events during the year. With the appointment of Mrs. Kerr in 1945 as the advisor to women students, the issue of women's athletics was for the first time given special attention. Arrangement was made to have one hour twice a week of exercise in the West Hall. The president and his wife – Mr. and Mrs. Dodge – had offered women students free use of the tennis court reserved for the president of the university. Swimming was popular and during the second half of 1930s women students engaged in swimming occasionally. The faculty beach was at their disposal twice a week in addition to the regular access they could have to the student beach. In 1940s the faculty and student beach merged and started serving increasing number of swimmers from the university community and by the end of 1940s most Beiruti girls attending the university regularly engaged in swimming.

Another developing sport in the 1940s was skiing, and chaperoned ski-trips to resorts became increasingly popular. By the second half of 1940s, several trips per season were organized by the Athletics Department in cooperation with a local sportswear shop. Although skiing demanded substantial financial, transportation and time resources, which were scarce in this war-marked decade, skiing was an opportunity for women student's to try their hand at a developing sport which later become very popular in the country. In addition, women students participated in several other sports in the form of mixed doubles. These sports included bowling, archery, ping-pong, badminton and tennis – by far the most popular sport of AUB alumni and alumna.

Conclusion

In 1947, the American University of Beirut – which reluctantly opened its doors to women in 1920 – marked the twenty-fifth anniversary of coeducation. Although the jubilee was a product of "the experiment of allowing women to enter Upper Classes of the School of Arts and Sciences, as well as the professional schools" (Report of the President 1947: 3), officially the university was proud of its achievement – the championing of coeducation. However, the first twenty-five years of coeducation at the university setting presented its women students with numerous challenges.

In order to brave some of these challenges, only one of which was the male atmosphere of study, women students at the American University of Beirut began to organize in the mid-1920s. The Women Students' Organization proved to be particularly useful in the beginning, during the consolidation phase. During the first two decades of its existence it served as a liaison with the rest of the university community and opened opportunities for women students to participation in campus life. In the late 1920s, WSO created a liaison with the only club accessible to women students – the Brotherhood – and strategized the way to participate in the welfare activities of fighting illiteracy. In so doing they took advantage of decreased male students' interest in issues of poor youth and night school expansion projects desire by the university authorities. During the 1930s, women students and WSO made the prominence choice – taking up the social events and activities within the broad framework of the welfare as a means to gain wider experience range and larger exposure. Thus, they asserted their role under the realm of welfare activities while gaining more of social exposure and experience and also venturing into new fields of activity such as journalism and music. Additionally, they maintained a strong involvement with their base – the Women Students' Organization – and related social activates. During the 1940s, the university further promoted civil welfare and social work. It was expected that women students would continue their strong engagement with the Civil Welfare Society, where their place was essential and guaranteed. However, women students gradually drifted away from the CWS and followed their interests, becoming prominent and active in Debating Club and the International Relations Club. Although a number of them continue to participate in welfare activates, these activities seized to be the dominant and marking component of their involvement on campus. The Women Students' Organization stopped being the only means and way by which women students could gain access to the campus life. In addition, participation in CWS did not serve to contain women students' participation in sharing of campus space but rather facilitated access to other clubs and campus activities in pursuit of participation. In this sense, women students capitalized on the tradition of women's involvement in welfare to widen the scope of future possibilities.

Over the three decades, women students grew from rarities on campus to form a significant and active – yet still small – segment of the student body, although even in the 1940s their presence occasionally caused freshmen to fall from the university wall, as male students sought a glimpse of their female colleagues. Women students used various strategies in acting upon their drive to change the realities they faced on campus and responded critically both to the university authorities and to their male peers, navigating through the glass web of possibilities and constraints. Thus, they were not mere recipients of administration's good will opening the university gate for them. Instead they were active agents of changes within the missionary educational institutions they were enrolled in. By participating in the limited campus space and building a bigger one, they actively solicited and facilitated changes. By writing their experiences they left a significant historical and social document which illuminates the struggle for inclusion on the academic and social environment of the American University of Beirut.

This study contributes a first step towards pointing out the importance of reading sources other than those produced by missionaries, university administration and faculty – conveniently found in missionary archives outside the region – when discussing women students in the missionary institutions of higher education. The writing of women students left a strong imprint of their presence on campus and are important documents for further study. In addition, oral histories, could lead to further enriching of our knowledge of the Mandate period. Integration of students' writings during the time of their study into studies of the educational experiences in the missionary schools opens new topics for further exploration such as women's participation in sport, music and male students' views of their female colleagues. The use of sources other then those produced by missionaries or mission-related personnel dislocates the study from the framework of medium – message – recipient. Such diversification of frameworks will enhance our understanding of the women's agency in the coeducational university settings positioned between the constraints and opportunities offered by tradition, class and religion in a colonial setting and beyond.

Notes

1. The Latin phrase means "History is the mother of [all] studies."
2. In the second half of the 1920s it became a practice to ask most faculty members to set aside a time and a day when they are "at home" for the students. These were a kind of office hours in professors' private residences. Women students inverted the concept and decided to be "at home" for the wives of the faculty members.
3. With the exception of janitors, who could and had to enter and direct the cleaning of "the sacred precincts," and carpenters, electricians and plumbers came when needed.
4. Library facilities were at the disposal of the student of the American Junior College including the borrowing privileges. Thus, students coming from that school were generally acquainted with the library.
5. The Brotherhood was one of the oldest societies on campus. It was aimed at offering an opportunity for coming together and discussing social problems of various countries. The society included all of the religions represented on campus but was not irreligious and aimed at the betterment of character.
6. *Al Kulliyah* has taken the place of the *Students' Union Gazette*, which was a source much less rich in the content and less regular in publishing. From 1911 to 1932 there were nine volumes of the *Gazette* and they are now available online from the website of the Libraries' section on Archives and Special Collections' section of the university's web site: http://www.aub.edu.lb.

References

Abu-Izzedine, A. (2003), Interview with the author, Beirut.
"American University of Beirut Notes" (1921), *News Letter*, 2(6).

"Around the Campus" (1948), *Al Kulliyah Alumni News Bulletin*, 23(2): 8.

"Co-acting" (1937), *Al Kulliyah Review*, 4 (3): 1.

Cohen, V. (1936), "The Women Students," *Al Kulliyah Review*, 3(15): 1–2.

Cortas, W. (1947), "Women's Education," *Al Kulliyah Review*, 22(8): 4–5.

Da Cruz, L. (2004), Interview with the author, Beirut.

Druby, A. (1946), "Psychology on Campus," *Al Kulliyah Review*, 10(3): 19–20.

Faculty Minutes (1927), American University of Beirut, 6.

Fleischmann, E. (2002), "The Impact of American Protestant Mission in Lebanon on the Construction of Female Identity, c. 1860–1950," *Islam and Christian–Muslim Relations*, 13: 411–26.

Lerner, A. (1934), "Manners on the Tennis Court," *Al Kulliyah Review*, 1(2) : 4.

Minutes of General Faculty American University of Beirut, (1920), 5.

Müge Göçek, F. and Balaghi, S. (1995), "Introduction," in F. Müge Göçek and S. Balaghi (eds), *Reconstructing Gender in the Middle East*, New York: Columbia University Press.

Okkenhaug, I. M. (2002), "She Loves Books & Ideas, & Strides along in Low Shoes Like an Englishwoman": British models and graduates from the Anglican girls' secondary schools in Palestine 1918–48," *Islam and Christian–Muslim Relations*, 13(4): 461–79.

Report of the President (1947), American University of Beirut.

Shukair, L. (1938), "Ladies and Gentlemen," *Al Kulliyah Review*, 5(9): 12.

Thompson, E. (2000), *Colonial Citizens: Republican Rights, Paternal Privilege, and Gender in French Syria and Lebanon*, New York: Columbia University Press.

"Who Cheers for Veracity" (1936), *Al Kulliyah Review*, 3(10): 1.

Zaphiriadis, J. (1946),"The Lady Students," *Al Kulliyah Review*, 10(1): 10–11.

5

Women's Voluntary Social Welfare Organizations in Egypt

Beth Baron

Introduction

Social welfare activities have been acknowledged in works on Middle Eastern women's rights movements and on gender and nationalism, for feminists often had strong social agendas and female nationalists nearly always coupled their work for the nation with social reform.[1] Indeed, one cannot read through works on women's movements and on gender and nationalism without noting the active engagement of the female protagonists in philanthropic endeavors (on Egypt, see, for example, Marsot 1978; Badran 1995). Yet this commitment and activity has rarely been the main story. Rather, it has been used to demonstrate other points, such as the feminists' concern for the poor and the reach of their movements, women nationalists' fervor and desire to uplift the nation, or women's search for an outlet for their energy and a path to wage-earning jobs and professions. None of this is necessarily wrong. Only more could be said about these voluntary social welfare projects.

My own work followed this pattern. A final chapter in *The Women's Awakening in Egypt Culture, Society, and the Press* on women's organizations saw their involvement in charities from 1890 to 1920 as a road to something else, a path to professional or political enhancement. "Charitable work came to be seen as a legitimate outlet for women of means as they learned new skills... Through voluntary associations, women expanded the parameters of permissible activities and increased their mobility." And, "elite women identified social welfare as a neglected field and fertile ground for building a power base and pushing toward the center of politics" (Baron 1994: 175, 171). In *Egypt as a Woman: Nationalists, Gender, and Politics* (Baron 2005), which covers the period through the 1940s, I suggest that social welfare work was not always a path to politics but sometimes a path from it, with women turning to social welfare work when pushed out of nationalist politics. A final chapter in *Egypt as a Woman* examines the philanthropic work of the Islamic activist Labiba Ahmad (1870s–1951) in the context of her religious nationalism.

Women's nationalist, feminist, religious and social politics cannot be easily disentangled, as women moved among and between these endeavors, seeing them as intimately connected. A range of figures, including Huda Sha'rawi, Esther Fahmi Wisa, Labiba Ahmad and others worked on several fronts, often simultaneously. The press of the period confirms this, containing numerous references to new charities, fundraisers and workshops side-by-side with discussions of women's rights and resistance to the British occupation. Yet ultimately female activists set priorities, with feminists primarily concerned with women's rights, nationalists with independence, Islamists with religious renewal, and social welfare activists with poor relief and public health (see Gallagher 1990: 54, whose work provides a good model on writing the history of women's social welfare work). Thus feminist, nationalist, religious and social politics need to be viewed both together *and* apart, to the extent possible.

The elite background of many of the Egyptian philanthropists, who as one author noted "were blessed with wealth" (Marsot 1978: 275), caused other observers to condemn their efforts as ineffectual, misbegotten or worse. They have been both lauded and attacked, yet there has been little serious historical reconstruction of their programs or analysis of the part they played in providing poor relief in Egypt. The social welfare activities of elite women were not only a central part of their lives but also a crucial chapter in the history of public health and social welfare in Egypt. This chapter moves women's social welfare activism to the center of inquiry, to examine it in the context of social welfare movements, as part of the history of "poverty and charity" in the Middle East (see Bonner, Ener and Singer 2003) and as a chapter in Egyptian women's history. The time frame considers women's voluntary social welfare work from the early 1900s through the 1960s.

A Patchwork of Providers: Private, State and Foreign

Scholars of European and US history have offered useful conceptual tools for analyzing women's social welfare work. The writing on this is voluminous, particularly from the 1990s, and is central to the field of US women's and gender history (see Ginzberg 1990; McCarthy 1990; Koven and Michel 1993; Sklar 1993; McCarthy 2001). These works consider the class backgrounds, motivations and methods of female philanthropists and "social justice feminists" (Sklar, Schuler and Strasser 1999). Their works make clear that the relationship between women and the state, and the state and social welfare, is pivotal to understanding social welfare. The literature suggests that the state picks up what women started, with women remaining instrumental in shaping and enforcing state policies and programs as they moved from volunteers to professionals with the growth of the welfare state system.

Yet for Egypt, like other areas of the Middle East, the interplay of state and private forces in providing social welfare is not the only story to be told, for there was another set of important actors in the field. These included missionaries, colonial officers and their wives, Western feminists, among others, who provided a range of social services. At first glance, it seems that women's welfare societies arose in Egypt as a nationalist reaction to foreign inroads in the field of social welfare. But to stress this simplifies the complex relationship between local and foreign social welfare activists, who competed, cooperated and relied upon one another to launch and sustain programs. This was true even as the ideological underpinnings of state, private and foreign social welfare programs shifted over time.

Mine Ener sketched transformations in poor relief in her *Managing Egypt's Poor and the Politics of Benevolence, 1800–1952* (2003). Prior to the nineteenth century, she tells us, providing benevolence was a religious obligation which individuals and the community fulfilled through acts of charity and the establishment of trusts. The rulers and elite had a special social obligation to take care of those in need and demonstrated largesse and power through the funding of soup kitchens, hostels, hospitals and the like. During the nineteenth century, the state increasingly appropriated religious functions and funds, taking over trusts and the care of the poor. Ener speaks of "managing" rather than "controlling" the poor, suggesting agency on the part of the recipients who received assistance and who "astutely negotiated" the state system of poor houses. The impulse to provide for the poor may have initially been a religious obligation, but the service was now increasingly divorced from religious institutions.

Under the British occupation from 1882, state "management" of the poor in Egypt continued. Like their predecessors, the British espoused a policy that seemed more concerned with keeping the poor out of view or off the streets than with providing meaningful services or training, and colonial authorities allotted less than 1 percent of the budget to health and welfare. Eager to have private individuals and groups bear the burden of providing social welfare, the British left the field wide open to private initiatives. Public health and social welfare thus remained a patchwork of state but mostly private Egyptian and foreign initiatives. The haphazard approach of the colonial authorities to social welfare was reflected in the distribution of services among various ministries with a reliance on efforts from missionaries, colonial wives and local elites.

Missionaries who had come to Egypt in the nineteenth century faced a ban on proselytizing among Muslims and had shifted their strategy from conversion to social transformation. They established a vast network of orphanages, schools and hospitals, and were joined in this effort by colonial wives and officers. The missionaries and colonial wives of the nineteenth and early twentieth centuries were increasingly replaced from the 1920s by representatives of large foundations such as Rockefeller and Ford. The rise of the big foundations reflected a new chapter in American philanthropy, as the foundations, some of which commanded huge resources, pushed their own ideological and social agendas. US government aid would follow the foundations into Egypt, but only later in the twentieth century.

The women's social welfare organizations that emerged from the late nineteenth century were often organized along religious and communal lines, though their lay leadership challenged traditional religious leaders. Intercommunal groups also appeared, playing a role in the secularization of society, and both communal and intercommunal organizations formed an important part of civil society. The volunteers who established these associations showed remarkable skill in navigating between the state and international agencies. The shifts and turns in this story are best told by focusing on a few examples. The stress here is on four voluntary welfare societies that devoted themselves to health and welfare. (Health and welfare are the focus rather than education, which is an enormous topic that has had some coverage and needs separate treatment.) The approach taken here diverges from the emphasis on the discourse of social reformers and family planners evident in the work of a cluster of young scholars (for more on the discourse of social reformers, see Shakry 2002). Rather, this chapter examines the founding of women's social welfare associations, their visions and programs, and the relationship of these associations to the Egyptian state and private donors.

Mabarrat Muhammad 'Ali al-Kabir (Muhammad Ali Benevolent Society)

The Mabarrat Muhammad 'Ali al-Kabir was founded in the early 1900s by royal women seeking to make a "humanitarian contribution" to the Egyptian nation in the wake of a high wave of infant mortality. Colonial wives had started a foundling home in 1898 in memory of the late Lady Cromer and subsequently started dispensaries as well. As Huda Sha'rawi, founder of the Egyptian Feminist Union, recounts in her memoir: Princess 'Ayn al-Hayat discussed her idea for founding a dispensary after Huda had declined an invitation to a tea for the new Lady Cromer. The latter, wife of the British high commissioner, had wanted to thank those Egyptian women who had participated in the founding of the Lady Cromer Refuge, among them Huda's late mother. Princess 'Ayn al-Hayat confessed to Huda she was ashamed that "we Egyptians" did not undertake such "splendid projects" (Sha'rawi 1981: 119–20 1986: 94–5; see also Mahfouz 1935: 106). At a subsequent meeting of princesses and aristocratic women, participants each pledged £50 pounds or more, with Khedive 'Abbas Hilmi's mother pledging £120 annually, and the Khedive and his wife also promising support. The pledges plus sales of a stamp added up to

£E3,000 (Egyptian pounds), which was the capital with which the society started. The stamp, which was distributed to ministries throughout the country for sale, showed a woman hugging a poor girl, reflecting the founders' maternalist vision of their benevolent role. Yet in relying on contributions of time as well as money and establishing a voluntary association to steer the project, the Mabarra marked a departure from earlier royal charitable projects.

Princess 'Ayn al-Hayat died shortly thereafter, but Princess Nazli Halim took over the project and with the assistance of aristocratic women such as Huda Sha'rawi moved their plans forward. A building was rented close to the palace on Shari'a al-Baramuni in the 'Abdin district of Cairo. An Egyptian architect renovated it and society members furnished it with donations: Huda gave beds, her brother gave desks, and one of the princesses gave sheets. The dispensary opened in 1913 in a ceremony attended by the wife of the Khedive. A "Miss Crouser," an Irish specialist in childcare, ran the unit, which was staffed by Egyptian and European physicians who volunteered their time. The society raised funds through elaborate galas in royal and aristocratic homes, which became events of great social occasion. The members of the Mabarra, who were well connected and wedded to elite notions of social prestige and "performance" of charity, assured the future of the organization (see Sha'rawi 1981: 121–3; Baron 1994: 240, notes 19 and 20).

While royal patronage of the association remained important and gave the group visibility, the day-to-day operations were in the hands of a paid staff, which was supervised by elite volunteers on the executive committee. Huda Sha'rawi at one time headed that committee, but after World War I Hidiyya Afifi (1898–1969) assumed control as treasurer and from that point effectively ran the Mabarra for nearly half a century. A product of a French convent school (Notre Dame de la Mère de Dieu), Hidiyya was tied to Sa'd Zaghlul, head of the Wafd Party, through marriage to the law professor Baha al-Din Barakat (Seton 1923: 30–1; Marsot 1978: 271–5). When she took command of the Mabarra, she pushed to expand the society's operations. According to the annual report for 1920, while the government operated twelve children's dispensaries throughout the provinces, in Cairo the field was left to "the useful work" carried out by "charitable committees" of the Mabarrat Muhammad Ali. The Mabarra ran a dispensary at Manshia and opened a new building at Madbuli, on the border of Bulaq (UK Foreign Office 1921: 77). The dispensary in 'Abdin eventually became a hospital with an outpatient clinic. Mabarra committee members oversaw the operation of the clinics and hospitals, inspecting them regularly.

Using its connections, women of the Mabarra encouraged donations of land and money to build new facilities. Government hospitals existed in major provincial towns, but these did not serve smaller towns or remote villages. Yet the government refused to broaden its services to outlying regions: "A general provision of such by the State ... would impose too great a financial burden upon the Government, and this local need must fall to be met by local effort," wrote the high commissioner in 1921. Noting the "evidence of an increasing public interest in the provision of hospital treatment for the poor is shown by the readiness of the prominent residents in many localities to give land and money to provide hospitals and to help in collecting funds for their maintenance," he was probably seeing the hand of the Mabarra at work (UK Foreign Office 1920: 83–7, 1921: 76).

Under Hidiyya Afifi Barakat's guidance and with the support of the government, the Mabarra continued to build hospitals and clinics. In the 1940s, it added emergency relief to its repertoire when faced with war and epidemics, a story which Nancy Gallagher (1990) has chronicled. During the bombing of Alexandria in 1940 and 1941, women from the Mabarra set up soup kitchens and shelters for refugees. In 1944, Mabarra leaders drew attention to the severity of the malarial epidemic and sent teams to the south to assist in emergency relief. In coordination with the Ministry of Health, which set guidelines for their work, they divided the field with the newly formed Women's Committee of the Egyptian Red Crescent Society. The first Mabarra group that went out to Luxor included Amina Sidqi, Firdaws Shitta, Mary Kahil, the Mabarra physician Dr. Benyamin, as well as two nurses, Abla Sa`id Ahmad and Ni`matullah Amin. The Red Crescent team, which was based at Isna, included women such as Nahid Sirri, Princess Chevikar's daughter Lutfiyya Yusri, Layla Shawarabi, Gertrude Butrus Ghali and Celine Cattawi, plus a palace physician. The volunteers delivered food, clothing and medicine to the sick and dying in the villages surrounding Luxor. They worked long stretches, setting up soup kitchens that fed up to 4,300 people a day and transporting food and medicine to villagers too sick to come to the larger towns for help. They soon built bases of operation and food distribution in other towns (Gallagher 1990: ch. 3; for contemporary accounts of the Women's Red Crescent, see "Shabbat al-Hilal al-Ahmar" 1945: 36–8, 1948: 40–4).

In the field and understaffed, the volunteers recognized the magnitude of the crisis and also understood that food and medicine, and their intervention, were not enough to stem the epidemic. Princess Chevikar, who then headed the Mabarra, drew attention to the crisis through a series of press conferences calling for support of the women's relief efforts. The politics of public health in the 1940s proved daunting. The British tried to defend their rather abysmal record on public health from the outset of the occupation in 1882, to deny their complicity in conveying the malarial mosquitoes to Egypt by air transport, and to keep American medical and technological competition at bay. The Wafd Party wanted to portray its own efforts from 1942, when the outbreaks of malaria began, as effective, and opposed foreign intervention, which would contradict their claims. King Faruq hoped to capitalize on the catastrophe to drive the Wafd, which the British had forced on him in 1942, from power. On their part, Chevikar and the volunteers from the Mabarra encouraged the king to press the Minister of Health to recall the Rockefeller Foundation expert in eradication. During the period that the Rockefeller team worked on eradicating the mosquitoes, they received help from the women of the Mabarra and the Women's Committee of the Red Crescent (Gallagher 1990: ch. 5).

The Mabarra continued to support the Rockefeller Foundation, which sought to turn the success of the eradication campaign into a more permanent presence in Egypt and a headquarters for their Middle East division. When Egyptian ministers proved unreceptive, officials turned to the women from the Mabarra and Red Crescent for guidance. They continued to back one another in political skirmishes, and in the field, specifically in a delousing campaign in 1946 to combat relapsing fever (Gallagher 1990: 101–2, 109). In 1947 when cholera broke out in the Delta, the government turned again to the women's relief organizations for help. The Mabarra and Women's Red Crescent Society responded by distributing supplies and clothing and by setting up vaccination centers. The Mabarra, now under the presidency of Faruq's sister Princess Fawziyya, started fourteen such vaccination centers, which inoculated hundreds of thousands of people (Gallagher 1990: 135–6).

Women involved in social welfare services developed a keen political sense and learned to work with government officials and foreign foundations. They were also well attuned to the needs on the ground. After coming face to face with the extent of rural poverty in Egypt during the eradication and inoculation campaigns, the Mabarra extended its programs and opened dispensaries in Minya, Tanta, Sidi Salim and Zaqaziq in the late 1940s. By the time the monarchy was overturned in 1952, bringing an end to Princess Fawziyya's presidency and royal patronage, the Mabarra operated twelve hospitals and eighteen dispensaries. Hidiyya Barakat assumed the presidency of the organization that she had essentially run for over forty years, administering over a hundred full-time male employees, seventy-six full-time female employees and twenty-two volunteers (Badran 1995: 121, from *Oeuvre Mohamed Ali*; see also Gallagher 1990: 170). The Mabarrat Muhammad ʿAli was one of the first non-governmental organizations founded in Egypt and provided a significant share of health and emergency relief at a time when the Egyptian state lacked the means or will to provide such services.

Jamʿiyyat al-Marʾa al-Jadida (The New Woman Society)

An alliance of middle- and upper-class Christian and Muslim notable women active in the Women's Wafd Central Committee (WWCC) founded a philanthropic organization in 1920. Calling it a "moral and charitable society" and "the first of its kind," they named it the New Woman Society (Jamiʿyyat al-Marʾa al-Jadida) after Qasim Amin's famed turn-of-the-century book of that title ("Fi Mashghal al-Mar'a al-Jadida" 1928: 183; "Jam`iyyat al-Mar'a al-Jadida" 1921: 67–76). The American visitor Grace Thompson Seton, who met some of the female founders of the society, claimed they "represented the brains, culture, and wealth of the country," and characterized their ambition as "no less than to stimulate and control the welfare work of the whole nation" (Seton 1923: 47).

Members ratified the charter of the society in April 1920. The charter divided the society into three sections: founders, distinguished members, who paid £12 per year in dues and voted a higher committee to supervise the finances and functions of the society, and general members, who elected the administrative officers to a board. The administrative officers were elected for three years, with the first term starting in 1920. The society recruited respected members of the community, announcing that only ladies of "good reputation" need apply and others would be excluded without explanation. Fees for general membership were set at 120 `ursh. As articulated in the group's charter, the mission of the society was to help Egyptian women advance through charitable projects and good works. They took as their main mission the raising and educating of poor girls.

The administrative board met weekly. It initially consisted of Amina Sidqi, wife of Dr. Mahmud Sidqi and daughter of Ismail Sidqi, an Egyptian economist, politician and sometime prime minister as president; the wife of Ahmad Shakir as vice-president; a daughter of Hussayn Thabit as treasurer; and Jamila `Atiyya, the daughter of Mahmud `Atiyya, as secretary. Distinguished members included `Alwiya Sharif, Esther Fahmi Wisa, Fatima Sami, Zaynab Rifat and Ni`mat Hamdi, plus the wife of Dr. Habib Khayyat, Raghib Iskandar and `Abd al-`Aziz Hilmi, and the daughters of Hussayn Thabit, Rahib Ahmad and Iskandar Ibrahim. More than a few were daughters or wives of physicians, and all were of the elite. Huda Sha`rawi served as honorary president, a role which essentially meant she was the main benefactor. The charter of the group clearly spelled out its structure and mission, and shows the formal nature of the organization as well as its commitment, at least on paper, to democratic processes ("Jam`iyyat al-Mar'a al-Jadida" 1921: 67–76; the program is also reproduced in al-Subki 1986: 203–7).

By the time the story of the society broke in the monthly journal al-Mar'a al-Misriyya, the group had already raised and invested a significant sum of money. The funds were used to set up a handicraft workshop and training school in the Munira section of Cairo. The editor of the journal praised the group for their industriousness and circumspection, for they had produced results rather than chased publicity ("Jam`iyyat al-Mar'a al-Jadida" 1921: 67–76). When Muhammad Tawfiq Rifaat Pasha, Minister of Education, visited the complex in the late fall of 1920, it was already in full swing, and he congratulated the group on its good work ("Jam`iyyat al-Mar'a al-Jadida" 1921: 36–7; Seton 1923: 48–9; Baron 1994: 172–3; Badran 1995: 51).

Seton visited the "Girls' Club" in the early 1920s. She described being taken to a "decayed old palace" in a poor quarter in Cairo where girls were taught "rug-weaving, embroidery, dress-making, lace-making and household work in order to learn a trade and become self-supporting." They were also given elementary instruction and lessons in simple hygiene "such as the care of teeth, eyes, skin and hair according to modern standards" (Seton 1923: 47). Jamila 'Atiyya, secretary of the society, oversaw the school with special help from two Thabit sisters – Amina and Wajida – as well as from Fatima Sami. The workshop contained between 150 and 250 girls, with some 50 living in residence ("Jam'iyyat al-Mar'a al-Jadida" 1923: 273; Seton 1923: 47). Seton noted that a visit to the facilities of the New Woman Society as well as to those of the Mabarrat Muhammad Ali "leaves one with the same impression as would a sismilar visit to Hull House in Chicago, or a settlement house in the Whitechapel district of London" (Seton 1923: 46).

Girls who benefited from charitable institutions sometimes served as foot soldiers for their benefactors. During a large meeting in January 1922 to protest British occupation policy, girls from the New Woman Society workshop sang nationalist songs (Badran 1995: 83). In a protest coordinated with the WWCC at the opening of the Egyptian Parliament in April 1924, girls from the society held up placards in French and Arabic attacking the British occupation and colonial efforts to separate Egypt and the Sudan in addition to demanding women's rights to education, divorce, monogamy and the vote (*Al-Lata'if al-Musawwara* 1924: 4; Sha'rawi 1981: 296–7, 1986: photo on p. 133). Whether the working-class girls carrying the signs understood or spoke French is not clear.

The New Woman Society established branches in provincial towns, including one, for example, in Zaqaziq early in 1922. The founder of that branch, the wife of 'Abd al-Baqi Kafifi, sent in seventeen *gallabias* for students in the society's workshop, sealing the tie between branches with a gift ("Jam'iyyat al-Mar'a al-Jadida bi al-Zaqaziq" 1922: 215). Other gifts to the society were reported in the press; giving was meant to generate publicity, garner good will or mark an auspicious occasion. Upon the death of her husband in the spring of 1922, Huda Sha'rawi gave £50 toward clothing for the students of the workshop. At the same time, Sharifa Riyad donated a quantity of valuable jewelry ("Jam'iyyat al-Mar'a al-Jadida" 1922: 262). Later that year and upon the occasion of the departure of Safiyya Zaghlul ("Mother of the Nation") to join her husband in exile in Gibraltar, Wajiyya Muhammad Musa of Minya gave £40 for clothing for the girls in the workshop ("Akbar Dakhiliyya" 1922: 405). The workshop was also meant to generate its own funds through the sale of the items of clothing, carpets and other handicrafts it made and potentially be self-sustaining.

Money was also raised in annual charity bazaars, which many flocked to and others found frivolous. These were generally held in the palaces of the elite and ran for a few days. In April 1923, the society held a three-day bazaar (two days for women only, one day for both men and women) in Munira in the palace of Mahmud Sami Pasha, a deputy in the Ministry of Communications. The bazaar included displays of handicrafts made at the workshop as well as food, sweets, flowers and musical entertainment. It made close to £1,300, the bulk of which came from the benefactor and her family ("Jam`iyyat al-Mar'a al-Jadida" 1923: 272–4). The following year, a European seamstress supervised sewing of women's and baby's clothing for a special fair ("Mashghal Jam`iyyat al-Mar'a al-Jadida" 1924). In 1928, the annual bazaar of the New Woman Society was held under the patronage of the Queen and raised £1,386 ("Fi Mashghal al-Mar'a al-Jadida" 1928: 183).

In elections in 1927, there was some reshuffling of administrative posts. Amina Sidqi retained the presidency, Fatima Sami became vice-president, the wife of Muhammad Musa took over as treasurer, the wife of Hasan Khalil Shanab became secretary and the wife of Ratib Pasha became the new honorary president ("Jam`iyyat al-Mar'a al-Jadida" 1927: 148). The change in honorary president that year (and possibly as early as 1924) might have marked the break Sha`rawi had had with the Wafd and the unraveling of the Women's Wafd Central Committee (Baron 2005: ch. 7). Already in 1924, the Egyptian Feminist Union (EFU) had opened its own dispensary for poor women and children, and a handicrafts workshop in Sayyida Zaynab, a densely populated lower-class quarter (Badran 1995: 99–100). That probably marked the withdrawal of Sha`rawi's patronage from the New Woman Society. The EFU workshop taught girls with an elementary education Arabic, French, arithmetic, hygiene, drawing, morals, religion and manual crafts (including needlework, sewing, rug-weaving and weaving of stockings, flannels and scarves). The dispensary operated alongside the workshop and was meant to serve women and children, teaching mothers hygiene and healthcare. Approximately two hundred people came daily to the dispensary, which received support from the government and from physicians who volunteered their time. Both operations were moved to Habbaniyya on Qasr al-`Ayni Street when the EFU relocated there in 1932. After the move, many medical cases were referred to the Qasr al-`Ayni hospital, which was close by, and eventually, in a budget crunch, the EFU closed the dispensary. Although a daycare facility was later opened, social work was an arm of the EFU but not its main purpose ("Dar Ittihad al-Nisa'i" 1925: 7, see photos of girls in the workshop on pp. 15–16; Arafa 1973: 33–6; Sha'rawi 1981: 298–9; Badran 1995: 99, 111–13).

By the 1940s, the New Woman Society workshop had become known for its production of carpets, handiwork and beautiful dresses, which "equaled the best" of foreign clothing styles ("al-Nahda al-Niswiyya fi Rub` Qarn" 1949: 14). By then the workshop had prepared poor girls for artisanal work and handicraft professions for over two decades.

Esther Fahmi Wisa and the Work for Egypt Society (Jam`iyyat al-`Amal li-Misr)

Esther Fahmi Wisa came from a leading Coptic notable family and was among the founders of the New Woman Society. Like many women in that group, she had marched in the ladies' demonstrations in March 1919, rallied to the side of the Wafd, and helped to found the Women's Wafd Central Committee in January 1920. When Huda Sha`rawi broke with the Wafd in 1924 and resigned as head of the WWCC, Esther stayed the course and helped establish the Sa`dist Ladies' Committee, which functioned for many years as the women's auxiliary of the Wafd Party. Having been schooled by an English nanny and American Presbyterians in Asyut, she spoke articulately to small and large gatherings at home and abroad and wrote articles for the press. She also acted as an intermediary with British officials, including Lord Allenby and others. The British high commissioner, Miles Lampson, described her in 1932 as "a prominent Wafdist lady, much interested in charitable works," and later as "a well-meaning enthusiast, much given to good works." By 1937, her son tells us, she had become disillusioned with the male political elite and declined to revive the Women's Wafd when approached by Mustafa Nahhas, successor to Sa`d Zaghlul as head of the party. (For full references, see Baron 2005: ch. 7.)

Esther had always split her energies between nationalist politics and social welfare work and was involved in a constellation of philanthropic organizations. These included the Young Women's Christian Association (YWCA), an organization that had been started in England in the 1850s, became internationalized in the 1890s, opened its first branch in Cairo in 1905 and came under the direction of Regina Khayyat in 1923. Its mission was to provide spiritual guidance and accommodations for young women along Christian lines. Esther served in numerous official capacities: as secretary of the Alexandrian board, ex-officio for Alexandria on the General Council from 1933 to 1936, chairman of the Executive General Council from 1937 to 1948, and president of the Alexandrian branch from 1942 to 1983. The group held an annual bazaar to raise funds, and Esther later hosted an annual charity dance at her home as well as the two-day summer meeting of the Executive Council. She also served on the boards of the Women's Committee of the Egyptian Red Crescent and the Coptic Ladies' Society, and worked for the Home International affiliated with La Maison des Jeunes Filles in Geneva (Wissa 1994: 251–3; Badran 1995: 114).

Hans Weiss, who surveyed conditions of "street waifs" in Alexandria for the Rockefeller Foundation in 1930, met "Madame Fahmy Wissa Bey." He described her as the woman leading the social welfare movement in Alexandria. Esther requested that a young woman be trained "so that Alexandria might also have a worker who could organize social work along modern lines in that city." She had considered studying social work in the United States herself but her family obligations – she had five children – ruled this out (Weiss 1930). Egyptian women like Esther proved savvy in seeking government and foreign assistance, and followed developments among American foundations. At the time, the journal *al-Mar'a al-Misriyya*, edited by a Coptic compatriot, Balsam `Abd al-Malik, noted the establishment of the Ford Foundation ("Mabarrat Mahmuda li-Mister Ford" 1930: 131).

Although Esther was involved in a range of philanthropies, she dedicated the bulk of her energy to the Work for Egypt Society and was the force behind the founding of the organization in 1924. Like the New Woman Society, it established a formal structure, published by-laws and established multiple branches, promoting the ideal that privileged members of society should give financial and moral support to poor families. The branch in Alexandria built and maintained an outpatient clinic at Schutz Ramleh, a suburb, on land it had purchased. The clinic employed a full-time general practitioner and nurse, with part-time specialists visiting several days a week. Patients were treated free of charge and provided with medicines. The society also had an educational arm, which gave mothers lessons in hygiene and provided childcare for working mothers ("al-Jami`yyat: Jamiyyat al-`Amal li-Misr" 1927: 48–50; "Ba`d al-`Utla" 1929: 296–7; Wissa 1994: 254–8).

Money was raised from subscriptions, annual plays, concerts, film showings, public contributions, subventions and a lottery. In 1928, in its fourth year, the Alexandrian branch of the society had a net income from the charity show of £E1,031 (after taxes) plus £E83 from subscriptions and donations. The expenses for the year, which included medicine and salaries, were £E863. The society was a corporate body whose accounts were audited annually after it came under the supervision of the Ministry of Social Affairs (Wissa 1994: 254–8).

Labiba Ahmad and the Society of Egyptian Ladies' Awakening (Jam`iyyat Nahdat al-Sayyidat al-Misriyyat)

Labiba Ahmad (1870s–1951) also marched in the women's demonstrations of March 1919, signed the petitions and rallied for the Wafd. She may have been involved in the work of the Mabarra before that, because her husband was closely tied to the royal court and was briefly master of ceremonies for Khedive `Abbas Hilmi II (r. 1892–1914). After the 1919 revolution, Labiba remained close to Safiyya Zaghlul and to the inner circle of female Wafdists, but instead of joining the Women's Wafd Central Committee, she struck out in another direction. In 1919 or so she founded the Society of Egyptian Ladies' Awakening (Jam`iyyat Nahdat al-Sayyidat al-Misriyyat), an association with an Islamic nationalist vision. Her work was "inspired by God" and a desire to "uplift the nation." The society's first project was an orphanage: Labiba and her colleagues gathered together 170 orphaned or abandoned girls from the area around Sayyida Zaynab, their base of operations, and opened the home in 1920. Labiba vowed to raise the girls and teach them the commandments of Islam. (For full references to the section here and below, see Baron 2003: 239–54.)

Not much is known about the orphanage other than the need for such an institution. Given the stigma of illegitimacy in Egyptian society (which was taken as proof of illicit sexual encounters), undesired infants were abandoned. The Lady Cromer Home (or Foundling Hospital) was originally founded in 1898 in a wing of Qasr al-Aini Hospital to take in abandoned babies. In 1902 it admitted 85 children, of whom 32 were later adopted; two years later, the hospital admitted 131 abandoned babies. Mortality was high among the group for the infants had been found shortly after their birth in deserted buildings or on waste ground (UK Foreign Office 1903: 53; "Malja' al-Itfal wa al-Wilada" 1920: 353–7). A Muslim women's welfare organization – Wafd Khalil Agha – was subsequently established in connection with the hospital to, among other things, find homes for the orphans, though strictly speaking adoption was not legal in Islam (Seton 1923: 49). The refuge still carried the name of Lady Cromer in 1920, though by then it was funded by the Egyptian government and some called it the Children's and Birthing Home ("Malja' al-Itfal wa al-Wilada" 1920: 353–7).

Labiba's group may have taken note of the fact that missionaries and colonial wives had established orphanages throughout Egypt raising them in a Christian context, and that the state ran only a few institutions at most. By starting an orphanage, Labiba Ahmad could guarantee contributors that the girls would be raised in a Muslim setting, would learn Islamic tenets and would also be groomed to be good nationalists. Like the girls of the workshop of the New Woman Society, the girls of the Society of Egyptian Ladies' Awakening marched in demonstrations carrying banners.

Raising orphans meant caring for their various needs: feeding, clothing, healing, educating and training them. Appeals were made for donations of clothing, and physicians, including her son, volunteered their services. A workshop was established to teach the girls handicrafts and housekeeping so that they would have skills and vocations. There was an appeal for lecturers to teach the girls morality. When Labiba subsequently decided that poor girls in general needed training to save them from falling into professions like prostitution, the society looked for a larger space. It rented the palace of the late ʿAbd al-Qadir Pasha Hilmi in Sayyida Zaynab and opened the doors to the new "Institute and Workshop of the Women's Awakening" in 1923.

The Society of Egyptian Ladies' Awakening did not use the same strategies for fundraising as some of their contemporaries. Bazaars and dances were too Western for their taste, even if they were segregated affairs. Instead, they started the journal *al-Nahda al-Nisa'iyya* (The Women's Awakening) to publicize their values and mission and made appeals through the press to Islamic circles. Labiba also tried other fundraising tactics. She sold a book of wisdom to raise funds and tapped into a network of governing officials as well as an Islamic circle that generously supported her venture. The workshop, too, in time probably became self-sufficient, as not only did it train girls, but also the girls produced items that could be sold.

Tracing the girls of the orphanage and workshop is difficult as their stories are not recorded in the brief reports of the society in the press. Some photos of the girls appear in *al-Nahda al-Nisa'iyya*. One shows a small child who accompanied Labiba on a trip to see off a friend sent into exile. Others show them marching with the society's banners in demonstrations or at the opening of the new workshop and institute.

Toward a Welfare State

The British colonial state was stingy in funding social services. Once Egyptian notables gained a greater measure of control over the state in 1923, they sought to undo some of the damage done by the neglect of this field. They turned their attention first to increasing the provision of state education, for education made loyal citizens and good nationalists, and only hesitantly addressed public health and welfare issues. The Egyptian state moved incrementally in the 1930s and 1940s toward broadening social services. There were reorganizations of ministries and departments, with the appearance of a Ministry of Social Affairs in 1939. One of the charges of the new ministry was to monitor private social welfare organizations. In practice this often meant giving subventions and auditing them annually. The ministry had limited funds to launch new initiatives and tended to work in cooperation with private groups. There was little legislation in this sphere during this period, aside from some protection of women's and children's labor, and in general the pace of socio-economic reform was slow.

The 1952 revolution did not result in an immediate transformation of the state's social welfare policy. Although the end of the monarchy removed an important layer of the patronage network (royal women), many of the women's social welfare organizations had assets that had been built up over the course of decades, and the societies continued to operate orphanages, workshops, clinics and hospitals. The 1950s showed a tightening of state control, continuing the pattern of characteristic of earlier years: under the provisions of Law no. 384 of 1956, all private social welfare organizations came under government supervision. This did not immediately mean a complete loss of autonomy. But eventually the state nationalized many foreign and private institutions, including most women's voluntary social welfare organizations, as part of its commitment to provide a wide spectrum of social services. The women who had been deeply involved in social welfare experiments since the 1920s experienced the new regime's injunctions in different ways as their institutions faced a variety of fates.

In 1962, the director of the Ministry of Social Affairs in Alexandria told Esther Fahmi Wisa's family that she thought the Work for Egypt Society's aims were "old-fashioned" and "irrelevant to the Ministry's plans for the development of social affairs." Having eyed the premises of the society, she planned to transform the space into a handicraft school for girls. While Esther and her board wanted to fight liquidation or to direct their assets to an institution of their own choosing, her children cautioned against putting up a fight. In the end, the Work for Egypt Society lost the property they had administered for thirty-eight years and, in spite of a promise to the contrary, the name associated with the space (Wissa 1994: 258).

The Mabarra operated its twelve hospitals and eighteen dispensaries until 1964, when all major hospitals were nationalized and its clinics were taken over as well. By its own count, it treated some 13 million patients in its last two decades, designating one-quarter of the beds in the hospitals for free service and providing treatment in the clinics for free or for nominal fees. Hidiyya Barakat stayed on as the only volunteer to work alongside government officials. By that time, the New Woman Society had merged with the Mabarra, and the new group turned its attention and what remained of its assets to developing orphanages and childcare centers. After Hidiyya's death in 1969, her daughter assumed her place as head of the group (Marsot 1978: 272–4; Gallagher 1990: 171).

Labiba Ahmad died in 1951, before the revolution. Her workshop, had it lasted until then, would have been confiscated, as most education and training centers came under the control of the state. On the other hand, if the orphanage had survived, it might have been allowed to continue. A 1965 list of member organizations and centers of the Joint Committee of Family Planning, which were all based around Cairo, included "Renaissance of Women," which was one possible translation of the group's name. Labiba's group may have survived and refashioned itself as a provider of family planning services (Hussein 1965).

Tentative Conclusions

Women's social welfare work underwent a metamorphosis from the 1900s to the 1960s. Royal, aristocratic and elite Egyptian women had always engaged in charitable giving. From the beginning of the twentieth century, they became involved in starting and running voluntary philanthropic associations that sponsored clinics, workshops, orphanages and the like, and they dedicated time and resources to the smooth functioning of these operations. When war and epidemics challenged the state welfare apparatus, these women moved into relief work, forming teams that went throughout Egypt to help clothe and feed refugees and fight disease and epidemics and advocate policy.

The state's neglect of social welfare gave women's groups ample space to launch programs and follow their own particular recipes for improving the conditions of the poor. At the same time, the state capitalized on the free services of these volunteers and intervened only to set guidelines, inspect sites and check financial records. When government officials needed their expertise and assistance, they were not averse to calling upon them. These social welfare activists in turn negotiated with the state for permissions, subventions and support. The mutual dependence worked for a few decades, giving the government a cheap way to provide limited welfare services and the women freedom to work without professional training. When the state expanded its reach in health and welfare in the 1960s, this collaboration ended. The properties of most women's voluntary social welfare organizations were taken over in a bid to monopolize and expand the scale of social services offered by the state. In revolutionary times, most of the volunteers were also discredited for having refused to address or to challenge the underlying causes of the poverty they were trying to ameliorate.

To what extent did this group of social welfare activists have an impact on the social policies of the state from the early 1900s through the 1960s? Although they were advocates of the poor, these volunteers lacked the power to enact a broad program of social legislation. Their advocacy in the political arena needs further exploration. But with the exception of some bills to regulate women's and children's labor in the 1930s, there was little social legislation in Egypt until after the revolution. The volunteers had a larger influence on social welfare practices than they did on policy. Some of the social welfare institutions they started, such as hospitals, dispensaries and workshops, endured for years and served as models. They also established a record of achievements in a new field, opening the door of the profession of social work to women. A coterie of women soon staffed the Ministry of Social Affairs and reached its upper echelons. The social welfare activists also forged links with foreign foundations, which set precedents for alliances between a generation of development specialists running NGOs and Western aid providers. While the development specialists would later disparage the relief projects of an earlier generation of social welfare activists as misguided if not outright reactionary, those professionals built their programs on decades of social welfare work in which women volunteers had started from scratch, used the tools at hand, taken risks and attempted to build projects that were local, self-sustaining and ahead of their times.

Dedication

This chapter marks the beginning of a new research project on social welfare in Egypt. I had hoped to be accompanied in this journey by Mine Ener, who set the groundwork for subsequent studies in this field with her pioneering work *Managing Egypt's Poor and the Politics of Benevolence, 1800–1952* (2003). She died in tragic circumstances in the summer of 2003. I would like to dedicate this chapter to her.

References

"Akbar Dakhiliyya" (1922), *al-Mar'a al-Misriyya*, 3, November.

Arafa, B. (1973), *The Social Activities of the Egyptian Feminist Union*, Cairo: Elias Modern Press; (1954), BA thesis, American University at Cairo.

"Ba`d al-`Utla" (1929), *al-Mar'a al-Misriyya*, 10, October 15.

Badran, M. (1995), *Feminists, Islam, and Nation: Gender and the Making of Modern Egypt*, Princeton, NJ: Princeton University Press.

Baron, B. (1994), *The Women's Awakening in Egypt: Culture, Society, and the Press*, New Haven, CT: Yale University Press.

—— (2003), "Islam, Philanthropy, and Political Culture in Interwar Egypt: The Activism of Labiba Ahmad," in M. Bonner, M. Ener and A. Singer (eds), *Poverty and Charity in Middle Eastern Contexts*, Albany, NY: State University of New York Press.

—— (2005), *Egypt as a Woman: Nationalists, Gender, and Politics*, Berkeley, CA: University of California Press.

Bonner, M., Ener, M., and Singer, A. (eds) (2003), *Poverty and Charity in Middle Eastern Contexts*, Albany, NY: State University of New York Press.

"Dar Ittihad al-Nisa'i" (1925), *al-Hisan*, 1, December 2.

Ener, M. (2003), *Managing Egypt's Poor and the Politics of Benevolence, 1800–1952*, Princeton, NJ: Princeton University Press.

"Fi Mashghal al-Mar'a al-Jadida" (1928), *al-Mar'a al-Misriyya*, 9, March–April.

Gallagher, N. (1990), *Egypt's Other Wars: Epidemics and the Politics of Public Health*, Syracuse, NY: Syracuse University Press.

Ginzberg, L. (1990), *Women and the Work of Benevolence: Morality, Politics, and Class in the Nineteenth-Century United States*, New Haven, CT: Yale University Press.

Hussein, A. (1965), "Voluntary Efforts in Family Planning," paper delivered to a conference on Family Planning, May 5–7, box 12, Population Council Papers, Rockefeller Archive Center.

"al-Jami`yyat: Jamiyyat al-`Amal li-Misr" (1927), *al-Mar'a al-Misriyya*, 8.

"Jam`iyyat al-Mar'a al-Jadida" (1921), *al-Mar'a al-Misriyya*, 2, February.

—— (1922), *al-Mar'a al-Misriyya*, 3, June.

—— (1923), *al-Mar'a al-Misriyya*, 4, May.

—— (1927), *al-Mar'a al-Misriyya*, 8, March.

"Jam'iyyat al-Mar'a al-Jadida bi al-Zaqaziq" (1922), *al-Mar'a al-Misriyya*, 3, May.

Koven, S. and Michel, S. (eds) (1993), *Mothers of a New World: Maternalist Politics and the Origins of Welfare States*, New York: Routledge.

Al-Lata'if al-Musawwara (1924), April 21.

"Mabarrat Mahmuda li-Mister Ford" (1930), *al-Mar'a al-Misriyya*, 11, April.

Mccarthy, K. (1990), *Lady Bountiful Revisited: Women, Philanthropy and Power*, New York: Rutgers.

—— (ed.) (2001), *Women, Philanthropy, and Civil Society*, Bloomington, IN: Indiana University Press.

Mahfouz, N. (1935), *The History of Medical Education in Egypt*, Cairo: Government Press of Bulaq.

"Malja' al-Itfal wa al-Wilada" (1920), *al-Mar'a al-Misriyya*, December.

Marsot, A. (1978), "The Revolutionary Gentlewomen in Egypt," in L. Beck and N. Keddie (eds), *Women in the Muslim World*, Cambridge, MA: Harvard University Press.

"Mashghal Jam'iyyat al-Mar'a al-Jadida" (1924), *al-Mar'a al-Misriyya*, 5, November.

"al-Nahda al-Niswiyya fi Rub' Qarn" (1949), *al-Taliba*, 12(2) March.

Seton, G. (1923), *A Woman Tenderfoot in Egypt*, New York: Dodd, Mead.

"Shabbat al-Hilal al-Ahmar" (1945), *al-Taliba*, 8, May.

—— (1948), *al-Taliba*, 11 July.

Shakry, O. (2002), "The Great Social Laboratory: Reformers and Utopians in Twentieth Century Egypt," PhD dissertation, Princeton University, Princeton, NJ.

Sha'rawi, H. (1981), *Mudhakkirat Huda Sha'rawi*, Cairo: Dar al-Hilal.

—— (1986), *HaremYears: Memoirs of an Eqyptian Feminist* (1879–1924), trans. M. Badran, London: Virago.

Sklar, K. (1993) "The Historical Foundations of Women's Power in the Creation of the American Welfare State, 1830–1930," in S. Koven and S. Michel (eds) *Mothers of a New World*, New York: Routledge.

—— Schuler, A. and Strasser, S. (eds) (1999), *Social Justice Feminists in the United States and Germany: A Dialogue in Documents, 1885–1933*, Ithaca, NY: Cornell University Press.

al-Subki, A. (1986), *al-Haraka al-Nisa'iyya fi Misr 1919–1952*, Cairo.

UK Foreign Office (1903), 407/161, no. 7, Cromer to Lansdowne, "Annual Report of 1902," Cairo, February 26.

—— (1920), 371/6337/8320, *Egypt: Annual Report*, London: Foreign Office.

—— (1921), 371/7766/14446, *Egypt: Annual Report*, London: Foreign Office.

Weiss, H. (1930), Letter to Dr. Durham, May 6, folder 524, box 38, series 3, Bureau of Social Hygiene, Rockefeller Archive Center.

Wissa, H. (1994), *Assiout: The Saga of an Egyptian Family*, Lewes, Sussex: Book Guild.

6

Nineteenth-century Protestant Missions and Middle Eastern Women: An Overview

Heleen Murre-van den Berg

Introduction

One of the most characteristic aspects of both Roman Catholic and Protestant mission work in the nineteenth century is the enormous amount of time, energy and money that was channeled into activities directed towards women. The missions in the Middle East were no exception to this rule. Although earlier Roman Catholic mission work in this part of the world did not ignore the women of the communities they worked with, work especially directed at women and girls was sparse compared to the nineteenth century (Heyberger 1994: 339, 470–4; Langlois 2001; Verdeuil 2001). For especially the latter decades of the nineteenth century, however, the sources suggest that activities organized for women and girls accounted for considerably more than half of the personnel and time available and that the number of females influenced by missionary activities must have been larger than the number of boys and men. In this chapter I intend to give an overview of the large variety of the work initiated by Protestant missionaries for women and girls between 1820 and 1914, coupled with a tentative assessment of the reception of these activities by the women of the Middle East.[1]

Although Protestant mission work in the Middle East in many respects was similar to mission work in other parts of the world, some of its characteristics were unique. These included the missionary activities among the ancient Christian communities of the Middle East, and the difficulties surrounding mission work among Muslims. These two issues influenced many of the choices made by the missionaries in the field. A third unique feature of these missions was the fact that they took place in a region that held a special position in the minds of the Protestants as the birthplace of Christ and Christianity.[2] The large variety of missionary groups in the Middle East as a whole, and in Palestine in particular, should be attributed to this special position of the "Bible Lands" in early nineteenth-century Protestantism. However, much as these beliefs influenced the choice of stations and the distribution of missionary funds by home administrators, the practical issues in the Middle Eastern missions do not seem to have been much affected by it.

Historical outline

The two organizations that dominated Protestant mission work in the Middle East were the Church Missionary Society (CMS) based in London, and the American Board of Commissioners for Foreign Missions (ABCFM) based in Boston.[3] From 1815 onwards, these two organizations sent their missionaries to the region and continued to dominate the scene for the next hundred years.[4] The CMS was strong in Egypt, Palestine and Persia, the ABCFM in Persia, Lebanon and Turkey. In addition, the London Jews Society (LJS) supported work in Istanbul (1826) and Jerusalem (1833) (Gidney 1908; Tibawi 1961; Crombie 1991). From 1842 onwards, the Anglo-Prussian bishopric in Palestine cooperated with the LJS in working among Jews, and with the CMS in working among Eastern Christians. Probably the first missionary school for girls was established around 1824, when the wives of the ABCFM missionaries Goodell and Bird started a little school in Beirut (Tibawi 1966: 32).[5] In 1835 the first unmarried female teachers arrived (ABCFM), Rebecca Williams in Beirut and Betsey Tilden in Jerusalem (Tibawi 1966: 65–6, 74, 82–4, 86). In the 1840s, more female teachers followed, among them Fidelia Fiske in Iran, and the number of girls' schools continued to grow, especially in the ABCFM missions.

In the 1850s and early 1860s, the Kaiserswerth Deaconesses from Germany founded orphanages and schools for girls in Jerusalem (1851), Smyrna (1853) and Beirut (1861); besides these, hospitals were opened in Jerusalem (1851), Constantinople (1852), Alexandria (1857) and Cairo (1884) (Disselhoff 1886: 105–35). Next to these, other nursing projects were established, such as Miss Wordsworth Smith's The Palestine and Lebanon Nurses' Mission (Richter 1970 [1910]: 206). Over the century, the deaconesses' organization was to grow into one of the most important in connection with work among women. There were more organizations supporting women's work in the Middle East: the Female Education Society (FES) and the Society for Promoting Female Education in the East (SPFEE), which initially had sent their (female) missionaries mainly to India, started to send missionaries to the Middle East, for instance working with the CMS in Nazareth, Palestine (Murray 2000: 66–90; see also Richter 1970: 244). The British Syrian Mission (also known as the Ladies' Association for Social and Religious Improvement of Syrian Females) started as a private initiative by Mrs. Elisabeth Bowen Thompson and Mrs. Augusta Mentor Mott in Syria (around 1860), and developed into a fully fledged girls' school system with thousands of pupils (Tibawi 1966: 156–7; Richter 1970: 203; Melman 1992: 178).

Other private initiatives were Caroline Cooper's schools for girls in Palestine of 1848 (Tibawi 1961: 150, 208; Melman 1992: 184ff.) and Mary Whately's "ragged schools" in Egypt of 1861 (Whately 1863a, 1863b; Cale 1984). In these years, other Protestant organizations also began work in the Middle East, such as the American Presbyterians in Egypt (Watson 1898; Richter 1970: 345–8), the Scottish Presbyterians in Palestine (Marten 2002), the Free Church of Scotland in Syria (Tibawi 1966: 155; Richter 1970: 205), the Society of Friends in Palestine (Richter 1910: 257) and the Lutherans and Anglicans in Urmia, Persia (Coakley 1992; Murre-van den Berg 1999; Joseph 2000). In 1870, the Presbyterian Board of Foreign Missions took over ABCFM work in Syria and Persia (Brown 1936), and the Dutch started mission in work in Egypt (Vlieger 1892).[6] All these missions supported some form of female education, and most missions did additional work among women.

When in the 1870s and 1880s the work of unmarried female missionaries became both increasingly popular and widely acceptable,[7] work among the female half of the population increased even more, since most of these missionaries worked almost exclusively for women, as teachers, evangelists, doctors and nurses.[8] Another characteristic of mission work in these later years was the fact that some of the larger stations functioned almost as family businesses, being occupied by missionary families of several generations interconnected by marriage. In such groups women played important but often informal roles, with wives, daughters, sisters and nieces of the leading male missionaries taking responsibility for large parts of the work.[9]

As indicated in the introduction to this chapter, the characteristic population mix of the Middle East made for mission work that in some respects was significantly different from that in other parts of the world. Although the initial aim of the Protestant missions was to convert Muslims (and in some circles, Jews) to Christianity, it was the Eastern Christians who in the period up to 1870 attracted the largest number of missionaries. The most obvious reason for this was the fact that Muslim governments as well as local religious authorities made it rather difficult for Protestant missions to direct their activities towards the Muslim population, whereas mission activities among Christians were accepted by the governments and often initially welcomed by local Christian leaders. Partly as a response to this situation, and partly as a result of the evangelical rejection of "ritualistic," "hierarchical" and "nominal" Christianity (familiar elements from Roman Catholic Protestant polemics), the "reawaking" or "reformation" of the Eastern Christians was seen a necessary step towards the long-term goal of conversion of Muslims and Jews. It was only some of the smaller missions (like those of Mary Whately in Egypt and the LJS in Palestine) that consistently worked among Muslims or Jews, whereas most other missions worked among the Christian communities of the Middle East. From the 1870s onwards mission work among

Muslims again became the focus of the larger organizations, of the Presbyterians in Iran, the CMS in Iran and Egypt, and the new Arabia Mission of the American Dutch Reformed Church in southern Iraq and the Arabian Peninsula, all of which gave considerable attention to work among females (Al-Sayegh 1998; Doumato 1998; Francis-Dehqani 2000). Increasing numbers of female missionaries and work more and more aimed specifically at the women of the Middle East thus went hand in hand with increasing attention for the Muslim population.[10]

The Variety of Missionary Work

Protestant mission work in the nineteenth century consisted of a large variety of activities that were ultimately intended to induce Muslims, Christians and Jews to convert to the evangelical version of the Christian faith. At least six categories of mission work can be distinguished: formal or public preaching; informal preaching or teaching ("conversation"); caring for children of the local population; education; translating and printing; health care.[11] In addition to the conversionist aim, most if not all of the nineteenth-century missionaries were also committed to certain civilizational aims, which in their view belonged intrinsically to the evangelical lifestyle.[12] In particular the work for women was motivated by more or less explicit ideas about "evangelical motherhood," in which women were portrayed as the driving force behind the new Christian family.[13] These ideas were transmitted to the women and men of the Middle East through all aspects of missionary work, parallel to the conversionist aim.

Formal or Public Preaching
"Formal" or "public" preaching, despite being ABCFM administrator Rufus Anderson's preferred missionary method (Hutchison 1987; Harris 1999; Murre-van den Berg 2000), in practice was the least important missionary method in the Middle East. In most stations, missionaries had an opportunity to preach only in the context of the newly established Protestant congregations; in addition, female missionaries were excluded from public preaching or speaking in almost all mission stations. This suggests that the influence of such preaching was mostly restricted to a small circle of women and men who had converted to Protestantism or were at least sympathetic to the missionary message. Although the actual contents of missionary sermons have to my knowledge never been the subject of serious study, one might assume that a call for repentance and conversion on the one hand, and maintaining a Christian lifestyle on the other, constituted the main part of the message. To what extent male missionaries conveyed explicit messages about evangelical domesticity and the role of women and men to their congregations remains to be seen.

Informal Preaching or Teaching

Informal preaching or teaching, on the contrary, played a large part in the missions of the Middle East and was considered by most of the missionaries, male and female, to be the core of their mission work, even if it often took place in spare time between formal teaching, healing and writing. "Conversational preaching," as it was often called, was a particularly appropriate term for women's meetings in private homes (so-callled "harem visits") and informal gatherings of women in the countryside initiated by a missionary teacher or a local Bible woman. Especially in the later decades of the nineteenth century, this line of work was the strong point of the female missionaries, who, unlike their male co-workers, generally seem to have been less involved in organized activities such as literary work and preaching. In some cases, conversational preaching combined with strong personal relationships was another key method of fostering conversions, especially among the Christian population. A missionary teacher such as Fidelia Fiske in Urmia (Iran) used every opportunity to talk about the evangelical message with the girls in her seminary, and became famous for the large number of conversions among her pupils (Porterfield 1997: 68–86; Robert 1997: 109–15; Murre-van den Berg 2001). Among non-Christians, however, conversions were scarce. Elisabeth Anne McCaul Finn, the wife of the British Consul in Jerusalem between 1845 and 1863, was not formally a missionary but spent much of her time visiting the women of the Jewish community talking to them about Christianity – with hardly any conversions to show for it.[14] Later in the nineteenth century, female missionaries in Persia and Arabia saw "visiting" as the best opportunity to preach the Gospel to those Muslim women who lived largely secluded from the outside world. While they seem to have been received warmly by the local women, almost no conversions are reported. In general, therefore, the work was seen as preparatory, as a "means to conquer the deep-rooted antipathy, and superstitious fear of the Persian women, thus helping the missionaries to come into close relation with them, and bringing into their dull and dark lives some rays of new hope and heavenly light" (Richter 1970: 327). Although the missionaries tended to write more about their conversionist than their modernist agenda, it seems likely that they also used these homely contacts to convey the ideals of evangelical motherhood and domesticity to the women they encountered.[15]

Caring for Children of the Local Population

The raising of local children in missionary families, although not often described as a separate activity, formed an important part of missionary work all over the world. Initially, children were frequently brought to missionaries as a sign of trust, and soon the missionaries encouraged such temporary adoptions as a good opportunity to convey to these children the evangelical truths in all its aspects. A few local children in missionary families often formed the nucleus of the small boarding schools that were established in the 1840s, like the girls boarding with the De Forest and Whiting families in Beirut and Abeih (Tibawi 1966: 115–16). It was in the 1850s and 1860s that the Kaiserswerth Deaconesses introduced girls' orphanages in which, although the conversionist and civilizational aims remained important, immediate relief from poverty and destitution formed the prime incentive, especially after the intercommunal wars in Lebanon in 1860 (Disselhoff 1886: 106–12, 122–30; Richter 1970: 202, 268).

Education

Formal teaching, from primary schools to college education, was the most visible aspect of missionary work directed towards girls and young women, and has received considerable attention in mission studies so far.[16] Many of the larger missionary organizations, especially the ABCFM, maintained a network of primary schools in the countryside surrounding the mission station. The CMS had a similar system in Palestine and Egypt. Not a few of these schools were coeducational and closely resembled earlier Christian and Muslim denominational schools in the region. In later years, these schools either became more closely linked to the missionary educational system (because graduates from the mission schools taught there) or were disbanded or completely taken over by local teachers. An interesting variant of such primary schools were Mary Whately's "ragged schools," which she established for poor Muslim girls in Cairo and elsewhere in Egypt. The "ragged school" was a concept derived from missionary work in British towns, aimed explicitly at the lower classes. In some ways more like the boarding schools in other missions, her day schools tried to inculcate concepts of cleanliness and domesticity in the girls, in addition to making them familiar with the Bible (Whately 1863a, 1863b; Richter 1970: 358).

It was the boarding schools in the mission stations that in many respects constituted the center of missionary educational work. These were the schools that had initially been set up by missionary wives in their own homes, but were subsequently taken over by single female teachers with a more or less formal training in teaching. In these boarding schools, girls learned to read and write (in the early years only a few of the girls had had any prior education), to be followed by a kind of secondary education including subjects such as geography, philosophy, history, moral philosophy, singing and sometimes English.[17] In addition, the girls were trained in a variety of domestic skills, including sewing and needlework. This was in line with the Mount Holyoke model, one of the first institutions for women's advanced education in the United States, where many female missionaries had been trained (Porterfield 1997). The first goal of these institutions was the conversion of the pupils, the second the formation of a new generation of Protestant wives and mothers who would transmit the new religious and domestic values to the coming generation.[18] Despite the concern for the religious and intellectual training of the future Protestant elite, the schools also attracted girls from families less connected to the Protestant communities, so much so that in a few cases, like the Female Seminary in Constantinople in the early 1860s (Merguerian 1990–1) and the schools in Tripoli in 1873 (Tibawi 1966: 198), the ABCFM administrators felt compelled to force the missionaries to open up new schools especially for Protestant girls.

The Kaiserswerth Deaconesses introduced a different model of education. Theirs was aimed at providing girls from the lower classes, of all denominations, with a basic industrial training to enable them to provide financially for their families.[19] In this context needlework and domestic skills did not belong so much to the extras of the evangelical housewife, but rather were valued as important skills in the labor market: the girls were expected either to work as domestic helps in the households of the rich or to make money by sewing, embroidery or laundering.[20] In Jerusalem, where the Talitha-Kumi institute became well established, earlier projects to help Jewish and Christian women to provide a living had already been started by Finn, Cooper and the LJS (Melman 1992: 183–8; Okkenhaug 2002a: 14–19). In 1868, the Women's Board of Mission initiated a somewhat similar practical project when they funded a school in Constantinople that combined schooling for females with community outreach and medical care (Merguerian 1990–1: 121).

In the same period, still other types of missionary education began to develop, often in response to requests from local communities of both Protestants and Eastern Christians. The Syrian Protestant College (for boys, later to develop into the American University of Beirut) was one of such initiatives that provided higher education for students from all parts of the population, rather than concentrating on Protestant youth (Tibawi 1967). For girls, similar ventures were undertaken, such as the American College for Girls (later the Constantinople College for Girls), the Female College in Beirut (Fleischmann 2002) and the girls' department of the Euphrates College in Kharput, the first higher institution that in 1875 was coeducational in the sense that boys and girls were offered identical programs, although they were taught in separate buildings (Merguerian 1990–1: 121, 1992–3: 51). These schools then became attractive to other segments of the population, and Muslims, especially Muslim girls, started to return to the mission schools.[21] The mix of pupils from different communities, together with a growing international outlook in the Ottoman Empire, led the Constantinople College to adopt English (which had been temporarily banned from the ABCFM mission schools in 1862) rather than Armenian as the language of instruction (Merguerian 1990–1: 121). The schools established by the Anglican Bishop Blyth and his family in Jerusalem from 1887 onwards also succeeded in attracting a mixture of pupils from the different groups in Palestine, not in the least because of their (rather unusual) non-proselytizing policy (Okkenhaug 2002a: 11). Even the Kaiserswerth Deaconesses, although thoroughly committed to the education of the lower classes, from 1862 onwards maintained a "Höhere Mädchenschule" in Lebanon intended for girls from the higher classes – with the explicit aim to generate surplus money from the school fees to be fed back into other projects (Disselhoff 1886: 128). In these types of schools, the conversionist aim faded more and more into the background – sometimes deliberately so (as in the case of the Blyth schools), sometimes without explicitly admitting it. Consequently, the modernizing aim of missionary education became a driving force of the schools, and to a large extent determined the curriculum and the informal teaching in and around the schools.

Translating and Printing

The missioniaries' activities in the area of printing and translating have sometimes been overrated, but they have undoubtedly contributed significantly (more so in the more remote regions than in the communities closer to the metropolises of the Middle East) to literacy in general and printing and publishing in particular.[22] Through their publications, the missionaries publicized the twin aims of the Western missions, and the titles in the missionary catalogues and contributions in missionary magazines display a peculiar mix of pious conversionist literature (usually translations of Anglo-Saxon evangelical books and tracts, but including some publications by missionaries or local converts) and publications extolling the accomplishments of Western culture (Kawerau 1958: 390–7). There is no doubt that women were included in the intended readership of the new publications as much as men.

Health Care

It was the extension of the health care system in the last decades of the nineteenth century, including a significant increase in female doctors and nurses, that became of great importance for Muslim women in the more remote regions of the Middle East. The missions in Persia (both in the cities and in the countryside), and especially those in southern Iraq and the Arabian Peninsula, made good use of these female agents, who were able to get in touch with women who until that time had had no contact with Westerners at all. Apart from benefiting from Western medical knowledge in regions where little medical expertise was present, these visits also provided the missionaries with ample opportunities to spread the Gospel. However, although the work was successful as regards the numbers of women treated in the hospitals and dispensaries, conversions to Christianity hardly ever took place.

Results of Mission Work

The most difficult question to answer is how all these activities influenced the women of the Middle East. Is it at all possible to weigh the disparate evidence and make conclusive judgments on such a varied and long-term undertaking as the Protestant missionary endeavor in the nineteenth century? It formed part of the growing Western influence in the Middle East in general and took place alongside rival Roman Catholic missions, whose modernizing agenda was not fundamentally different from that of the Protestants. Although it is therefore difficult to disentangle Protestant missionary work from the many other influences that stimulated women's awakening in the Middle East (Baron 1994), I would like to pay attention to a few areas where the missions' influences are clearly detectable.

The most obvious places to look for Protestant missionary influence are the communities of the converted. Although the Protestant communities were rather small, probably consisting of no more than about 30,000 members in all of the Middle East in 1908 (Richter 1970: 421), and most converts originally belonged to the Eastern Churches rather than to Islam or Judaism, the early converts are an important source for a better understanding of Protestant influence. Although it is somewhat risky to go by the few sources that have been explored so far, my own research on the early converts of Fidelia Fiske's Female Seminary in Urmia suggests that the first generations of female converts were attracted to the missionary message first and foremost because of its aspect of individual repentance and conversion (Murre-van den Berg 2001).[23] Evangelical conversion was a highly personal affair, nourished by close relationships with the missionary teacher and sustained by a continuing interaction with the teacher and others in the same circle. For women this aspect probably was more important than for men, because at least some of the women seemed to have perceived active participation in religion (and even partaking in "salvation") as a male privilege: "They used to dwell much on those words of Solomon, 'One man among a thousand I have found, but a woman among all these have I not found' but now they see their mistake, and that Christ died for women also" (Murre-van den Berg 2001: 41).[24] One might assume, therefore, that the active religious roles of the female missionaries might well have encouraged a further and more individual spiritual awakening and appropriation among women of the Eastern Churches.

The letters of Fiske's converts also indicate that conversion in the strict sense, that is accepting the evangelical version of Christianity, went hand in hand with a conversion to "evangelical modernity" (Van der Veer 1996; Makdisi 1997). The most striking example of such a modernizing influence is that of the young man Yuhannan, who wrote to Fiske that he did not want to marry the girl from the mountains his parents had chosen for him, because "if I take one of these who are so wicked, ignorant, immodest and disorderly, they will embitter my life." He rather preferred a particular girl of the Female Seminary, who "can help me, and strengthen me, in the work of God." Yuhannan's preferred wife, Sarah, daughter of the priest Auraham, herself later referred to the virtues of the evangelical housewife as "visiting the sick," "propriety, politeness, and courtesy to every one," "cleanliness and good order in the house" being "outward signs of Christianity," as well as "diligence in business, that we should not be dependent on others for assistance, but on the might of our own hands" (Murre-van den Berg 2001: 43). These same letters also indicate that the missionaries' influence on these women went further than change of heart and daily lifestyles: many of these women, including Sarah, followed in Fiske's footsteps by becoming teachers and missionaries themselves (Anderson 1873, vol. 2: 307–11; Murre-van den Berg 2001: 39–40). Such women have played important but largely undocumented roles in the spread of evangelical modernity in the Middle East. All histories make references to converts that became teachers and missionaries themselves, such as Tibawi's work on Middle Eastern women who became teachers in mission schools (Tibawi 1966: 82, 163, 198, 209) and Disselhoff's on various former pupils who became deaconesses or taught in their schools (Disselhoff 1886: 111–12, 122, 126–7, 129). However, so far no systematic study on the lives and careers of these early converts has been carried out.

Yet, the modernizing influence of the missionaries extended beyond the converts to evangelical Protestantism. The mission schools, from primary schools up to the colleges, usually had no problems filling their classes, which reflects the almost immediate recognition by the people of the Middle East of the importance of education for girls. In fact, although Protestant missionaries in their home publications often refer to local opposition or initial lack of interest when starting girls' schools, in practice it seemed to have been relatively easy to acquire at least a few pupils to start with. I know of no single mission station where it proved impossible to establish a girls' school, and after a slow start more pupils were usually queuing up than the missionaries could accept. Later, opposition directed against the missionaries' message itself often led to the establishment of rival schools for boys and girls, rather than a return to earlier informal educational systems.[25] Although the influence of these schools on these generations of Christian, Jewish and Muslim girls cannot be easily measured, it is striking that many of the women who played crucial roles in the "women's awakening" in Egypt were educated at Syrian mission schools founded in the second half of the nineteenth century, both Protestant and Roman Catholic (Baron 1994: 16–26). This indicates that the schools not only produced a new female readership in the Middle East, but also stimulated women to write and publish themselves.[26]

Not only through these schools, but also through the missionary publications and perhaps also through "conversational preaching," the missions were one of the factors that stimulated Middle Eastern women to rethink their roles in family and society. Changes occurred in both areas: women were increasingly seen as "professional" and primary child-raisers, coinciding, however, with a growing acceptance of public roles for Middle Eastern women.[27] As noticed by others, the female missionaries themselves provided the examples for the ambiguous relationship between these two types of roles: some female missionaries remained single and found their destiny in their teaching or medical careers, others were already married, or married after some years of teaching or other professional occupations.[28] The same types of life-paths may be seen among the graduates of the mission schools.

Missionary education prepared some women for more than interesting professional careers. Especially in the new nationalist movements, whose rise was to a certain extent also connected with the missionary experiment, women rose to positions of leadership by conscious choice or by historical accident. An interesting example of such a career is Surma d'Bait Mar Shimun (1883–1975), who was born in to the leading family of the Assyrians in Kurdistan and was educated largely by an Anglican missionary, William Henry Browne. The combination of an aristocratic background and Anglican "imperial" education made her into the perfect leader of the Assyrian people after World War I had not only driven the Assyrians from their ancient homelands in Eastern Turkey, but also robbed them of most of their male leadership.[29]

A final question to be asked is to what extent the missionaries' spirituality influenced the religious life of the women of the Middle East. Did the women who did not convert take away with them something of the "Protestant" type of religious life? I came across the interesting example of Halidé Edib from Istanbul. Halidé, a woman from a wealthy and politically well-connected family in Istanbul, was a pupil of the Constantinople College for Girls in the 1890s. In her memoirs she reflects on her two periods in the college. Although she never felt tempted to convert,[30] she describes the college's influence on her spiritual development, on the one hand opening up "new vistas,"[31] and inciting deep religious emotions,[32] on the other showing the limits of Christianity.[33] She summarized her quest as follows: "I struggled to fit all the new outlook of life, acquired through my education in the college, into Islamic experience and belief" (Edib 1926: 192).[34] To what extent her experience is representative of her generation of Muslim students in the missionary colleges is difficult to say, but it seems not so different from the type of experiences expressed by later generations of students in the schools in Beirut and Jerusalem. In all these cases, the missionary message of evangelical conversion was explicitly rejected, but important aspects of the religious message, especially in connection with individual spiritual agency, were accepted and internalized.

Conclusion

This overview of Protestant missionary activities aimed at the women of the Middle East in many ways remains unsatisfactory. Despite the wealth of studies already available, an overview such as this confronts us with the fact that with respect to many of the organizations and many of their activities our knowledge is rather superficial. Although education in general has received a good deal of attention, the differences between the various types of missionary schools, and between schools supported by different missionary societies, have hardly been studied, whereas the contents of the important aspect of "conversational preaching" remain largely hidden from our sight. The ambiguous policy of raising local children in missionary families and orphanages has also hardly been studied so far. This is even truer when those who undertook these activities were the women of the Middle East themselves. Their contribution to these missionary activities has hardly been documented and analyzed. Despite all this, however, there can be no doubt that the Protestant missionary movement dedicated a large part of its resources to what it thought to be the uplifting of the women and girls of the Middle East, and there is also little doubt that in many instances these activities were received positively by the local population, mainly Eastern Christians, but also Jews and Muslims. Via spiritual empowerment on the one hand, and education and modernization on the other, the missionaries contributed to the awakening of the women of the Middle East in the late nineteenth and early twentieth centuries, and thus to the shift in gender relations that fundamentally changed the social and political structures of the Middle East.

Notes

1. Due to the great variety of missions featuring in this overview, I have limited myself to published materials, most of which consist of secondary studies from the twentieth century, although a number of published primary sources of the nineteenth century have been taken into account. For the difficulty of retrieving the voice of the women of the Middle East, see in particular Fleischmann (1998).
2. On Protestant "geopiety" in the nineteenth century, see Melman (1992) and Vogel (1993). On the characteristics of Middle Eastern missions in general, see Murre-van den Berg (2005).
3. Note that many of the smaller missions are not mentioned in the following overview. Some of these can be traced via Richter (1970 [1910]); other small (often private) missions have not made it to the official histories. Note too that Richter is somewhat hesitant about the American approach to female education: "So Americans are inclined

to extend to Oriental women, too, a fuller measure of educational advantages than seems desirable or proper to a German mind" (Richter 1970: 133).

4. The first CMS missionary was William Jowett at Malta; the first ABCFM missionaries were Pliny Fisk and Levi Parsons, who arrived in Syria in 1819. On the CMS and ABCFM, see the official histories by Anderson (1873), Stock (1899) and Strong (1910).

5. The early missionaries seem to have been largely unaware of the existing forms of female education in the Middle East, such as the *kuttabs* where Muslim boys and girls learned the Koran, some schools in the Christian communities, as well as some government-sponsored schools in Egypt (see Tucker 1999: 82–3). On the rather ambiguous aims and results of the Egyptian governmental "School of Midwives," established in 1832, see Fahmy (1998). On Constantinople, see Merguerian (1990–1: 107).

6. Vlieger (1892: 33) gives the impression that schooling for girls in the Dutch mission was rather different from that for boys. For the latter, elaborate and apparently high-level examinations are described, whereas a visit to the girls' school mentions needlework only. Although this can be due to the observer (a male German scholar), it seems very possible that the level and actual program of the boys' and girls' schools were quite different.

7. The CMS sent its first unmarried women missionaries as late as 1887, although single woman missionaries of the FES and SPEE often worked in CMS mission stations (Murray 2000: 72). The ABCFM sent its first single female missionaries in the 1830s, whereas the interdenominational Woman's Union Missionary Society Board was established in 1861 because American women disagreed with the policies of the main American mission boards. In 1868, the Woman's Board of Missions was founded, which supported ABCFM work only, among other things by sending single female missionaries (Robert 1997). For the number of female versus male missionaries in the Presbyterian Mission in Persia around 1908, see Richter (1970: 326): sixteen unmarried and twenty married females, in total, thirty-six women versus twenty-three men. On British female missionaries, see Semple (2003).

8. In this period hospitals with training facilities for doctors and nurses were introduced all over the Middle East, often with separate women's wings. An example is the hospital in Urmia (Iran) that was built in 1880 and to which a women's wing was added in 1890, headed by Dr. Emma T. Miller (Murre-van den Berg 1999: 70).

9. On the CMS Stuart family, see Murray (2000: 75–6); on the Anglican Blyth family in Jerusalem, see Okkenhaug (2002a: 9–11). Similar types of relationships probably existed among the Shedd and Cochran families in Urmia, and the Bliss, Jessup and Dodge families in Beirut (both ABCFM).

10. It is unlikely, however, that the two developments are directly linked. Some of the reasons for the shift to Islam are, first, the less antagonistic attitude of Muslim governments towards Western missionaries because of increasing Western influence in general and the British occupation of Egypt (1882) in particular, second, a growing awareness of the fact that both the awakening of the Eastern Christians and the new Protestant communities would not by itself attract Muslims to Christianity, third, the attractiveness of higher education and professional medical care (hospitals) for

Muslims, and fourth, the arrival of a new generation of evangelical missionaries who were not encumbered with attachments to the local Christians.

11. In general, the missions did not consider material support for the poorer parts of the population to be their immediate responsibility. Only under specific circumstances such as the massacres of 1860 in Lebanon, the Armenian massacres at the end of the nineteenth century, as well as during World War I, orphanages and income-generating projects were established to alleviate the suffering of the local population. On a smaller scale, however, similar projects were started when converts lost their regular income because of conversion to Protestantism.

12. Through the nineteenth century, the relationship between these two aims was subject to intense discussions. In ABCFM circles, the civilizational aims were seen as secondary to the conversionist aim for most of the nineteenth century, whereas towards the end of the nineteenth century the civilizational aspect became of equal importance: see Hutchison (1987) and Harris (1999). On similar discussions in British missions, see Stanley (2001).

13. Since the mid-1980s, there has been a large range of literature on this topic, discussing its limits and inner tensions; see Hill (1985), Porterfield (1997), Robert (1997), Fleischman (1998) and Okkenhaug (2003).

14. On Finn's activities in Jerusalem, which amounted to considerably more than just visiting, see Melman (1992: 179–90). See further Finn's fictional work based on her stay in Jerusalem (Finn 1866, 1869).

15. On this type of mission, see Doumato (1998: 332–3) and Francis-Dehqani (2000: 99, 111). For several descriptions of such visits, see Rice (1922: 80–3, 94, 97–8); the missionary Mary Bird is quoted reporting: "The Princess gave me no opportunity of talking about religion, but I hope prejudice is giving way" (Rice 1922: 97–8).

16. Education in general has always been the most easily quantifiable and describable element of mission history; early mission historians such as Anderson (1873), Richter (1970 [1910]) and Stock (1910) were eager to include relatively large amounts of materials on educational projects. Their works, together with the two studies by Tibawi (1961, 1966), remain invaluable, also for the field of female education. In studies concerned with mission and gender, education has understandably been a primary focus; see the studies mentioned in notes 7 and 13. In addition, see Merguerian (1990–1).

17. Despite the relatively large amount of studies on missionary education, it is rather difficult to assess the contents and level of the schooling offered in the various mission schools. On the curriculum in the Armenian schools, see Merguerian (1990–1: 111–12, 1992–3: 45). On the girls' school in Beirut, see Tibawi (1966: 125), on Fiske's school in Urmia, see Porterfield (1997: 70) and Robert (1997: 111–13).

18. Muslim girls had attended the boarding schools in the earliest phase, but left when the schools became more professional in the 1840s, compare, for example, Tibawi (1966: 82) on the school in Beirut.

19. It seems that the schools of the deaconesses attracted slightly more non-Christians than those of the Americans, but the numbers were small; compare Disselhoff (1886: 126) on the school in Beirut (date uncertain, towards 1880s): 31 Druse, 2 Muslim and 2 Jewish girls out of a total of 800 girls.

20. Compare also the discussion by Labode (1993: 126–44) on the importance of domestic training in Anglican missions in South Africa, different from both the Kaiserswerth model and the ABCFM model.

21. According to Tibawi (1966: 287), Muslims in Syria removed their children from the mission schools in the 1890s, partly because of the emerging Ottoman school system, and partly because the government strongly discouraged sending children to "foreign schools" (Edib 1926: 153). In Egypt, according to Baron (1994: 135–6), Muslim girls in mission schools were few around 1890, whereas around 1810, 30 percent of the female students were Muslim. This was a higher percentage than that of Muslim boys, probably due to better educational possibilities for boys outside the missionary schools. In 1909, the American College for Girls was opened in Cairo, with twenty-nine students, seventeen of whom were Muslims.

22. See an assessment of the missionary contribution to Arabic printing by Roper (1998), and for the Armenian situation see Merguerian (1998). Influence of missionaries on publishing and printing has been the most extensive among the Assyrians of north-western Iran: compare Murre-van den Berg (1999) and Kawerau (1958).

23. There are indications that part of the attraction of Catholicism in the earlier period was also related to the individualization of religion: "La distinction: conscience individuelle et comportement social du catholique" (Heyberger 1994: 511–22).

24. This is not to suggest that women did not participate in religion before the nineteenth century; however, it was in ways rather different from those introduced by the missionaries, compare Murre-van den Berg (2004).

25. Compare the establishment of Armenian schools in Istanbul (Anderson 1873, vol. 2, 231) and Coptic schools in Egypt (Baron 1994: 133). Compare also the somewhat exaggerated assessment of the influence of the missions on female education in the missionaries' own circles by Richter (1970):

> It was said at that time that there was not a girl in all Syria who could read and even educated Muhammadans asserted that one might as well try to teach a cat to read as a girl. The missionaries were thus the pioneers of female education. Looking to-day at the hundreds of girls' schools belonging to Muhammadans, Greeks, Maronites and Jews, which cover Syria from Aleppo to Jerusalem, we realize the change that has taken place in public opinion, a result of the example set by the missionaries. (Richter 1970: 191)

26. In the Neo-Aramaic missionary magazine of Urmia (*Zahrire d-Bahra*, "Rays of Light"), women are among the first local contributors (Murre-van den Berg 2001). Because many early publications were anonymous much more research is needed to assess both the local contributions in general and those of women in particular.

27. On these developments, see especially the discussions by Abu-Lughod (1998), Janjmabadi (1998) and Shakry (1998). These authors do not link these developments within the Islamic world to missionary influence per se, although Western influence in general is recognized as one of the factors.

28. On the ambiguous relationship between these two aspects, see Fleischmann (2002). See further Okkenhaug's chapter on the graduates of the Anglican girls' school St. George College in Jerusalem (2002a: 298–323), describing a slightly later period.

29. Her biography is still to be written; the best source so far is Coakley (1992). Her own work (Surma 1983 [c. 1920]) tells us little about herself. Compare also the reference in Stark (1951):

    > So that they really have a very strong position, and they are being led by a remarkable woman, the Lady Surma, aunt of the young head of the nation who is a religious chieftain. She and her nephew are sitting up at a place called Amadia (old Roman fortress) in the north, and refusing all blandishments to come down. I think they have every chance of forcing people's hands so long as they make reasonable demands: on the other hand they seem to want quite unattainable things, such as a mountain kingdom of their own, when there are no uninhabited mountains to give them. [June 15 1932]. (Stark 1951: 265–6)

30. "and the Old Testament stories the teacher told us about David and his time sounded to me so like Battal Gazi stories that I did not associate them with anything religious" (Edib 1926: 149–50).
31. "Some of the already strong tendencies of my thought also now found new vistas into wider paths" (Edib 1926: 149–50).
32. "She [Miss Fensham] merely told the story of Christ's birth and his mission in the simplest possible language, just as she felt it herself, and it was like a marvelous spiritual flame which passed from her into one's heart, purifying and warming and arousing intense emotion" (Edib 1926: 194).
33.
    > My contact with Christianity gave me a sense of its hard intolerance as a directing influence in the lives of its devotees, while the historical developments through which it has passed seemed to me almost contrary to the teaching conveyed by the life of Christ himself. Individuals excepted, Christianity set up barriers which shut out non-Christians from a possibility of ultimate bliss more than did any other religion. (Edib 1926: 192)

34. More of this type of influence is found in the later period; compare Fleischmann (2002) and Okkenhaug (2002b).

References

Abu-Lughod, L. (1998), "Feminist Longings and Postcolonial Conditions," in L. Abu-Lughod (ed.), *Remaking Women: Feminism and Modernity in the Middle East*, Princeton, NJ: Princeton University Press.

Al-Sayegh, F. H.(1998), "American Women Missionaries in the Gulf: Agents for Cultural Change," *Islam and Christian–Muslim Relations*, 9(3): 339–56.

Anderson, R. (1873), *History of the Missions of the American Board of Commissioners for Foreign Missions to the Oriental Churches*, 2 vols, Boston, MA: Congregational Publishing Society.

Baron, B. (1994), *The Women's Awakening in Egypt: Culture, Society, and the Press*, New Haven, CT and London: Yale University Press.

Brown, A. J. (1936), *One Hundred Years, A History of the Foreign Missionary Work of the Presbyterian Church in the U.S.A., With Some Accounts of Countries, Peoples and the Policies and Problems of Modern Missions*, New York: Fleming H. Revell.

Cale, P. S. (1984), "A British Missionary in Egypt: Mary Louise Whately," *Vitae Scholasticae, The Bulletin of Educational Biography*, 3: 131–43.

Coakley, J. F. (1992), *The Church of the East and the Church of England: A History of the Archbishop of Canterbury's Assyrian Mission*, Oxford: Clarendon Press.

Crombie, K. (1991), *For Love of Zion, Christian Witness and the Restoration of Israel*, London: Hodder and Stoughton.

Disselhoff, J. (1886), *Jubilate! Denkschrift zur Jubelfeir der Erneuerung des apostolischen Diakonissen-Amtes und der fünfzigjährigen Wirksamheit des Diakonissen-Mutterhauses zu Kaiserswerth am Rhein*, Kaiserswerth: Verlag der Diakonissen-Anstalt.

Doumato, E. A. (1998), "Receiving the Promised Blessing: Missionary Reflections on 'Ishmael's (mostly Female) Descendants," *Islam and Christian–Muslim Relations*, 9(3): 325–37.

Edib, H. (1926), *Memoirs of Halidé Edib*, New York and London: Century Company.

Fahmy, K. (1998), "Women, Medicine, and Power in Nineteenth-Century Egypt," in L. Abu-Lughod (ed.), *Remaking Women: Feminism and Modernity in the Middle East*, Princeton, NJ: Princeton University Press.

Finn, A. E. (1866), *Home in the Holy Land*, London and Edinburgh.

—— (1869), *A Third Year in Jerusalem: A Tale Illustrating Customs and Incidents of Modern Jerusalem*, London: James Nisbet.

Fleischmann, E. L. (1998), "'Our Moslem Sisters': Women of Greater Syria in the Eyes of American Protestant Missionary Women," *Islam and Christian–Muslim Relations*, 9(3): 307–23.

—— (2002), "The Impact of American Protestant Missions in Lebanon on the Construction of Female Identity, c. 1860–1950," *Islam and Christian–Muslim Relations*, 13(4): 411–26.

Francis-Dehqani, G. (2000), "CMS Women Missionaries in Persia: Perceptions of Muslim Women and Islam, 1884–1934," in K. Ward and B. Stanley (eds), *The Church Mission Society and World Christianity, 1799–1999*, Grand Rapids, MI: Eerdmans and Cambridge: Curzon Press.

Gidney, W.T. (1908), *The History of the London Society for Promoting Christianity amongst the Jews, from 1809 to 1908*, London: London Society for Promoting Christianity amongst the Jews.

Harris, P. W. (1999), *Nothing but Christ: Rufus Anderson and the Ideology of Protestant Foreign Missions*, New York and Oxford: Oxford University Press.

Heyberger, B. (1994), *Les Chrétiens du Proche-orient, au temps de la réforme catholique*, Rome: École Françaises de Rome.

Hill, P. R. (1985), *The World their Household: The American Woman's Foreign Mission Movement and Cultural Transformation, 1870–1920*, Ann Arbor, MI: University of Michigan Press.

Hutchison, W. R. (1987), *Errand to the World: American Protestant Thought and Foreign Missions*, Chicago and London: University of Chicago Press.

Janjmabadi, A. (1998), "Crafting an Educated Housewife in Iran," in L. Abu-Lughod (ed.), *Remaking Women: Feminism and Modernity in the Middle East*, Princeton, NJ: Princeton University Press.

Joseph, J. (2000), *The Modern Assyrians of the Middle East: Encounters with Western Christian Missions, Archaeologists, and Colonial Powers*, Leiden: Brill.

Kawerau, P. (1958), *Amerika und die orientalischen Kirchen: Ursprung und Anfang der amerikanischen Mission unter den Nationalkirchen Westasiens*, Berlin: Walter de Gruyter.

Labode, M. (1993), "From Heathen Kraal to Christian Home: Anglican Mission Education and African Christian Girls, 1850–1900," in F. Bowie, D. Kirkwood and S. Ardener (eds), *Women and Missions: Past and Present Anthropological and Historical Perceptions*, Providence, RI and Oxford: Berg.

Langlois, C. (2001), "Les Congrégations françaises en Terre sainte au XIXe siècle," in D. Trimbur and R. Aaronsohn (eds), *De Bonaparte à Balfour: La France, l'Europe occidentale et la Palestine, 1799–1917*, Paris: CNRS.

Makdise, U. (1997), "Reclaiming the Land of the Bible: Missionaries, Secularism, and Evangelical Modernity," *American Historical Review*, 102–3: 680–713.

Marten, M. (2002), "The Free Church of Scotland in 19th-century Lebanon," *Chronos. Revue d'Histoire de l'Université de Balamand*, 5: 51–106.

Melman, B. (1992), *Women's Orients: English Women and the Middle East, 1718–1918. Sexuality, Religion and Work*, Ann Arbor, MI: University of Michigan Press.

Merguerian, B. J. (1990–1), "The Beginnings of Secondary Education for Armenian Women: The Armenian Female Seminary in Constantinople," *Journal of the Society for Armenian Studies*, 5: 103–24.

—— (1992–3), "Saving Souls or Cultivating Minds? Missionary Crosby H. Wheeler in Kharpert," *Journal of the Society for Armenian Studies*, 6: 33–60.

—— (1998), "The ABCFM Press and the Development of the Western Armenian Language," *Harvard Library Bulletin*, 9(1): 35–49.

Murray, J. (2000), "The Role of Women in the Church Missionary Society, 1799–1917," in K. Ward and B. Stanley (eds), *The Church Mission Society and World Christianity, 1799–1999*, Grand Rapids, MI: Eerdmans and Cambridge: Curzon Press.

Murre-van den Berg, H. L. (1999), *From a Spoken to a Written Language: The Introduction and Development of Literary Urmia Aramaic in the Nineteenth Century*, Publication of the De Goeje Fund no. XXVIII, Leiden: Brill.

—— (2000), "Why Protestant Churches? The American Board and the Eastern Churches (1820–1870)," in P. N. Holtrop and H. McLeod (eds), *Missions and Missionaries*, Woodbridge, Suffolk: Boydell Press for the Ecclesiastical History Society.

—— (2001), "'Dear Mother of My soul': Fidelia Fiske and the Role of Women Missionaries in Mid-Nineteenth Century Iran," *Exchange*, 30(1): 33–48.

—— (2004), "Generous Devotion: Women in the Church of the East between 1550 and 1850," *Hugoye: Journal of Syriac Studies*, 7(1), http://syrcom.cua.edu/Hugoye.

—— (2005), "The Middle East: Western Missions and the Eastern Churches, Islam and Judaism," in *Cambridge History of Christianity*, Volume 8, Chapter 26, Cambridge: Cambridge University Press.

Okkenhaug, I. M. (2002a), *The Quality of Heroic Living, of High Endeavor and Adventure: Anglican Mission, Women and Education in Palestine, 1888–1948*, Leiden: Brill.

—— (2002b), "'She Loves Books & Ideas, & Strides along in Low Shoes Like an Englishwoman': British Models and Graduates from the Anglican Girls' Secondary Schools in Palestine 1918–48," *Islam and Christian–Muslim Relations*, 13(4): 461–79.

—— (2003), "Introduction to 'Gender and Nordic Missions in the Nineteenth and Twentieth Centurie'," *Scandinavian Journal of History*, 28(2): 73–82.

Porterfield, A. (1997), *Mary Lyon and the Mount Holyoke Missionaries*, New York and Oxford: Oxford University Press.

Rice, C. C. (1922), *Mary Bird in Persia*, 2nd edn, London: Church Missionary Society.

Richter, J. (1970 [1910]), *A History of Protestant Missions in the Near East*, New York and Edinburgh: Oliphant, Anderson.

Robert, D. L. (1997), *American Women in Mission: A Social History of their Thought and Practice*, Macon, GA: Mercer University Press.

Roper, G. (1998), "The Beginnings of Arabic Printing by the ABCFM, 1822–1841," *Harvard Library Bulletin*, 9(1): 50–68.

Semple, R. A. (2003), *Missionary Women: Gender, Professionalism and the Victorian Idea of Christian Mission*, Woodbridge, Suffolk: The Boydell Press.

Shakry, O. (1998), "Schooled Mothers and Structured Play: Child Rearing in Turn-of-the-Century Egypt," in L. Abu-Lughod (ed.), *Remaking Women: Feminism and Modernity in the Middle East*, Princeton, NJ: Princeton University Press.

Stanley, B. (ed.) (2001), *Christian Missions and the Enlightenment*, Grand Rapids, MI: Eerdmans.

Stark, F. (1951), *Beyond Euphrates: Autobiography: 1928–1933*, London: John Murray.

Stock, E. (1899), *The History of the Church Missionary Society: Its Environment, its Men and its Work*, 3 vols, London: Church Missionary Society.

Strong, W. E. (1910), *The Story of the American Board: An Account of the First Hundred Years of the American Board of Commissioners for Foreign Missions*, Boston, MA: Pilgrim Press.

Surma d'Bait Mar Shimun (1983 [c.1920]), *Assyrian Church Customs and the Murder of Mar Shimun*, New York: Vehicle.

Tibawi, A. L. (1961), *British Interests in Palestine, 1800–1901*, Oxford: Oxford University Press.

—— (1966), *American Interests in Syria, 1800–1901*, Oxford: Oxford University Press.

—— (1967), "The Genesis and Early History of the Syrian Protestant College," *Middle East Journal*, 21: 1–15 199–212.

Tucker, J. E. (1999), "Women in the Middle East and North Africa: The Nineteenth and Twentieth Centuries," in G. Nashar and J. E. Tucker, *Women in the Middle East and North Africa: Restoring Women to History*, Bloomington, IN: and Indiana University Press.

Van der Veer, P. (1996), *Conversion to Modernities: The Globalization of Christianity*, London: Routledge.

Verdeuil, C. (2001), "Travailler à la renaissance de l'orient chrétien: Les missions latines en syrie (1830–1945)," *Proche-Orient Chrétien*, 51: 267–316.

Vlieger, A. de (1892), *De Hollandsche Zending in Egypte*, Neerbosch: Vereeniging tot uitbreiding van het Evangelie in Egypte.

Vogel, L. I. (1993), *To See a Promised Land: Americans and the Holy Land in the Nineteenth Century*, University Park, PA: Pennsylvania State University Press.

Watson, A. (1898), *The American Mission in Egypt, 1845 to 1896*, Pittsburgh, PA: United Presbyterian Board.

Whately, M. L. (1863a), *Ragged Life in Egypt*, London: Seeley, Jackson, and Halliday.

—— (1863b), *More about Ragged Life in Egypt*, London: Seeley, Jackson, and Halliday.

7

The Paradox of the New Islamic Woman in Turkey

Jenny B. White

Introduction

One of the more remarkable aspects of the rise of a politically engaged Islamist movement in contemporary Turkey has been the social and political mobilization of large numbers of conservative women who had not previously been active in the public sphere. Women's activism was crucial in propelling the various Islamist political parties of the 1980s and 1990s to power, culminating in the 2002 election of the Justice and Development Party. This has given rise to discussions about "the new Islamic woman," educated, active in society, politics and national debate, and challenging the secularist elite on their own ground by presenting an alternative modern, elite image and identity. The central symbol of the "new Islamic woman" was a particular style of *tesettür* veiling, signaling an accompanying lifestyle. During the 1990s the definition of the new Islamic woman slipped the leash of ideology and was transformed by a globalized commercial marketplace that created an "Islamic elite" lifestyle out of reach of poorer activist women. Poorer women were able to be the new Islamic woman as students, workers or activists until they married or had their first child. At that point, their lack of financial resources pulled them back into the patriarchal confines of the home as their only viable means of security. Based on ethnographic research carried out between 1994 and 2002, primarily with Islamist activists in Ümraniye, a working-class neighborhood of Istanbul, I suggest that Islamist ideology and practices regarding women, while opening doors in some directions, nevertheless are charged with contradictions about women's place in family and society. Women's choices are further conditioned by their social class status, exacerbated by global market forces.

The Paradox of the New Islamic Woman

Turkish women's opportunities and choices are affected by the economic conditions of their environment, whether they view themselves as Muslim, secular or Islamist.

Within the boundaries of economic possibility, there is a broad space of movement within which women can strategize and manipulate existing options and pursue new opportunities. The Islamist movement of the 1980s and 1990s populated this space with many new options for women. This included opportunities to gain an education or professional training, work outside the home, and participate in political activism. The "new Islamic woman" took part in previously male-dominated activities in the public sphere, whether political activism or shopping. However, the Islamist movement's expectations of women represented a paradox, as it was also strongly asserted that women's primary duty was to remain at home and dedicate herself to her family, a lifestyle that in Ümraniye often involved restrictions on movement outside the home. Additionally, an apolitical, bourgeois "new Islamic" lifestyle developed, defined by commodities and supporting a broad palette of Islamic dress and behavior. These contradictory sets of lifestyle choices were encoded in the multiple meanings of *tesettür* veiling that could be invoked under different circumstances, as political symbol, marker of modesty and as fashion. *Tesettür* is a distinctive form of veiling that developed in the 1980s – an oversize headscarf with matching tailored coat or suit. The colors, patterns and clothing styles that make up *tesettür* respond to tastes in fashion and are continually transformed.

While Islamist ideology and activism opened doors for women, these tended to be revolving doors for lower-class women, who were often unable to sustain an activist or professional life or to support a middle-class "new Islamic" lifestyle. After a period of activism, at marriage or motherhood they retreated to the security and seclusion of the patriarchal family home, where the "commodities" that counted were virginity, honor, obedience and motherhood. This touches on a general disconnection between women's aspirations, ideological ideals, and the social and cultural environment within which women must act. While the Islamist movement provided women with strategic opportunity, within the constraints of class, it also presented a paradox of contradictory expectations that supported both activism and patriarchy.

Tesettür veiling is a key symbol of the Islamist movement, but despite its centrality, *tesettür* is rent by the same multiple, contradictory meanings as Islamist lifestyle choices. *Tesettür* bears a heavy symbolic burden: it denotes egalitarianism among Islamist followers, party populism and resistance against the Westernized secularist elite that controls religious expression in Turkey's public arenas, for instance, forbidding headscarves in schools and the civil service. Göle (1996) has argued that wearers of *tesettür* are engaged in identity politics, that is, a bid to acquire elite status for an Islamic lifestyle that would put it in competition with a Western lifestyle in the definition of social status. Certainly, *tesettür* in Ümraniye was a "city look" that had developed its own fashion momentum. This gave it a cachet of upward mobility. Islamist fashion also implied moral uprightness and other qualities that residents found attractive, especially in the opposite sex. *Tesettür*'s association in the media and in public displays with the Islamist social movement also added to its value within the community, at least among Islamist supporters.

However, there was no evidence that *tesettür* had any effect on the actual social status or economic position of its wearers in Ümraniye. Indeed, the relative freedom of action that the Islamist movement afforded women within the economic and social restrictions of Ümraniye might simply be part of the life cycle for young unmarried women or married women before they have children. This is quite a different image from that drawn by studies of Islamist elites – the editors, writers, intellectuals, middle-class activists, Islamist Yuppies – that are perceived to be engaging in identity politics.

The paradox of the new Islamic woman lies in two sets of superimposed meanings: the Islamist challenge to the status quo, and Islamist support for the principle that a woman's place is in the home and her role is to take care of her husband and family. Islamists have attempted to deal with this paradox by differentiating "Islamist" practices from those of the masses. Islamist practice is regarded as superior because it is "conscious," unlike the unconscious adherence to tradition that is presumed to explain these same practices among the masses. Much like secularists who attempt to distance themselves from certain behaviors and values by attributing them to the "Other" (rural, patriarchal, uncivilized) Istanbul, Islamists attribute the restrictive, patriarchal nature of shared practices to the "Other" Muslims. This constitutes a kind of Islamist elitism quite distinct from the more neutral "elite status" envisioned in the discourse of identity politics.

This "enlightened" explanation of veiling, seclusion and women's proper place in the family, however, does little to change the fact that women are subject to the constraints accompanying these practices. In many instances in Ümraniye, a practical seclusion at marriage was "chosen" because of a lack of other credible options for establishing and maintaining a family. Even educated women may have difficulty finding the resources to establish a professional life. Family life is a powerful source of support, protection and comfort, although it exacts a great price from women in the curtailment of their choices, activities and movement outside the home. Not surprisingly, Islamist female activists and male activists in Ümraniye emphasized different sides of the paradox when asked about their own goals within the movement. Women were interested in the means by which the Islamist movement could allow them to challenge the status quo; men envisioned an ideal in which women were wives, mothers and homemakers. Some wanted the possibility of a polygynous marriage (illegal under secular Turkish law). Next I describe the lives of women in Ümraniye, their choices and constraints, and the role that the Islamist movement played in these.

Managing Virtue

Nurcan, her sister-in-law and I had a discussion one day in Ümraniye about why Nurcan's 8-year-old daughter needed to learn not to mix with boys and why she should begin wearing a headscarf. The conversation started with the new eight-year minimal school requirement newly announced by the government and the resulting expectation that boys would be together in classes with girls, their heads uncovered, for all eight years. That is, unprotected girls would be thrown together with boys after puberty. This would be a disaster for her niece, the sister-in-law insisted, because something was bound to happen. "People have no brakes. If you put them in a situation like that, something bad will happen." In other words, women could be blamed for bringing trouble on themselves because they were available or in the wrong place at the wrong time. It was up to society to set the boundaries and keep people's behavior straight, through constant vigilance and social disapproval, ostracism or punishment. If unrelated men and women were alone for any length of time for whatever reason, it was assumed that "something happened." It must have, because people had no self-control and society had not been there to keep them apart.

If the impetus to maintaining one's virtue is located in behavior, then behavioral signals become important markers of unapproachability and inviolability. Ironically, it is the very act of covering the body, of veiling, that has allowed women like those in Ümraniye the first step across the threshold to a public life of work and political activism. Islamic foundations gave scholarships and funded gender-segregated dorms that allowed young women from conservative, poor families to pursue higher education. Veiling itself established a kind of mobile honor zone from which young women could interact with male students and teachers without fearing loss of reputation. Islamic corporations established training centers and issued professional certificates for men and women. This allowed some women to establish professional footholds, however, precarious.

Tesettür, unlike other forms of veiling, has a cachet of politically correct respectability. A man molesting a woman in *tesettür* would be more than a scoundrel; he would be a traitor to a national movement whose intellectuals argue that an Islamic lifestyle is not only respectable and reputable, but also morally superior to a Western lifestyle. The honor of the nation is at stake, not merely the honor of an individual woman. Women in *tesettür* reported being able to move freely through the city without fear of harassment, unlike women in Western dress, who often complained of being mauled in buses and harassed by men on streets outside their neighborhoods. Implicit in *tesettür* style is participation in a national social movement that lends the wearer a heightened sense of status, both moral (vis-à-vis secularists) and social (vis-à-vis women who merely cover, but do not veil). However, despite its political cachet, behind the social force of *tesettür* one can discern the familiar principle of <u>himaye</u>, guidance and protection by (and from) men.

Neither political cachet nor norms of respectability explain the newer, more assertive, even revealing styles of *tesettür* veiling that have emerged. How does one reconcile the revelation of the female shape in a form-fitting dress or suit, with the act of hiding one's hair under a *tesettür* scarf? Two answers come to mind. First, veiling is a form of seduction, simply by virtue of the fact that it emphasizes what is hidden. This is no secret to observers of women in other Islamic countries, where the discreet but effective twitch of a veil speaks as loudly as any Victorian ankle. Veiled young women sometimes engage in a self-conscious checking for strange males, a kind of preening, demonstrating publicly their virginity and moral standing. It is a kind of flirtation, with overtones of sexual danger in looking.

Second, Islamic veiling in Turkey has taken on a life of its own as commercialized fashion. Ideally, to be fashionable, women should purchase new *tesettür* headscarves regularly to keep up with the patterns and colors of the moment. There are also suits and dresses, to be worn under special coats with matching headscarves. Many married women in Ümraniye were unable to keep up with the fashion and washed and ironed their one or two good scarves until they were threadbare. Young women, like adolescents everywhere conscious of their standing among their peers, were more likely to be sporting the latest fashion. Elite Islamic women attended *tesettür* fashion shows. Navaro-Yashin (2002) described an Istanbul fashion show at which expensive Islamic fashion styles were demonstrated by runway models. A well-off Islamic woman at the fashion show complained that when she began to veil at age 39, the sales assistants at the shops she had frequented didn't recognize her and, because of her veil, began to treat her as someone who wouldn't be able to afford to buy anything in the store. The woman was happy that a more fashionable and recognizably elite *tesettür* style was emerging that allowed her to retain a middle-class identity while following the dictates of her faith.

In other words, *tesettür* reflects contradictory cultural and politico-cultural philosophies, the latter associated with Islamist ideology; it is also deeply conditioned by socio-economic forces. Indeed, as fashion, the style can be worn without the wearer evincing any overt interest in politics or in political Islam. As a populist uniform and symbol of aspirations for upward mobility, *tesettür* unites people despite differences in social class or political motivation; as fashion, it divides those who can afford to keep up with the latest styles and buy the best quality materials from those who cannot.

Islamist Elitism

The symbolic content of *tesettür* veiling is highly contradictory. On the one hand, it incorporates ideas about an "Islamic modernity" in which women are educated and professionally and politically active. On the other hand, it refers to values like patriarchal hierarchy, gender segregation and women's primary role as mothers and their place in the home. And at other times, it is simply a fashion that implies the wearer is urban, stylish and upwardly mobile, in intent, if not in fact. This multiple symbolic load puts women in an awkward situation, when first one, then another, set of meanings is invoked. In other words, while the distinctive style of Islamic self-presentation is a key symbol of the Islamist movement, these styles also have a deep cultural resonance in everyday life.

Gender segregation and veiling, as practiced in the everyday lives of working-class people, carry multiple meanings, reflecting gender and class as much as religious or political identity. For these people, daily hardships deriving from unemployment, poverty, lack of adequate infrastructure and educational and health care facilities create fundamental conditions within which family-oriented practices may be the only viable portals to survival. For women in particular, obedience to family, submissiveness and gender-appropriate behavior like veiling and segregation are important for claiming the social and economic safety net of community membership and family support. These sets of practices can be referenced to a non-elite Muslim identity, as well as to an elite Islamic identity. Islamists point to motivation as the crucial marker of difference.

Islamists have approached the difficulty of distinguishing an "Islamist" practice by differentiating the commonplace cultural and religious "tradition" of veiling from veiling that is done as a deliberate act of pious reflection and political activism. Islamist activists attempt to distance their own cultural actions from those of the surrounding population by claiming that their own veiling is more conscious, more thought out (*şuurlu*). The head of the Islamist Virtue Party Women's Branch in Ümraniye said: "My mother is covered (*kapalı*), in traditional covering. Now, our covering is, of course, different from our mothers' covering. Ours is more purposeful, more researched, more conscious than that in our neighborhood."

Islamist intellectual discourse (and academic discourse on that discourse) further supports a distinction between "conscious" veiling representative of "cultural politics" and an everyday veiling tainted by everyday motivations. Veiling because it is required by "tradition" or by patriarchal authority is not the same as "conscious" Islamist practice. The Islamist project aims "to introduce the 'real Islam' to social groups with lower levels of education and culture who otherwise experience 'folk Islam'" (Göle 1996: 113). This top-down approach, reminiscent of secularist Turkish social engineering, relies on the leadership of educated elites and their modeling of elite styles and lifestyles. In her study of Islamist women, Göle tellingly insists that the contemporary actors of Islam are "not marginal, uneducated, frustrated groups," but rather university students, future intellectuals and professionals, new elites that she says have moved Islam from the periphery to the center (Göle 1996: 96, 92). *Tesettür* style, as it is advertised, is rooted in the fashions of the Ottoman elite, not the customs of covering practiced by the masses.

Islamists strategically (and consciously) wield cultural symbols, like veiling, in an attempt to gain social distinction for an Islamic lifestyle. Veiling also hides social distinctions between believers, although this clearly yields a contradiction, to be discussed below. Islamists have attempted to associate such social behaviors as veiling and gender segregation with the meaning complex of urban/modern/educated, challenging social hierarchies that had associated these behaviors in the past with rural/backwards/uneducated. Ideally, this would give veiling the cachet of an elite marker distinct from mass behavior and provide a unifying cultural marker for the party and the movement.

Many Islamic women want to use Islam to liberate themselves from conventional patterns of life and patriarchal constraints. While supporting women's centrality in the Muslim family, they believe that Islamic doctrine also supports women's becoming educated, working and being politically active. Islamic feminists, as some call them, actively disseminate their ideas in publications and the media. Islamic feminists, however, vary in their prescriptions for the ideal Islamic life. Some emphasize appearance and clothing and a woman's role as wife and mother in a bourgeois household, and agitate for change within those parameters. Others desire improvement of women's lives within an Islamic framework. These views of women are not incompatible, but rather differ in degree of emphasis. Indeed, it is not unusual to encounter Islamist activist women who hold both views simultaneously, promoting the centrality of woman in the family while attending university, engaging in professional work outside the home, editing a magazine, or canvassing for votes. As we shall see, non-elite Islamist women may subscribe to these ideas as well, but are not as free to voice these ideas or to act on them, nor are these ideas necessarily shared by non-elite Islamist men.

Despite efforts by the Islamists to distinguish *tesettür* and its associated lifestyle from their "traditionally lived" context and make of them markers of a different, "consciously" lived Islam, *tesettür* remains associated not just with the Islamist movement, but also with everyday urban life. *Tesettür* is worn by a great variety of women, from middle-class matrons like those attending the fashion show to poor migrants in the urban slums who wish to display modesty, religious devotion, urban cachet and the image (if not always the practice) of upward mobility. Some modern, middle-class secularists, although not veiled, lead consciously Islamic lives generally associated with veiling. They may pray and practice a modified yet still gender-segregated use of space. This further complicates any association of clothing and lifestyle with a fixed sociopolitical meaning.

In some respects, the term "Islamist elite" itself is a misnomer, since what is most often referred to is educational status, not necessarily economic status. Two major studies of Islamist women (Ilyasoπlu 1994; Göle 1996) took as their subjects educated women who were politically or professionally active, but whose families were migrants and lived in neighborhoods like Ümraniye. Although these women wore *tesettür* and gained status from their education, they were unlikely to be economic elites. Few from a migrant, poor or working-class background have the means to actually move upwards economically. The families of Islamist businessmen and Islamist Yuppies enjoy a very different lifestyle from the educated, politically active "elites" of Ümraniye. Education, however, is available to the masses, both men and women, thanks to early republican reforms and to some financial assistance by the true economic elites of the Islamist movement, either through direct assistance or funneled through foundations and the party.

Since cultural differences are associated with class distinctions in Turkey, the differentiation between common, everyday Muslim practice and elite Islamist practice inevitably implies attempts at de-proletarianization. For instance, popular Islamist novels and magazines aimed at an audience of working-class, lower-middle-class and migrant women often focused on Islamic interpretations of modesty, veiling, gender segregation and traditional female roles as wife, mother and homemaker (Acar 1995: 50). This earned the disapproval of Islamist intellectuals who disparaged such "discourses of 'cheap radicalism and populism'" as an "amalgamation of 'Islamicization and proletarianization'" and "the birth of an 'Islamic arabesque'" (Göle 1996: 113), connecting the popular working-class *arabesk* musical style held in contempt by secularist elites to the implied working-class character of "traditional" Muslim practice.

There is a fundamental contradiction in the Islamist assumption that a "new" politicized, egalitarian Muslim value system can be impressed upon an unenlightened, class-bound, patriarchal Muslim lifestyle and raise it to a higher level. These fields of value and practice already intersect; one is embedded within the other; politics and culture are merged in practice. The attempt to establish one as separate from the other, "elite" Islamic practice as different from – and superior to – the everyday Islamic practice of the masses, leads to a form of Islamist elitism that holds out to non-elite women implicit promises of socio-economic mobility and professional opportunity, and then betrays that promise. For Islamist women, *tesettür* and Islamist activism opened new routes of mobility and action but, in the end, their world is bounded by the requirements of economic survival and cultural respectability that cling to veiling like the smell of smoke that cannot be washed out.

Women in the Party

One manifestation of the implicit contradiction between conscious activist intentions and the varied cultural expectations hidden under the canopy of populism is the different constructions of women's rights, privileges and motivations by activist women and their male colleagues within the Islamist Welfare Party in the 1990s. While many activist women I interviewed in Ümraniye were engaged in the Islamist project in order to carve out new areas of autonomy within the traditional expectations of their community, male activists in the next office were motivated in part by a desire to reinforce traditional female roles and to enhance their own autonomy vis-à-vis women, for instance, by supporting polygyny, which is illegal in secular Turkey. The women were very much interested in using party activism to advance the position of women, particularly through education and work outside of the home. As the head of Ümraniye's Welfare Party Women's Branch, put it, "I too used to be just like other women in this neighborhood. I sat around and ate and talked, ate and talked. But now I've found myself. I've become active and productive." She firmly believed that women should work outside the home, get an education, and enter the professions. In her study of Islamist activists, Arat also found that women felt empowered by political work. Some saw it as a path "to prove ourselves to ourselves." Others felt that through their activism they had gained back the status, autonomy and authority they had lost when they decided to veil and found themselves under patriarchal "house arrest." If unable to attend university, party activism was a form of education, a legitimate vocation, an identity and a way to expand one's networks (Arat 1999: 36–9).

Female Welfare Party supporters were extraordinarily successful in popular mobilization and it is widely acknowledged that they were in large part responsible for Welfare Party's success in working-class neighborhoods like Ümraniye in the 1994 and 1995 elections. In the month before the 1995 elections, in Istanbul alone, the Welfare Party's women's commission worked with 18,000 women and met face to face with 200,000 women (Arat 1999: 67). They worked person-to-person, building cells of local women attached to the Women's Branch that, in turn, was guided by the party and took its direction (and much of its financial support) from there. By 1997, women made up a third of party membership in Istanbul (Arat 1999: 23).

However, at the time almost no women were represented in the party administration and the women's branches and commissions had no formal status within the party. This latter fact clearly irked some of the women activists, but they assured me that this would change in the near future. Although the lack of formal connection between the Welfare Party and its Women's Branch could be attributed to state laws forbidding political parties from forming special interest branches, it did not explain the lack of women in formal party administration.

Male party activists generally deflected questions about the lack of women in the party's formal administration by retraining the question on the issue of banning headscarves in university. This disguised internal divisiveness with the artful unity of political symbolism. Another means of not answering this divisive question was to blame the lack of democracy in the system: a government that refuses education to women on the grounds of their wearing a headscarf is undemocratic. However, when pressed about the importance of education for women, these same male activists stated simply that women's main role was to be mothers and homemakers and that women should be educated because it would make them better mothers.

Within the party, there were contradictory views about whether women should work outside the home and whether they should receive training to do so. In an interview, Recep Tayyip Erdoπan, then mayor of Istanbul, underscored his belief that women should be fully involved in social and political life, but with several reservations.[1]

> Some work is not suitable for women; it goes against their delicacy, like the work women did behind the iron curtain – working in construction, laying roads and so on. It's natural for them to do other work. They could even be managers of managers... Women's right includes political work. But I support struggle (*mücadele*), not a quota system... A quota means you are helping people; it's an insult to women.

On the other hand, the mayor also believed that "Working at home is safer for women. They often get no insurance when they work outside the home. If they are young, they may be molested in workshops and other workplaces. This way they aren't oppressed by the employer."

I asked him whether this meant he believed all women ideally should work at home. He shook his head emphatically and explained,

> Those women who have the talent and the education, those who are engineers and so on, anyway find work. If women have graduated from high school, they should be able to work. But for the others, staying at home at least gives them the possibility of making their own trousseaux [with money earned from the sale of handicrafts]. But it's a stopgap solution. You can't solve the unemployment problem that way.

Both the mayor and male activists, in other words, differentiated between women who were educated and might work at a profession and women who were not educated and would be better off at home than in a job where they could be oppressed and molested.

However, local male activists in Ümraniye in their discussions and in practice added the requisite that even educated women's first priority was husband, home and children and that they should stop working when they married or after the birth of a child. Veiling and the segregation of women within the home meant that women reserved their beauty, their attention and their labor for their husbands and family. Many of the men categorically resisted the idea that women could or should work outside the home after marriage. This corresponded to the reality of life in much of Ümraniye, where women were under the protection of their family and under the authority of family males. They worked for their family and did not travel far afield from their homes. I know of several cases in Ümraniye where educated professional women and activists were required by their new husbands or husbands' families to remain at home after marriage or after having their first child. In some cases this resulted in greatly constrained mobility, including being required to ask permission to leave home to visit nearby family and friends or to shop at the grocery. A common theme in popular Islamist fiction is the quandary faced by Islamist women when they marry and lose the "voice" they had as activists, students and professionals. Non-Islamic women's popular fiction also takes up this theme; Kemalism, like Islam, is shot through with contradictions in its expectations of women.

Although activist women in Ümraniye agreed with the idea that women's first responsibility was to make a home for husband and children, they also had very firm ideas about the need for education and work, and not only to make a woman "a better mother." The head of Ümraniye's Welfare Women's Branch: If a girl's family doesn't send her to school, "what will that girl do at home?... She'll go either to a textile workshop or wait at home for her fate (*kismet*). That a man should come, see her, like her, and start a family. Why should it be like that?" She will sit at home and "be a consumer, not a producer. But if that girl finishes high school, finishes university, maybe she will work somewhere in some area, and find herself contributing to the country's economy by working." In this, as in some of their other expectations, Islamist feminists and women activists were out of step with the Welfare Party and, in some ways, constituted their own stream of the Islamist movement in the 1990s.

Despite their isolation from the center of power and policy-making, female Welfare Party supporters were extraordinarily successful in popular mobilization. They worked person-to-person building social cells attached informally to the party's Women's Branch. These same women used the Koran to explain and justify what were, in some respects, universalist, modernist, even feminist ideas about women's roles that challenged local norms.

Veiling as perceived by women (whether elite or working class) differed appreciably from veiling as understood by men in the Islamist movement. Activist women in the Welfare Party consciously wielded veiling and gender segregation as central political symbols to try to forge new social identities and concrete possibilities for women within and outside of the movement. The interpretation of these cultural forms by male Welfare Party (and its successor, Virtue Party) activists, however, was influenced by the everyday context of veiling and segregation, in which male control over women's sexuality and movement through space has primacy over women's autonomy and control over their bodies. Dissonance within the party was controlled by populist rhetoric, the judicious use of unifying symbols in neutral contexts, and avoidance of language that would acknowledge cleavages. Party leaders deflected public statements on divisive issues, allowing differences in the lower ranks between men and women activists to be attributed to personal points of view.

Tesettür was a political symbol that unified members of the Islamist movement and Welfare Party. It also hid class differences among members of the party and itself became a symbol of upward mobility and urban lifestyle, even if the reality contradicted the symbol. Women activists desired mobility – social, physical and professional. Yet *tesettür* also signified the opposite of mobility: that the proper place of women was in the home. As a fashion, *tesettür* revealed the yawning gap between those who could afford an elite lifestyle, including couture veiling, and those for whom veiling – and associated behaviors like segregation and obedience within a patriarchal hierarchy – were crucial for respectability and security. While the gap between rich and poor, educated and uneducated, was obscured by Islamist populism, the desire to make an Islamist lifestyle an elite lifestyle led Islamists to distance themselves from the masses. This opened the door to a form of Islamist elitism that celebrated economic and status differences, while simultaneously denying them.

Acknowledgments

This chapter is based on Chapter 7 of J. B. White (2002) *Islamist Mobilization in Turkey: A Study in Vernacular Politics*, Seattle, WA: University of Washington Press.

Note

1. Interview with the author, June 29, 1998, Istanbul.

References

Acar, F. (1995), "Women and Islam in Turkey," in S. Tekeli (ed.), *Women in Modern Turkish Society: A Reader*, London: Zed Books.

Arat, Y. (1999), *Political Islam in Turkey and Women's Organizations*, Istanbul: Turkish Economic and Social Studies Foundation.

Göle, N. (1996), *The Forbidden Modern: Civilization and Veiling*, Ann Arbor, MI: University of Michigan Press.

Iliyasoŋlu, A. (1994), *Örtülü kimlik: Islamcı kadın* kimliŋinin oluŋum öŋeleri, Istanbul: Metis Yayınları.

Navaro-Yashin, Y. (2002), "The Market for Identities: Secularism, Islamism, Commodities," in D. Kandiyoti (ed.), *Fragments of Culture: The Everyday of Modern Turkey*, London: I. B. Tauris.

8

Visions of Mary in the Middle East: Gender and the Power of a Symbol

Willy Jansen

Introduction

In the nineteenth and twentieth centuries, visions of Mary were reported all over the world. Some sites became famous, like Lourdes, drawing millions of pilgrims. Visions in the Arab world, like those beheld by a Palestinian girl in 1874 in Jerusalem, or experienced by thousands of people in Cairo in 1968, are less widely known, but did have an important local impact. Several authors have noted that such apparitions of Mary often took place in periods of stressful social change. In this chapter the two cases of visions in Jerusalem and Cairo are studied in relation to contemporary social changes in the Middle East. The images and discourses concerning the apparitions are described and contextually analyzed as part of gender politics, intertwined with issues of ethnicity and religion. It is argued that these visions enabled groups of women to give alternative meanings to the symbol of Mary, which empowered them to change their identities and to take on new religious, economic and social roles.

Few of the many pilgrims who flock to Jerusalem know of the visions of Mary that a Palestinian girl had here in 1874. Somewhat more people have heard of the apparitions of Mary above a Coptic church in Old Cairo in 1968, although this site never reached the fame of Lourdes or Guadalupe. The apparitions in Jerusalem and Cairo, nevertheless, deserve our attention here, not for devotional reasons or to judge their present day attraction, nor to take part in the debate on their authenticity, but because they can inform about the relation between gender, religion and change in the Middle East. The apparitions of the Virgin Mary reported worldwide in the nineteenth and twentieth centuries often took place in periods of stressful social change and were both expressive of and contributive to that change. Here, the stories of the apparitions of Mary in the Middle East will be analyzed for the meanings they have for the visionaries and devotees, and how these are connected to changes in gender. They will be looked at from the theoretical perspective of comparative symbology, the intersection of gender with other identities, and feminist Mariology. I have asked whether and how these visions of Mary, and the revival and re-imaging of the symbol of Mary, have empowered women in changing identities, and taking on new social and economic roles. It is argued that the multiplicity of meanings underlying the symbol of Mary provided women with alternatives to the dominant gender notions. Moreover, the specific social, political and religious circumstances allowed that these meanings were actively appropriated to enlarge women's room to maneuver.

The Visions of Mary in Jerusalem

The Virgin Mary is said to have appeared in Jerusalem in 1874 to Sultane Marjam Danîl Ghattas (1843–1927), a young Arab Christian from the mixed Muslim-Christian community of Ain-Karim near Jerusalem. Brought up by a father who worked for the Franciscans and a mother devoted to Mary, and educated by French Catholic sisters, Marjam Ghattas was well prepared for Marian devotion. In 1858, at age 15, she entered the convent of the Sisters of Saint Joseph under the name of Mary Alphonsus.

The apparitions started on January 6, 1874, when Sister Mary Alphonsus was saying the Rosary.

> She perceived a bright light and the Queen of the Holy Rosary standing before her with outstretched arms and a large rosary in her hands. The crucifix of the rosary rested on her bosom and the decades fell about her on either side in a semicircle down to her feet. The fifteen Our Father beads were of stars, and between these stars were the fifteen Mysteries of the rosary. On the head of the Blessed Virgin glowed a crown of stars. At the feet of the apparition she saw on either side seven stars representing Mary's Joys and Sorrows. (Stolz 1968: 16)

This same vision repeated itself when she customarily said the rosary in the Milk-Grotto in Bethlehem in May 1874. The visions became stronger in 1875 and on the Feast of Epiphany, January 6, the seer read in letters of light above Mary, who appeared accompanied by countless virgins dressed like herself in blue and white: "Sisters of the Rosary – The Congregation of the Rosary" (Stolz 1968: 18).

The repeated message of the Virgin was that she wanted a Congregation of the Rosary founded. Some friends of Mary Alphonsus, among whom her sister, Regina, had been discussing the formation of an all-Arab women's congregation and asked her to found such a Congregation of the Rosary. But the visionary was hesitant and it took some new apparitions of Mary urging her to continue despite her lack of means. The Virgin asked her: "When are you going to begin the Congregation of the Rosary? Carry out my instructions. Do you not understand what I want? The Congregation of the Rosary will appease for evil and ease worldly misfortune" (Stolz 1968: 20). The Lady also blessed her and the maidens of the Rosary with a stole and conveyed them her strength: "Then extending her hands over them as a Bishop does at Confirmation, she continued, 'I strengthen you in the name of my joys, sorrows and glories'" (Stolz 1968: 20). The seer also had visions of Saint Joseph, who allowed her to leave his Congregation in order to found another, and of the Virgin showing her that Father Tannûs was to be the spiritual director and formal founder of the Arab Congregation of the Rosary. In the end, the Virgin's request was fulfilled and a congregation of all Arab nuns (the Sisters of the Rosary or *Rahbât al-Wardiyya*) was set up, and later a convent and a chapel were built (Jansen 2004).

Her fellow sisters learned about the visions only after her death in 1928. They became wider known when, in the 1930s, Stolz wrote Mary Alphonsus' life story based on the diary she had kept at the request of her confessor and on interviews with other sisters. The English version, kindly given to me by the sisters, was published in 1968. The historians of the Catholic Arab community in Palestine recognize the important role of the Sisters of the Rosary but pay scant attention to the visions that led to their foundation. Médebielle (1963) provides a picture of Sister Mary Alphonsus with a caption that she was "favored with heavenly graces" but only Duvignau (1981) and Goichon (1972) describe the visions, leaning heavily on Stolz (1968). The visionary was proclaimed Venerable in 1994.

The biography by Stolz contains both a description and a visual reproduction of Our Lady of the Holy Rosary as seen by Sister Mary Alphonsus (Stolz 1968, opposite p. 12). Mary is dressed in a simple white gown and headscarf, and a darker (blue?) cloak, standing on a cloud with her arms outstretched downward. She has a youthful, friendly and open face that looks directly at the viewer. A halo of stars encircles her head. She holds a round rosary with the crucifix resting on her bosom. Stars surround her.

The apparitions in Jerusalem show several similarities with apparitions of Mary elsewhere, in particular France. First, the closeness in time should be noted. Throughout the nineteenth century apparitions were reported in France, and broadcast abroad, such as the visions of Catherine Labouré, a 24–year-old novice in Paris in 1830, those of Mélanie Calvat and Maximin Giraud, 15 and 11 years old, at La Salette in 1846, and of Bernadette Soubirous, 14, of Lourdes, who saw the Virgin about three dozen times in the presence of thousands of people in the year 1858. Because Mary Alphonsus was educated by the French Sisters of St. Joseph and entered their convent in the same year that the apparitions in Lourdes took place, she must have heard about them and been familiar with the images of Mary. That these images were indeed present in the Middle East can be learned from the punishment she received from the parish priest for her "pseudo-visions": he forbade her to "look at pictures of the Blessed Virgin or to deck her altars" (Stolz 1968: 21).

Another parallel can be found in the gender of the visionary. In most, albeit not all, cases Mary was seen by young women or children. Although churchmen were at times hesitant to accept them as carriers of messages of God, for the general public the innocence and purity associated with these categories apparently supported the belief invested in them. It brought the seers closer to the Immaculate Lady, born without original sin. The Jerusalem visions also follow the European ones in the words Mary is heard saying: that Mary will appease for evil and ease worldly misfortune, that she wishes the establishment of a religious order or wants her followers to pray the Rosary (Christian 1996: 4–6).

Also in the iconography, parallels can be noted: the white dress with the blue cloak, the upright standing position of the Virgin, the direct gaze from a young open face, the emergence from a cloud, the halo around the head and the outstretched arms, can all be found already on the Miraculous Medal which was minted after Catherine Labouré's vision of Mary in Paris and of which by 1842 more than 100 million copies had been sold (Christian 1996: 4). More strongly than ever before, Mary was presented as Immaculate and Powerful (Pope 1985). The images focused less on Mary's motherhood or sorrow for her son, and more on her purity, her being born without original sin, her virginity, her chastity and above all her protective power. Especially the Parisian images exuded power: over the world as symbolized by the globe in her hand or under her feet; over evil by the snake crushed underneath her feet; and over humankind by the outstretched hands and the wide cloak held out for protection. This "new" image of Mary must have circulated in the Middle East, and it has influenced without doubt the visions of Mary Alphonsus. Her description is not based on the abundantly available traditional icons of Mother Mary with Child of the Orthodox Christians, or on the Mother-with-Infant image of Spanish origin cherished in the Ghattas house for its miraculous power (Stolz 1968, opposite p. 20). Instead, it shows the outstretched hands and open and erect stance of the Parisian image. It is significant for our later analysis that not the traditional but the more recent and modern French image of Mary figured in the visions of Jerusalem.

The Visions of Mary in Cairo

On April 2, 1968, an hour and a half after sunset, Muslim workmen at the bus garage of the Public Transport Authority in Tumanbay Street in the Cairene suburb of El-Zeitoun heard a disturbance in the street and came out to see what was happening. They saw a moving light on the dome of the Coptic church opposite the garage and thought it was a woman who had climbed on the roof in order to commit suicide. They cried out to her to be careful. Someone in the crowd cried, "Settana Maryam, Settana Maryam," and soon a big crowd of people gathered in the street to watch the luminous body that moved on the dome and to discuss whether or not they saw Our Lady Mary. The apparitions continued to occur until September 1970. The observers saw a glittering white cloud, which could take on the form of a bust or of a full body moving between and on the domes. She was always luminous, at times accompanied or preceded by celestial beings in the form of doves (Smith and Haddad 1989: 161; Stowasser 1994: 81; Hoffman 1997; http://www.zeitun-eg.org). On April 30, 1968, the apparitions lasted for a full two hours, enabling thousands of citizens and foreigners to see and photograph them. One of these pictures, by Wagib Rizk, was published in the Egyptian daily *Al-Ahram*, and can be seen with other photographs and videos on the Zeitoun website (http://www.zeitun-eg.org). The Coptic Orthodox authorities soon took up the cry from the street. According to Brady (1968) in the *New York Times* of May 5 1968, twelve clergymen of the Coptic Orthodox Church, including Bishop Athanasias, affirmed their acceptance of reported miraculous appearances of the Virgin Mary in Cairo.

The Coptic church dedicated to the Virgin Mary has since drawn many pilgrims who come to seek the Virgin's help and blessing. The word goes that she has miraculously cured blindness, paralyzed organs, cancer and dumbness (http://www.zeitun-eg.org, accessed August 18, 2003). Reference to these miraculous cures is frequently made to authenticate the apparitions, in arguing against non-believers or alternative explanations of the phenomenon, for instance that they are tectonic strain-induced luminosities preceding seismic activities (Derr and Persinger 1989).

Although the Virgin is not described as having spoken, several messages were attributed to her appearance. The priesthood understood the visions as having two missions:

The one [mission] that has been accomplished is the consolidation of faith at a time when heresy spread and when materialistic beliefs, i.e. communism and dissipation, deny resurrections, immortality, the existence of the soul and of God and of the Metaphysical. The apparition of the Virgin, then, was a strong urge that has strengthened the faith of the believers and disproved the claims of the skeptics. The apparition of the Virgin has consolidated the Orthodox creed. Had we been in the wrong, the Virgin would not have made Her apparition for a whole year over the domes of an Orthodox church. THE MOTHER VIRGIN HAS THUS MADE HER APPARITION OVER THE DOMES OF THE CHURCH THAT HAS PRESERVED FAITH FOR US! [Caps in original]. It is an act of Providence that the Virgin Mary Church at El-Zeitoun should become a sacred visiting-place at a time when the Copts were denied the right to visit the Holy Places in Jerusalem because of the occupation of the city. This apparition was also the herald of the forthcoming victory of our valiant army that crossed the canal and destroyed Ber-Lev line (1973). (http://www.zeitun-eg.org, accessed August 18, 2003)

Interesting in this extract and the rest of the narrative are the references made to acute religious and political conflicts that were relevant for the observers at the time. Several identities were at stake.

The first is the identity of believers versus non-believers. The speakers position themselves against the rationalists who do not believe in resurrection, the after-life, the soul, visions or even God. Another is the identity of Orthodox versus other Christians. In the repeated mentioning of the Virgin's choice for an Orthodox church, the implicit Others are the Roman Catholics (Latins) who had slackened their devotion to Mary while the Orthodox preserved the faith. Coptic Orthodox differ from Roman Catholics in particular in their views of Mary. The Orthodox are critical of the Latin dogma of Mary's Immaculate Conception and of the perception of Mary as co-redeemer (Armanios 2002: 124). But by renouncing Mary Immaculate Conception they implicitly renounce also the apparitions in Lourdes (1858) where Mary had announced herself to Bernadette as the Immaculate Conception thus confirming the dogma proclaimed three years before by Pope Pius IX. The occurrences in Cairo enabled Copts to reaffirm the meaning of Mary in Orthodox theology, and exalt Mary as *Theotokos*, mother of a Divine Son and all human beings (http://www.zeitun-eg.org; see also Van Doorn-Harder and Vogt 1997: 12).

The apparitions themselves, and the large-scale attention to them, expressed and reinforced the revitalization movement of the Coptic Orthodox Church, which started in the 1960s. They were embraced by the patriarchy as a means to increase contact between the clergy and lay people and for the Church authorities to gain more control over the beliefs and practices of believers. It fitted the Coptic traditions of belief in visions (Hoffman 1997) and of seeking the mediation of saints (Mayeur-Jaouen 1997: 220). The visions also strengthened the popular movement of a Christian minority under pressure. The Coptic share among the predominantly Muslim population of Egypt was dwindling, freedom of religious expression was at that time being curtailed in several ways, and the effect of the Islamic revival was closely felt (Coptic students were, for instance, harassed because they did not pray as Muslims did; Naguib 1996: 58; Martin 1997:16). The apparitions coincided conveniently with the disparate efforts to revive both the Coptic Church and the Coptic community.

It should be noted, however, that this was not done by seeking through Mary an identity distinct from Muslims. The first observers in Zeitoun were both Muslims and Copts. According to some reports, the Muslim employees of the garage had started to recite texts from the Koran that praised Mary when the luminosities were identified as Our Lady Mary. Muslims highly respect Mary. Her name appears thirty-four times in the Koran and altogether she is referred to in seventy verses as well as in many authenticated traditions (Smith and Haddad 1989: 162). Sura 19 carries her name as title, and describes the annunciation, Mary's sinless conception and the birth of Jesus (*Koran*, Sura 19: verses 12–37); and elsewhere she is celebrated as an example to the faithful because of her chastity, her trust in the words of her Lord and her devoutness (*Koran*, Sura 66: verse 12; Stowasser 1994: 67). Mary has been chosen by God above the women of the worlds and as one of the four ruling females in heaven. Islamic exegesis has stressed a number of Mary's virtues to be emulated by female believers. Women's circles throughout the Muslim world recite her Sura, believed to confer special blessings, and some women seem to pray through Mary, as through Fatima and other Muslim female saints, in moments of anguish (Stowasser 1994: 80–1). Muslims who know the Koran have thus heard of Mary and her virtues. The story goes that Farouk Mohammed Atwa, one of the Muslim bus drivers watching the lights, had held up to the Lady a seriously injured finger that needed amputation. The next day his doctor found a complete recovery. Such stories that Muslims believed in or were healed by Mary were used to argue the authenticity of the apparitions.

This unity in respect for Mary made it possible that in the narratives of the visions also a national Egyptian identity could be constructed. The appearance of Mary was seen as a message of comfort after Egypt's military defeat in the Six Day War of 1967. This blow to the nation had left many Egyptians ill at ease and in search of new meanings to their life. The apparitions were welcomed as a symbol of unity and support. However, Mary was not only a symbol to express religious identity for Copts and national identity for Egyptians but also a feminine identity for women. But before discussing the impact on gender some theoretical approaches will be explored.

Mary and Empowerment of Women: Theoretical Considerations

> The regular connection between Mary, the laity, the poor, and the colonized, in the rapid development of pilgrimages from visions and apparitions of the corporeal type, and from related miracles, points to the hidden, nonhierarchical domain of the Church, with its stress on the power of the weak, on communitas and liminal phenomena, on the rare and unprecedented, as against the regular, ordained, and normative. (Turner and Turner 1978: 213)

The narratives of the visions can fruitfully be analyzed from the perspective of comparative symbology, defined by Turner and Turner (1978: 78) as "the study of the verbal and nonverbal ways through which men seek a common understanding of their vital situation and social predicament." Not only men, but also women seek common understandings of their situation and predicament, but they do so from different positions of power. The concept of "religious regimes" was introduced by Bax (1987), to show that within the religious domain a variety of groups compete for access to the divine and recognition of their religious interpretation. As Christian said: "Apparitions spark little interest without people's general hunger for access to the divine" (1996: 7). Spiritual needs and wishes, or the search for communitas, are not necessarily devoid of power competition. In the negotiations over acceptance and interpretation of visions of the Virgin Mary, the main opposition was between the official Church, allied with religious orders, which promoted universal and inclusive devotional practices and beliefs in Mary, and lower clergy and common believers, who held on to localized, exclusive practices and interpretations. This observation has at times led to a theoretical simplification of a dichotomy between the formal belief system and folk-belief. Women, the ethnic Other or the disabled and diseased, were marked as particularly prone to folk-belief and superstition. Their belief in apparitions or in miraculous cures was often met with suspicion and rejection by Church authorities. Actually, the hierarchical dichotomy is less straightforward as it seems. The Catholic Church partly co-opted the movement from below and incorporated "folk-beliefs," when it saw its faith challenged in the nineteenth and twentieth century by secularist intellectuals opposed to the idea of the supernatural, or by social movements like communism. In these contexts, localized religious devotion was integrated and universalized by crowning Marian shrine images, proclaiming Mary as patron of dioceses or provinces, or by officially recognizing specific visions and supporting the establishment of shrines (Christian 1996: 2–3). These examples illustrate that there is a permanent interaction between the dominant religious regimes and the believers who claim religious agency on the local level.

The earlier extract from Turner and Turner (1978: 213) mentioned visions and pilgrimages as sites that stressed "the power of the weak," but also where an icon or image "is pressed into the service of loyalty to the universal Church" (Turner and Turner 1978: 78). There is indeed a tendency of the Church authorities to homogenize and universalize the image and meanings of Mary. This leaves, however, much to guess about the agency of the socially weak, of the meanings sought by the less powerful. It is important to understand how visions and pilgrimages to Marian sites can be empowering for the less powerful and to what extent the latter can impose their image and meaning of Mary. The female predominance among both the seers and the pilgrims is of interest here. Women's lack of a formal role within the Catholic Church can be compensated by a new intermediary role between heaven and earth, religious practices which better fit the devotional needs of women, and the claim of interpretative and authoritative power.

In the literature on Marian devotion from a gender perspective, contradictory stands have been taken. On the one hand it is shown that the symbol of Mary is upheld by the patriarchal clergy to female believers as the ultimate model for feminine virtues. Not only was it a strong model that held women submissive and obedient, but also it was an unattainable ideal for Catholic women. According to Warner (1978: 337): "the effect the myth has on the mind of the Catholic girl cannot but be disturbing ... by setting up an impossible ideal the cult of the Virgin does drive the adherent into a position of acknowledged and hopeless yearning and inferiority." The imposed ideals of womanhood were indeed experienced by many women as a straitjacket. On the other hand, this oppression and resulting feelings of inferiority should not be presupposed as a given but as something to be researched. Loizos and Papataxiarchis (1999) found that Marian imagery helps reinforce the norms of virginity for girls until marriage, and wifely devotion and sacrificial motherhood afterwards; yet, at the same time it presents a "triumphant, powerful image of womanhood" (Loizos and Papataxiarchis 1991: 225). It is the triumphant, powerful image of Mary that modern feminist theologians have sought out to use as emblem for reinforcing women's position in the Catholic Church and to counteract women's victimization by showing her agency (Ruether 1977; Halkes 1980; Maeckelberghe 1991; Dresen 1998). By foregrounding Mary's Magnificat (Gospel of Luke 1: 46–55) Mary was shown to be a strong, determined woman who takes action in situations of injustice. Especially women can see in her a symbol of resistance (Halkes 1980). The question of why women adhere to creeds that seem to deepen their subordination to men emerges, according to Bracke (2003),

at the crucial intersections of different impulses running through the field of women's studies and feminist theory. While one impulse wants to account for the structural constraints that shape women's lives, another impulse affirms women as agents, as subjects of their own lives, thus radically refusing these subjects to be constituted by oppression alone. (Bracke 2003: 336–7)

An analysis and conceptualization of the key symbols and the meanings attributed to them in specific situations by specific people, enables to show how gender is constituted at the crossroads of structural constraint and individual agency.

It is an intrinsic characteristic of symbols that they are multi-interpretable, their meanings are neither clear nor consistent over time and place, and influenced by the power position of the people holding them. Many have noted the numerous contradictions in the symbol of Mary, in which she was both servant and queen, virgin and mother, role model as well as unattainable ideal. It is exactly this multiplicity of meaning that allows alternative interpretations and (re)readings of the symbol to serve specific group identities. This leads us to ask for the Jerusalem and Cairo cases which interpretations related to specific models of femininity were given to the symbol of Mary and what effects that had for women.

The Power of Mary for Arab Women

Both apparitions coincided with the decision of a group of women to leave their homes and become active and independent in public life. How could they, given their specific context, find support in the symbol of Mary and the visions to break away from the dominant norms of their gender and bring about change?

Changing Gender in Jerusalem: Catholic Sisters of the Rosary
To establish a congregation, Mary Alphonsus and her group of friends needed allies in the community and with the Church establishment. Miracle healings convinced people around them of the power of the Virgin and the Rosary. In the visions she was told whom to approach in the Church: Father Joseph Tannûs, a young Arab priest. Tannûs had profited from the patriarchate's policy to establish a local priesthood. He was ordained as priest in 1863, and had become Chancellor of the Latin Patriarchate in Jerusalem in 1868. As a staunch defender of the integration of Arab Catholics in the Church, he used his close contacts with the patriarchs to support the women's demand for an Arab congregation. As her confessor, he asked Mary Alphonsus to write down all she saw, and on the basis of her visions, he wrote down the rules for the new congregation, hired a small dwelling for the sisters and most importantly gained the assent of the pro-Arab Patriarch V. Bracco for the foundation of the Congregation of the Rosary. The visionary also managed to gain approval for her cause from the pro-Marian Pope Leo XIII (Jansen 2004).

In their quest for a religious life in the world, the visionary and her followers balanced on a thin line between opposing identities in terms of ethnicity, religion and gender. On the one hand they courted the foreign powers: the French sisters who educated them, the Italian patriarch Bracco and the Latin Pope Leo XIII, who, since 1847, were all eager to restore the presence of the Latin Church in Palestine. To gain support of the Church the women stayed in line with the Church's perceptions of a women's congregation, and modeled their dress, organizational form, activities and even their image of Mary on European examples. On the other hand, they stressed their Arab identity, which fitted the rising resistance against the encroaching Western powers in a society havocked by disease and famine. Their Arab Congregation of the Rosary aimed to bring education, especially to girls, to various Arab countries, increase devotion to Mary by saying a perpetual rosary and do good works (Jansen 2004). They followed in the footsteps of Western congregations in the Holy Land, but at the same time claimed that they could do it better because of their ethnic background. Unlike the foreigners, they spoke the language and were familiar with the culture of those they taught and cared for.

The visions and Mary's request for an all-Arab congregation enhanced this self-respect and ethnic pride. One day Mary Alphonsus asked the Virgin:

"How is it that you are choosing us, poor despised mortals? Why do you not choose some one from the rich lands of Europe?" She smiled and said: "Remember, my daughter, that roses grow among thorns. In this very land I had my joys, my sorrows, and my glories. By you and through you, I want to reveal my power." (Stolz 1968: 34)

The Virgin thus shares with the women their native country as well as her joys, sorrows and glories. Through the Virgin their own ethnic/national identity is reconfirmed.

The resentment against foreign powers, and in particular English Protestant missionaries, was at a peak in the two years before the apparitions. In the winter of 1872/73 two girls of the English-run Protestant Orphanage in Nazareth had jumped off the roof of their school, to escape regular horsewhip beatings, forced hard labor, deprivation of food and water, and the wrath of the controversial headmistress, Miss Julia Rose. The small Christian community in Palestine was greatly upset with the Protestant mission. Rival church organizations jumped in to take on the schoolchildren who wanted to leave the school (Stockdale 2002: 1–9). The visions of 1874 by Mary Alphonsus reinforced not only a native Arab identity versus foreigners, but also a Roman Catholic identity versus the blemished Protestant one. They fueled the standing antagonism between Catholics and Protestants. National and religious identities intersected: Protestants in this context were considered more foreign than Roman Catholics, who already accepted Arabs in their clerical ranks.

In the multiple meanings given to Mary in the Jerusalem case, not only her Arab and Roman Catholic identity were put to the fore, but also certain specific gender aspects. Mary Alphonsus' vision was not modeled on the image of Mary as Mother that she knew from her youth in her parents' house or from Greek Orthodox icons, but on more recent nineteenth-century European versions of Mary as Virgin, which hailed her pure and virgin status, as well as her powerful protective qualities. Mary Alphonsus' description of Mary, which was materialized in a painting, depicts the Holy Virgin as standing straight and upright, facing fully the people, inviting them to seek protection under her cloak. Such a direct gaze and public stance was not considered appropriate for girls at the time. Yet, it well represented the aims of the young sisters who wanted to go out and face the world and offer strangers their help and support. Such a more autonomous gender model was difficult to develop and maintain in a situation where women were subjected to strict norms of marriage and motherhood. The divine intervention offered by the visions must have been welcome. By appropriating specific meanings of the symbol of Mary, they sought acceptance by Church and family, while at the same time exploring alternative gender scripts.

The main request of the Virgin, to found a congregation of active nuns, was quite revolutionary at the time. Women convents were non-existent among the

Arabs of Palestine, nor women publicly working in education and health care. It entailed changes in the gendered domains of sexuality, social relations, the use of space and economics.

Celibacy for women was very unusual, as was the control of women over their own sexuality. Chastity was one of the three vows taken by the sisters. This fitted the general norm of virginity for young unmarried girls, but new was the personal responsibility now demanded of mature, unmarried women to control their own sexuality. Rather than the father, brothers or husband, now they themselves became responsible for guarding their chastity. A task even more demanding because they would, more than any other girl or woman, move in public space.

Also the two other vows, obedience and poverty, at first sight did not seem to contradict dominant gender norms. Yet, it obscured the fact that the primary obedience of these women was not any longer towards their family but to God and the Church, and that poverty now was self-chosen, in order to better fulfill the powerful role of giver, rather than inflicted on them as dependants of males. Although the poverty experienced by the Sisters of the Rosary was at times extreme, they nevertheless gained economic decision-making power and later financial independence, first by making cards of pressed flowers for pilgrims, later by wisely managing school and hospital fees.

Once the congregation was established and generally accepted, the image of Mary as a determined, active, open-faced Virgin became less vital and was fused with other images. The painting in the chapel of the present convent on Rehov Agron in Jerusalem, fully renovated in 2000, depicts the Mother Mary with Child rather than the solitary Virgin. But it can be found towering large over the altar, rather than in its customary humble place to the left. The statue in the garden and the life-size painting in the living room of the Sisters' new guesthouse in Fuheis, Jordan, are reproductions of the Virgin of Lourdes, respectively the Virgin of Paris, rather than materializations of Mary Alphonsus' description of the Virgin.

The sisters changed not only their own gender destination, but also that of many other girls through their educational work. While in their teachings they inculcated dominant virtues like obedience, purity, cleanliness, domestic ability and subservience, their very active life showed that women could work, make independent decisions, give meaning to their life and live independently of men – an ambiguous message that gave room to many women for ambiguous emulation.

Changing Gender in Cairo: Coptic Sisters of Mary

A similar process of female empowerment through a reinterpretation of the symbol of Mary can be observed in Cairo, even though Egyptian and Coptic identities were more at stake than gender. Mary did not appear to one woman here, but to many people, nor did she explicitly demand a female congregation, but, as I shall show, the apparitions created an atmosphere conducive to the rise of an active women's group, the Daughters of Maryam (*Banât Maryam*) who took up new gender roles.

Part of the Coptic revival in the 1960s was that the clergy as well as dominant forces in society increasingly held up Mary as model to Coptic girls and young women. She is the most virtuous woman, with many attributes to be emulated: "holiness, purity, meekness, humility, faith, hope, love, obedience, endurance, patience, tolerance, fasting, praying" (M. Mikhail, quoted in Armanios 2002: 124). Such a combination of virtues fitted well with the dominant ideal of woman as "being entirely accountable to her spouse, her family, her God, and her community in terms of social and familial responsibilities" (Armanios 2002: 113). The use of Mary as a feminine model and the exaltation of a superior type of virtuous woman is not new in Coptic community. Nor is the recognition of two manifestations of female sexual identity: the woman as wife/mother or as perpetual virgin. New is the remarkable fascination with the latter in this period. Armanios (2002: 119) argues that the increasing exaltation of the female virgin-saint in modern Coptic culture is linked to the changing construction of sexuality in the Coptic community. The daily talk of Mary during the period of visions can have strengthened the impact of this subdominant model on Coptic women. How does this relate to the changing power position of Coptic women?

Since the 1960s also middle-class Coptic women started to gain access to education. Within a generation, there are considerable changes in gender relations. Compared with their illiterate, home-oriented, economically dependent mothers, young women now study, work, move around town and are confronted with national and international issues. Rather than being well anchored in their identity as women, many of the younger generation experience a personal sense of "not fitting" in the prescribed gender role. The world around them confronts them even more with their "misfit" as it questions their gender identity by hostile reactions to their use of public space and usurpation of men's scholarships or jobs. A similar experience by Muslim girls in the Middle East has been seen as an important factor contributing to their adherence to the Islamist movement (Macleod 1991; Jansen 1998). For Coptic girls, it seems likewise to have contributed to a religious revival. Whereas Muslim Egyptian girls frequently solved the identity conflict by taking on the veil, the Coptic girls chose a symbolic seclusion and identification with virgin saints or the Virgin Mary, or reacted by becoming religiously active. They went to work for the Church as "servants" (*khuddâm*) (Thorbjørnsrud 1997: 168).

Reinforcement of their religious identity offers security in a time when they doubt their gender identity in two ways. First, it restores their self-respect when they can function as pious, helpful, supporting women as is expected from them. As such they can follow the model of Mary as devout, obedient and devoted to others. Yet, at the same time the church-work is a way to express their individuality, independence and capacities. Among the fellow workers in the church (like the Egyptian Muslim women in Islamist groups) they gain companionship, support and encouragement for their own development, which they find lacking at home. Thorjbørnsrud (1997: 170–5) described a number of cases in which girls escape the frustrations of their home situation as well as the Islamist pressure of the wider Cairene society by their acceptable work for the Church. Without the veil, Coptic women have even more trouble than Muslim women to preserve their reputation. None of the authors in the volume edited by Van Doorn-Harder and Vogt (1997) explicitly refers to the apparitions of 1968 as an expression of and support for the religious revival that took place in that decade. But the apparitions, and the fierce debates on their authenticity and meaning, must have played a role in the identity politics and religious revival of the Coptic community at large, as well as for women who were crafting a new gender role. Moreover, a similar re-imaging of Mary can be noted. Van Doorn-Harder and Vogt (1997: 89) were surprised to find a mural painted by nuns of the Virgin Mary with long flowing hair rather than the normal modest headgear. The nuns said that they considered the latter a Muslim influence.

It is no coincidence that in the 1960s new meanings of virginity emerged, together with a more public role of young women. Dina El-Khawaga showed this in her description of the rise of a particular group of servants to the Church, the "consecrated virgins" (*al-mukarrasât*) (El-Khawaga 1977: 158–60). The foundation story of this active group of Coptic women, significantly called the *Banât Maryam*, the Daughters of Mary, resemble that of the Catholic Sisters of the Rosary.

At the beginning of the 1960s several young and older women in the diocese of Beni Suef expressed the wish to serve the community and to make a vow of celibacy. New in their request was not so much that they wanted to become nuns – female monasticism was well known in the Coptic community in Egypt – but rather that they wanted to live a form of active life. As El-Khawaga (1977: 158) indicates: "It was difficult for this new orientation to find its place in the already existing categories within the Coptic Church, where women had only one church vocation, that of contemplative nuns." The first community of "consecrated virgins" in Beni Suef called themselves the *Banât Maryam* and became active in building schools, a clinic, a home for children with learning difficulties and a variety of social projects; their success led other dioceses to promote the foundation of other groups. As grass-roots organizations, they differed considerably among each other in their work sector, way of living, naming or dress. The difference with the contemplative nuns was expressed in several ways: to facilitate their public work they wore gray ankle-length dresses with small gray veils or secular clothes with a headscarf rather than the traditional nun's outfit of a long black garb with a long black veil over a tight black skullcap. They were addressed as "my sister" (*tâsûnî*) rather than with the honorary title "our mother" (*ummînâ*), which was reserved for contemplative nuns, not only reflecting a lesser respect and status for the active sisters, but also offering a parallel to the Islamic "sisters" who were becoming active in that period in Egypt.

As in Jerusalem, the new group of sisters sought acceptance and guidance by the Church. The recognition by the patriarch Kyrillos VI of their community was half-hearted as he "did not want to give this model a general validity, but only to bless an effective group which already existed" (El-Khawaga 1977: 159). Little support was forthcoming. The consecrated virgins unwittingly had become involved in the intra-clerical conflict between centralizing and decentralizing factions, and between those who gave renewed value to the early Church and its institution as against adherence to the principle of "the church in the world" (El-Khawaga 1977: 160). In this modernization process, in which more lay people became involved in the Church and demanded the Church's preoccupation with the problems of the world rather than centralization and institutionalization, the Apparitions of Mary both expressed and reinforced the contemporary religious debate. Both sides sought and found support from Mary.

In the case of the Coptic active nuns it can be said that certain thoughts prevailed: by taking the name of Daughters of Maryam they chose to emulate Holy Mary, but especially in certain characteristics. Both contemplative and active nuns insist on a special connection with Mary (Van Doorn-Harder 1995: 48), but the active nuns select other elements: not just her holiness as mother of God, but also her active work for the community. According to the accounts of the life of Mary, she not only lived in the temple, where she prayed, but also provided services to the temple. Mary is a symbol that provides both meaning to the work of the active sisters and well as a profound sense of belief and belonging. It seems no coincidence that in the late 1960s, the time of the apparitions, the number of women seeking a life in service to the church and their co-religionaries multiplied.

Conclusion

The analyses of the apparitions of Mary in Jerusalem and Cairo show that they have multiple meanings for the visionaries and the believers concerned. This multiplicity is both expressive of and functional to a negotiation of power. A comparison of the apparitions in Jerusalem and Cairo showed how multiple meanings attached to Mary served certain groups of women in changing notions of gender, whether for themselves or others. The two cases showed similarities in that in each a group of women emerged, the Roman Catholic (Latin) Sisters of the Rosary in Jerusalem and the Coptic Orthodox Daughters of Mary in Cairo which each in their own way, and within the limits posed by their own time and place, managed to create for themselves a new role in society, with wide ranging consequences for many girls and women around them. The Sisters of the Rosary contributed significantly in elevating the education of Middle Eastern girls and in providing health care. The Daughters of Mary, unlike contemplative Coptic nuns, ventured out into the world and managed to be economically independent in the social projects in schooling, clinical health care, and services to drug addicts, unmarried mothers, individuals with learning difficulties and elderly people.

The adoration of the Virgin Mary and the practicing and preaching of patri-archal feminine virtues like obedience, virtuousness, virginity, sacrifice and self-effacement by nuns has frequently been criticized by feminist authors. Yet, by considering the visionaries and nuns also as active agents in their own right and not only as mere representatives of a dominant Church and executioners of its female models, we have discovered their emancipatory powers, both for themselves and for other women, and their value as agents of change.

References

Armanios, F. (2002), "The 'Virtuous Woman': Images of Gender in Modern Coptic Society," *Middle Eastern Studies*, 38(1): 110–30.

Bax, M. (1987), "Religious Regimes and State Formation: Towards a Research Perspective," *Anthropological Quarterly*, 60: 1–11.

Bracke, S. (2003), "Author(iz)ing Agency: Feminist Scholars Making Sense of Women's Involvement in Religious 'Fundamentalist' Movements," *European Journal of Women's Studies*, 10(3): 335–46.

Brady, T. (1968), "Visions of Virgin Reported in Cairo," *New York Times*, May 5.

Christian, W. (1996), *Visionaries: The Spanish Republic and the Reign of Christ*, Berkeley, CA: University of California Press.

Derr, J. S. and Persinger, M. A. (1989), "Geophysical Variables and Behavior: LIV. Zeitoun (Egypt) Apparitions of the Virgin Mary as Tectonic Strain-Induced Luminosities," *Perceptual and Motor Skills*, 68(1): 123–8.

Dresen, G. (1998), *'Is dit mijn lichaam?' Visioenen van het volmaakte lichaam in katholieke moraal en mystiek*, Nijmegen: Valkhof Pers.

Duvignau, P. (1981), *Une vie pour Dieu et les ames. S.B. Mgr. Vincent Bracco. Pariarche Latin de Jérusalem 1835–1889*, Jerusalem: Imprimerie du Patriarcat Latin.

El-Khawaga, D. (1997), "The Laity at the Heart of the Coptic Clerical Reform," in N. van Doorn-Harder and K. Vogt (eds), *Between Desert and City: The Coptic Orthodox Church Today*, Oslo: Novus forlag.

Goichon, A. M. (1972), *Jordanie réelle*, 2 vols, Paris: G-P. Maisonneuve and Larose.

Halkes, C. J. M. (1980), *Met Myriam is het begonnen: Opstandige vrouwen op zoek naar hun geloof*, Kampen: Kok.

Hoffman, V. J. (1997), "The Role of Visions in Contemporary Egyptian Religious Life," *Religion*, 27(1): 45–64.

Jansen, W. (1998), "Contested Identities: Women and Religion in Algeria and Jordan," in K. Ask and M. Tjomsland (eds), *Women and Islamization: Contemporary Dimensions of Discourse on Gender Relations*, Oxford: Berg.

—— (2004), "Arab Women with a Mission: The Sisters of the Rosary," in M. Marten and M. Tamcke (eds), *Christian Witness between Continuity and New Beginnings: Modern Historical Missions in the Middle East*, Hamburg: LIT.

Koran, The (1990), transl. by N. J. Dawood, London: Penguin.

Loizos, P. and Papataxiarchis, E. (1991), *Contested Identities: Gender and Kinship in Modern Greece*, Princeton, NJ: Princeton University Press.

Macleod, A. E. (1991), *Accommodating Protest: Working Women, the New Veiling, and Change in Cairo*, New York: Columbia University Press.

Maeckelberghe, E. (1991), "Desperately Seeking Mary: A Feminist Appropriation of a Traditional Religious Symbol," Pd.D. thesis, Rijksuniversiteit Groningen.

Martin, M. (1997), "The Renewal in Context: 1960–1990," in N. van Doorn-Harder and K. Vogt (eds), *Between Desert and City: The Coptic Orthodox Church Today*, Oslo: Novus forlag.

Mayeur-Jaouen, C. (1997), "The Coptic Mouleds: Evolution of the Traditional Pilgrimages," in N. Van Doorn-Harder and K. Vogt (eds), *Between Desert and City: The Coptic Orthodox Church Today*, Oslo: Novus forlag.

Médebielle, P. (1963), *The Diocese of the Latin Patriarchate of Jerusalem*, Jerusalem: Imprimerie du Patriarcat Latin.

Naguib, S. (1996), *Les Coptes dans l'Égypte d'aujourd'hui*, Brussels: Solidarité-Orient.

Pope, B. C. (1985), "Immaculate and Powerful: The Marian Revival in the Nineteenth Century," in C. W. Atkinson, C. H. Buchanan and M. R. Miles (eds), *Immaculate and Powerful: The Female in Sacred Image and Social Reality*, Boston, MA: Beacon Press.

Ruether, R. R. (1977), *Mary: The Feminine Face of the Church*, Philadelphia, PA: Westminster Press.

Smith, J. I. and Haddad, Y. (1989), "The Virgin Mary in Islamic Tradition and Commentary," *The Muslim World*, 79(3–4): 161–87.

Stockdale, N. L. (2002), "An Imperialist Failure: English Missionary Women and Palestinian Orphan Girls in Nazareth, 1864–1899," paper presented at WOCMES, Mainz, September 9–12.

Stolz, B. (1968), *A Handmaid of the Holy Rosary: Mother Mary Alphonsus of the Rosary. First Foundress of an Arab Congregation 1843–1927*, Jerusalem: Typ. PP. Franciscan. T.S.

Stowasser, B. F. (1994), *Women in the Qur'an, Traditions, and Interpretation*, New York and Oxford: Oxford University Press.

Thorbjørnsrud, B. (1997), "Born in the Wrong Age: Coptic Women in a Changing Society," in N. Van Doorn-Harder and K. Vogt (eds), *Between Desert and City: The Coptic Orthodox Church Today*, Oslo: Novus forlag.

Turner, V. and Turner, E. (1978), *Image and Pilgrimage in Christian Culture: Anthropological Perspectives*, New York: Columbia University Press.

Van Doorn-Harder, P. (1995), *Contemporary Coptic Nuns*, Columbia, SC: University of South Carolina.

—— and Vogt, K. (eds) (1997), *Between Desert and City: The Coptic Orthodox Church Today*, Oslo: Novus forlag.

Warner, M. (1978), *Alone of All her Sex: The Myth and the Cult of the Virgin Mary*, London: Quartet.

9

An Army of Women Learning Torah[1]

Leah Shakdiel

The Researcher Positions Herself

Midday, sunny, early spring 2000, a big clearing in a wood of eucalyptus trees. Young women in military uniform, caps duly fastened on their heads, cross the screen diagonally, starting from the top left corner, in straight lines, marching to the uppity sounds of the military band playing the well-known IDF [Israeli Defense Force] hymn. The small figures grow large as they approach the camera: some of them are in trousers, some in knee-length skirts, some in ankle-long skirts which are a novelty, obviously marking the extra religiosity of those wearing them, and the willingness of the army to sew for them this special garb made of the same familiar khaki cloth. Just before one of these latter women disappears out of the bottom right corner of the screen, a split second of motherly and patriotic pride: it's my daughter Racheli, gazing straight ahead most seriously, not at the camera.

It was the ceremonial conclusion of Racheli's basic training course. I was there with the other families and friends, but did not know at the time that an hour-long documentary about one of the two groups in that particular military track was in the making (not Racheli's group; that snapshot is her only moment on the screen). It was the second year of this new track, and filmmaker Pnina Greitzer thought it was news, not only for these girls' immediate communities. She named it Be'Ezrat Nashim, which literally means either "in the women's auxiliary section" (of the synagogue, following ancient practice in the Temple in Jerusalem) or "with women's help," and the latter meaning can even be read as a take-off on the ubiquitous idiom "with God's help." This seemingly intended pun triggers the problematization of the film's plot in several simultaneous directions; for me personally it facilitated a synthesis of my insider's perspective (the emic) with Greitzer's, an outsider (the etic). I ended up reading the film through its potential relevance to feminist research of female identity construction at large.

Weaving Gender Construction into Nation Construction: The Case of Zionism and Israel

The Zionist movement sprang in Europe towards the end of the nineteenth century, in the bosom of modernist revolutions in all spheres of life. As such, it carried with it, inter alia, not only the message of normalizing the Jewish people into the contemporary format of a nation-state in its historical homeland, with its revived historical language and a sustainable economy, but also the intertwined idea that personal and collective cultural identities must also be converted into forms that were perceived as compatible with that enormous change. Thus, in accordance with the modernist myth of the New Man, Zionism gave rise to images of the New Jew: no longer weak, vulnerable and effeminated by generations of internal (Jewish religious) and external (Anti-Semitic) oppression, this self-emancipated person was shaped like a Byronic hero, like a Greek Herculean statue, like a Soviet propaganda poster. That is to say, the New Jew was about as gender-neutral, and as culture-inclusive, as the New Man in Leonardo da Vinci's *Vitribionic Man* or Michelangelo's *Creation of Man*: this person was a muscular Greco-Nordic secular male (Elboim-Dror 1992–4; Boyarin 1997; Mayer 1999). And since national movements, just like other human projects, need females too, this meant that women from the start have had to deal with a double message – a rhetoric of inclusion, that claims to liberate them from antiquated obsolete religious patriarchy, at odds with practices of exclusion, that marginalize them, and allow them to penetrate the hegemonic ethos only within the boundaries of "the glass ceiling effect" (that is, only a few at a time, and only those who are more masculinized than the rest, and only temporarily, as long as we can use them to increase our "manpower" while in conflict with some menacing Others) (Hazleton 1977; Swirski and Safir 1991).

So it came to be that the more Zionistic the ideology of the woman, the more likely she has been to accommodate herself to these conditions (Shilo 1998). In the context of this chapter, this means that she has struggled for her right to share the burden of military guard, guerrilla and underground activities, and military service, with some success. Moreover, this explains why Israel focused on the inclusion of women in the IDF by law (1949), very close to its creation when the state was founded (1948); to the present day, Israel is one of the few states worldwide which have opted for compulsory conscription of women, albeit for a shorter period than the men's service, and with other leniencies (automatic release upon marriage) (Etzioni-Halevi and Illy 1993).

Images of pretty 18-year-old girls in uniform with guns have been exported fervently all over, and have served to hide from view the discomfort of an on-and-off debate questioning this practice. Liberal feminists have criticized the sexist relegation of women in the army to "pink-color jobs" only (secretaries, caretakers of male soldiers, teachers), the stereotypes that bar women from equal access to self-fulfilling military jobs such as combat pilots, and the ensuing disadvantage women have later in life when facing the same glass ceiling in Israeli politics, which favors ex-military leaders (Golan 1997; Izraeli 1997). Radical feminists have pointed at the normalization of sexual harassment practices in the army, at the militarization of Israeli society at large (including schooling practices and rituals) once women are co-opted into the system as supportive "fellows"-in-arms and later as mothers-as-brave-as-fathers, at the need to distance ourselves as women from the hegemonic ethos if we are to regain our political advantage as historical outsiders (Women in Black, The Four Mothers, New Profile, Coalition of Women for Peace, Women's Blockade Watch) (Mazali 2001; Lubin 2003).

But the first objection, and so far the most successful, to the imposition of military service on women, came from the Jewish religious parties, who declared the issue a casus belli, and forced the government to enable women coming of age (18) to resort to a bureaucratic procedure of automatic exemption, by signing an affidavit in the office of state-paid rabbis attesting "religion and conscience" as their reasons for objecting the draft (Welner 1952; Cohen 1988).[2]

This political achievement is remarkable for several reasons. First, it happened in a state that to the present day has recognized very few conscientious objectors to conscription, and this after lengthy and exhausting legal drilling (see, for example, Helman 1999). Second, when the Law of Compulsory National Service was passed in 1953, as an alternative civilian service for those not willing or not able to share the burden of active military service, it was clear from the start that it was an inapplicable dead letter, due to the explicit objection of rabbis to any form of legal coercion of women to serve the state.

The resulting parallel tracking of religious women of service age into earlier entry into marriage and motherhood, or the workforce, or higher education, should be seen against the backdrop of the perceived national "situation" – post-Holocaust on the one hand (and therefore still traumatized enough to cede to the Ultra Orthodox on matters of military service: see Chapter 2 by Yohai Hakak in this volume) and ongoing menace from the outnumbering Arabs in the region and their "brothers" inside Israel (that is, the consensus that neither conscription nor obligatory civilian national service can be imposed on all of Israel's Palestinian minority and certainly not on their female half).

Religious Zionism, Military Service and Women

This chapter focuses on Religious Zionism, a segment of Israeli society that has been torn from the start over the issue of gender roles, and therefore may serve as litmus paper that can bring to light certain undercurrents in the intricate dynamics described previously.

Historically, it started with some nineteenth-century rabbis in Eastern Europe and the Balkans, who translated ancient religious longing for Return of the Exiles to the Land of Israel into practical plans for resettling it. Groups of religious agricultural settlers, not only from Eastern Europe but also from Yemen, established colonies in this province while still under Ottoman rule. When Theodore Herzl published his tractate *State of the Jews* in 1896 and started convening periodically the World Zionist Congress (as of 1897), this matured into the founding of a political party within it (1902), the Mizrahi (Hebrew acronym for "spiritual center"), which consistently sided with Herzl, and his heirs in the General Zionist party, in their understanding of Zionism as a secular political liberation movement that leaves all issues of religion and culture to the different parties and their respective educational systems (Laqueur 1972).

This led the Mizrahi party to a milestone decision, backed by its rabbis' religious ruling, in 1926, to extend the suffrage (passive and active) to women, which enabled it to join the secular religious parties in the establishment of Jewish self-government in Palestine under the auspices of the League of Nations British Mandate rule (1918–48), while the Ultra Orthodox maintained their anti-Zionist politics (Zohar 1996). Few women have since joined the leadership of Religious Zionism, but this historic choice has affected the everyday life of this sector: the modernization of gender roles in all areas of life, in family lifestyles, dress code, schooling (mixed sex as well as single sex), the job and professional scene. That is, the modernist middle class has allowed the religious to develop their variant within it, and it has manifested as much gender freedom (and denied sexist practices) as its secular counterpart, including difficulties concerning aspirations of equal participation in defense and pre-state military underground (Rosenberg 2002).

It should be noted that the aforementioned Herzlian-cum-Mizrahi type of liberal Zionism ended up giving way to its fierce opponent, the more activist and intrusive Socialist Zionism led by Ben Gurion, who established himself as head of the movement by the 1930s, and influential first prime minister of the State of Israel from 1948 into the 1960s. During this second phase, Religious Zionism was engaged in unrelenting struggles, in two directions: to fight off hegemonic secular ideologies and defend the autonomy of its schools, settlements, budgets, immigration policies, community services – but at the same time it also competed for pushing its own agenda into the land and the state at large (Liebman and Don-Yehiya 1983). In the context of this chapter, it is important to note that by 1949 this political party had already been long split in two – the more-strict-religious Mizrahi (bourgeois city-dwellers) and the less-strict-religious socialist-activist haPo'el haMizrahi (with their own kibbutzim, moshavim and some city proletariat). When this party voted with the Ultra Orthodox in 1953 against compulsory service of women, its Zionist-activist part lost the inner political battle, but continued its practice as the religious mirror image of secular Zionist activism: nourishing a popular mixed-sex youth movement, established in 1929 (Bnei Akiva),[3] that explicitly educates towards the climax at age 18, when this self-appointed national elite volunteers to serve in the Nahal corps (Hebrew acronym for Pioneering Combat Youth) and eventually settle for life in kibbutzim, old and new, agricultural outposts of Zionism as land conquest. Thus, a small but steady minority of religious girls did serve in the army every year, mostly in religious Nahal units, with the backing of some bold rabbis (Admanit 1977; Cohen 1979, 1982).

I can illustrate this with my own story. In 1968, when I graduated at 17 from a high school in Tel Aviv, I was swept by my patriotic family and community and by my socialization in single-sex classrooms in a system that propagated gender equality and middle-class aspirations for individual excellence. All of this boiled down to one bottom line: I wanted to serve in the army. Alas, my widowed mother pulled on me the ultimate weapon (she had never used it before, nor after): "If Dad were alive, you would not do this to me." Dad had been a central figure in the Mizrahi politics, and, inter alia, opposed the conscription of women. The only religious females I knew who were going to serve in the army were Bnei Akiva "cool" girls. The organization of alternative civilian service for religious women was so sporadic at the time that all around me agreed I should not even do *that* to Mom, so I joined the majority of my classmates and went straight to university. This has remained with me ever since as an unfinished business.

By 2000, Israel – including its army, its women and its religious Zionists – has changed somewhat, though all of the above historical analysis is crucial if we are to understand present-day unfolding problematics. My daughter Racheli was born and bred into a family committed to visions of social justice, peace with Palestinians, and feminism. However, her religious Zionist generation should be characterized too;[4] I submit that it can be best explained as the product of two related processes, evident since the Six Day War in 1967.

The first is the saga of messianism, which fermented especially following the collapse of the old competitor, secular Zionism led by the Labor movement, as a result of the disaster of the 1973 war, and its replacement in 1977 by right-wing politics headed by the Likud party. Religious Zionist youth flocked energetically to settle the "liberated" territories, and this ideology took over almost the entire educational system of this camp, its youth movement, its synagogues and rabbis, and its parliamentary politics (Levine 1986). But this euphoria has suffered serious punctures since the first Intifada in 1988 (Palestinian uprising against the Israeli occupation), and at time of writing, even Ariel Sharon, a hawkish Likud prime minister, is talking of the necessity to pull out of the Gaza Strip and parts of the West Bank. Consequently, more and more religious Zionists have given up on their recent one-track politics (right-wing messianism) in favor of a return to the broader agenda – the production of modernized religion in a sovereign Jewish state.

The second process is the peculiar reawakening of women's issues in this camp, to the point of the frequent reference to it as "a revolution," in the media as well as in academic research. I claim that this second phenomenon is closely linked to the unfolding of the first "saga" as told above.

At first, the empowerment of women went hand in hand with the messianic trend (Rapoport, Penso and Garb 1994; El-Or and Aran 1995; Rapoport, Garb and Penso 1995): single-sex high schooling for girls with intensified religious education, often with boarding away from home in high school age, outdid mixed-sex public schooling in popularity; NGOs for organizing girls' national service were established, and one and even two years of volunteer work in needy schools or hospitals became the social norm; girls and women participated visibly in the settling movement, in all political practices. However, all of this assumed the dimensions of a "revolution" that draws the attention of society at large only from the late 1980s on, a timing that coincides with the dwindling of the settlers' movement: as if the messianic spirit, a crucial element for all types of social engineering, has started blowing in a different direction. It is since then that religious women have pushed for new positions of religious leadership; institutions for top-level Torah learning for adult women have been established; international and national political caucuses of religious women have drawn thousands to their conferences; written Torah scholarship by women has come out, a new phenomenon in the history of Orthodox Judaism; and the compound "religious feminism" has become subject of household incessant debates, weighing its perceived potential against its perceived "dangers" to family and community (El-Or 2002).

It is in this context that new formats for military service for women were devised, with the explicit aim of meeting the needs of growing numbers of religious women who are no longer satisfied with the norm of alternative national service; some rabbis, arguing that it is wrong to leave these girls with no religious guidance, started nuancing the old Halachic debate with careful "openings" (Shaviv 1983). One such unit, within the existing track of soldier-teachers in needy schools, is the "female soldier-teachers of Torah culture," which trains religious girls to teach Jewish culture in non-religious schools: the uniform sends the message that, contrary to civilian national service girls engaged in the same activity, these religious soldier-teachers are non-sectarian, and therefore enjoy more trust in the non-religious schools. But my daughter Racheli chose another track, even newer: the two senior Torah learning institutions for female high school graduates in Israel, Midreshet Ein haNatziv (originally founded by the Religious Kibbutz Movement as the counterpart of its men's yeshiva),[5] and Midreshet Lindenbaum in Jerusalem (originally founded by and for US-born young Modern Orthodox women in Israel), developed for the first time in Israeli history the female parallel of the "Hesder" (literally, "arrangement") with the army. The Hesder enables religious young men (since 1970) to combine their military service with Torah study, in a way that enables their rabbis to continue nourishing their commitment to religion in a combat unit which is socially protective; the Hesder for women equally combines Torah study with military service with rabbinical supervision, but in line with the aforementioned Halachic carefulness, the service track consists of teaching soldiers (mostly males) in need of either basic literacy or high school education.

Filmmaker Pnina Greitzer, a non-religious woman, documented the Ein Hanatziv second group through the winter of 2000, in the army, in their study hall in the kibbutz, in their rooms and in their homes. She interviewed not only them, but also their teachers, their rabbi, other rabbis, their mothers and ended up also researching the endeavor of the previous generation, my age group, towards the empowerment of women in the Torah world. The edited product is distinctly divided into two parts – the girls, then the older women – and ends with the girls, back to the finale of the scene chosen for the opening of the film. This structure posits the two parts like two stages of the religious feminist's life cycle, and projects each one of them on the other as suggested interpretation. It is from this angle that I chose to analyze the film, because it serves best my intention to bring into focus some insights about girlhood and female identity construction, that may resonate beyond the immediate context as expounded above.

Here is a final avowal and disclaimer. In 2003, a similar program was established in my town Yeruham, and I am on its staff. Besides, almost all persons of my generation included in this film, but not the girls portrayed, are personal acquaintances of mine. I shared my thoughts about the film with Greitzer, and she admitted I was not off-track, but I alone am responsible for the written result.

Realizing Two Dreams at Once

A long shot of a men's study hall, mostly black and white: dark heads, some beards, white shirts, dark trousers, dark covers of closed books, white open pages. Background buzz of human voices, learning with each other. The scene dissolves into a long shot of the girls' study hall: similar books, but the girls' clothes fill the screen with patches of color. Same steady buzz. Close up on a Talmud page, thick with script. Zoom in on the page, the selected phrase lightened up, as a voiceover announces emphatically: "Let the words of Torah burn rather than be given to women." Another page, same technique, "He who teaches his daughter Torah, it is as if he taught her frivolity." Cut. Two girls sitting on green grass, open books on their knees, in discussion: "He who teaches his daughter Torah it is as if he taught her frivolity. I understand that in those days it was a problem because women were not educated so it was a bad idea to teach them complicated stuff, they could not understand it. But today this is not so."[6] The girls recite the traditional blessing upon leaving the house of study: "We thank you God for giving us a share with the dwellers in the house of study, rather than with those at the street corner, we get up early and so do they, we get up for the sake of eternal life, and they get up for the sake of the passing moment."

Enrollment day. Fingerprints, injections, portrait photos, duffel bags, now it's time for getting uniforms. The try-out room is behind the flap-door, which is thrown open frequently as this girl or another comes out towards the counter, and asks the male soldier in charge for a different size of some clothing item. Everyone is excited and smiling. No'a, chewing gum, approaches the counter for a skirt: "Size 38." Soldier: "You don't need something longer?" "No!! It's too long! I need to make it shorter." "What?!" She climbs the counter and demonstrates so he can see: "Now it's down to here" – halfway to ankle – "I'll make it down to here" – below knee – "it's OK." Camera settles at the side, so all can see his head is bare, he is not religious. Soldier: "No this is not right. Religious girls should not be like the secular girls. You know, modesty (mocking at her)... When I was a kid, I attended yeshiva, by us, I know how it should be, you should think about those things!" No'a starts preaching: "This length is quite enough, modesty is a personal criterion." Another girl joins in: "It's wrong to judge people by how they dress. Besides, modesty is not only about dress, it's how you behave." The girls look triumphant, as if they had expected this and had practiced their lines. Soldier looks unconvinced, smiles ironically.

The title of this section is a quote of No'a's words, which were chosen as the summing up sentence of the film: yes, she is very pleased, this year she succeeded in realizing two very important dreams. She does not need to spell them out: the film intertwines throughout the two spheres the girls have recently moved into, two male territories, that of traditional Torah study the yeshiva way, and that of military service. All come from religious Zionist families that assume the need to "give to the state, in return for all the good that She gave you all these years," "to contribute to your people and to your country." All know that the move of women into the field of Torah study is part of a feminist age, which is both inevitable and welcome, in step with other doors that had opened for them in other spheres of life.

It seems that Greitzer lets No'a lead the narrative not only for her charm and verbal fluency, but also mainly because she of all the girls embodies a conscious move from the first stage of women's empowerment in this generation as analyzed previously, to the second stage. She grew up, she says, in a conventional girls' school and youth movement where she was told to wear skirts only and stereotyped trouser-wearing females as "not religious enough"; she is happy she chose to study on the kibbutz, where women who wear trousers "are so religious and ethical that I am like the ground they can walk on." This she sees as open-mindedness, and thinks that it is a great trade-off against the compromise of her previous principles that is represented by the trousers she started wearing. "We learnt a lot at school, but they digest it for you; it is only here that I started learning the real stuff, in depth, so that I know why I do things in religion." Rachel Keren, the head of the Midrasha, echoes this perception: "I don't spoon feed them, I just set the table, so they can be religious by choice."

The soldier described earlier expresses doubts concerning the probability of this intricate vision. Army life brings together people with varied backgrounds, and in this case there is a clash between his dichotomous worldview of an Israel neatly split into the religious and the secular, and the Israel that these girls set out to participate in. He gives voice to the more popular stereotypes, whereas they promote an opinion consciously held by a minority. The kind of religious society he grew up in is in line with the androcentric, exclusive and even sexist and misogynist texts that Greitzer presented in such stark contrast to the modernist ambitions the girls express while studying Torah. The kind of split he holds on to, even now that he is no longer part of that world, between the good women (accommodating themselves to the lusty male gaze) and the bad ones (the daring ones who play with fire), leaves him with a cognitive dissonance that has no room for these girls – they deviate, and therefore can only fall into the second category in his mind. The girls know that as soon as their training for their military job is over, they will have a clear edge over the likes of him in their classrooms, and they know that their role in the lives of their soldier-students will forgo the dispensation of specific skills and information into the sphere of modeling and value acculturation. This is not new: women have served in such military roles ever since 1948 (Horowitz 1982; Smooha 1984). What is new though is their female version of the religious Zionist, Hesder yeshiva boys, and they are eager to dispense the new knowledge concerning the exciting options represented in their very existence, and in the intrusion of their existence into the plain Israeli-ness of the military. This is their "frontier" – religiously, nationally, socially.

And they are a novelty that meets other objections as well, from within their own religious Zionist camp. The chief rabbi of the city of Ramat Gan, Ya'akov Ariel, a leading figure of the religious Zionist camp, is interviewed (as a balance to the Midrasha rabbi, who obviously supports the military service of women): "The Torah says, 'your camp should be holy'. I don't rule out women's soldiering abilities, I rule out the mixing with men. We have to decide, either the men should fight, or the women, not together." Ariel echoes here the threat of some Hesder yeshiva rabbis to pull their men out of the army if women continue to be sent to mixed sex combat units: though the service track of the Midrasha girls is shielded from the kinds of physical intimacy which is unavoidable in combat units, the debate over women's conscription engulfs the "civilianized" military jobs too. After all, the drama of the modern Jew as a Zionist takes place between male protagonists only: the Torah scholar with the weak body who was forced during years of exile to exercise his soldiering in the world of texts, the secular soldier hero renewing biblical national glory, and the religious Zionist who claims he can and should combine Torah with physical national renaissance. This latter one is hard enough to digest, and just like the other two, he expects his females to support him rather than complicate things further, for maleness is constructed through the systematic construction of femaleness as the necessary Otherness. All three have this in common – that they construct their respective "imagined community," the Nation of Israel, as collective masculinity, based on the exclusion of women (Anderson 1983).

Without a clue about these undercurrents, the girls sound well acquainted with the arguments voiced by their opponents, and are intent on proving that a strictly observant female Torah scholar who is also a soldier is not an oxymoron. They say their daily prayers devoutly in the military tent, learn how to chant the Book of Esther and hold their own reading on the festival of Purim followed by a carnival party in masks, discuss the dilemmas of pre-marital physical contact with boys. They are feminist resisters and innovators, and their tone is optimistic, happily girlish, curious, adventurous. Small wonder the Midrasha shows select scenes from the film during its public relations events, and for recruitment of the next batches.

Four: When, Not If, We Get Married and Have Kids

A quiet room full of books. Chana Urbach, 80 or more, remnants of a German accent: "My late husband and I, we learned Torah with the children, still, the boys learned more. But now I am happy to see my daughter Rachel as head of a women's Midrasha, and for my granddaughter Tehilla this road is open."[7] Medium shot on these other two women in the room. Chana: "A few years ago it was a novelty to hear a woman's voice reading the Book of Esther, soon enough it will be difficult to find a synagogue that does *not* offer this women's service. I can see the point of a man who is so religious he avoids contact with women, but I cannot understand those who accept women as doctors and accountants but not in the Torah world. This is dishonest, intellectually and morally."

Evening, a middle-class flat. Ya'ir wraps up in a big towel a laughing and kicking post-bathtub boy, about 6. A younger girl runs around in pyjamas. Tehilla sits at the table, baby in one arm, flapping through a big Talmud volume for the quote she wants for the interview, then settles on the sofa for a bedtime story. Tehilla: "When we got married, Ya'ir was in yeshiva, and I went to university. Now it's the other way around, he is in the academic world and I learn and teach Torah." Ya'ir: "Why should I feel threatened by her Torah scholarship? I can't understand those potential husbands who fear that their wives have an insight into that which they value as the heart and core of their faith. If she wanted to postpone childbearing because of her passion for learning, that would not be accepted, but it would be equally unacceptable if I said we should not have kids until I'm through with medical school. I am glad Tehilla does what she wants in life." Tehilla: "In this generation, it is still the women who feel more acutely the conflict of children and career." Ya'ir: "I am Tehilla's *rebetzn*."[8] The baby groans in his arms as Tehilla puts the older ones into bed. Ya'ir: "With all my feminism, I can't help you here, wait for Mom to feed you..."

Mid-morning, study hall of Matan (Hebrew acronym of Women's Torah Institute), Jerusalem. A couple of religious-looking men (teachers who are there as aids to independent study), the rest are women, all married as indicated by their head coverings, young or older, in various learning situations, singles, diads, small groups, sitting with books open, standing near bookshelf engrossed in discussion. One woman sits on floor next to baby on colorful mat with toys, open book on knees. Other women hold babies in arms. Tehilla: "This is my first child with no nursing problems!" Another woman: "What is the difference between men's Torah and women's Torah? Men swing this way as they learn" – she demonstrates

```
by bending forward and back again - "and women swing this
way" - she holds her baby close and moves sideways. Her
friends smile and all resume discussion of text.
```

This other part of the film provides the background for the girls' adventure in the Torah-cum-army program, in two directions. On the one hand, it explains how it all came about, by telling the story of recent generations of women in Religious Zionism wanting more than they had, reaching out for it, developing the ways and the means to have it. And on the other hand it also provides the optimistic scenario for the future lives of these girls, by demonstrating the kind of marriages they can expect, the homes they will build, the communities they will join. The film is scattered with brief glimpses of supportive males, but it zooms in on Mr. Perfect, Ya'ir, who epitomizes the possibility of complete gender role fluidity and mutual gender support, to the point of accepting the traditionally female role of the career enabler for his scholarly wife. As Rachel Keren says encouragingly to a cluster of mothers who came to the girls' Purim party in the Midrasha: "Don't worry that the girls will be too clever to marry! In Jerusalem, a Midrasha on a girl's résumé is already a big advantage!"

How sweet… But I want to problematize this a bit, by examining not only the harmonious continuity between these two life phases, but also the discord between them that emerges through the cracks.

Conscription for most soldiers, with the obvious exception of those entering a military career at the end of the compulsory service, is only a temporary stage, a late teens experience between school and "real life," a prolonged adolescent moratorium. As such, it has been mostly studied as far as men are concerned (Lieblich 1989; Kaplan 2000), whereas research of female identity formation tended to focus either on earlier (girlhood) or on later (career choice, motherhood) life stages. Reference to religious Zionist young women at this point in their life is particularly rare as yet, and it is not surprising that the little there is points at a difference between those choosing the army and those choosing the alternative civilian national service, which corresponds to the typology described previously: the former group's religiosity is more "open," and they are eager to plunge into new challenges, whereas the latter group adheres more strictly to religious practice, and aspires to conform to consensual social lines. One expression of this difference is a clearer, earlier focus of the second group on the aspired marriage partner – a Hesder yeshiva boy (Cohen-Amir 1995).

During a heated argument in the hall of study in the Midrasha, one of the girls' classmates, who opted not to join the program, says passionately: "It's cool to serve in the army, that's all, and it's not cool to do the alternative civilian service!" She rejects her friends' claims that by serving in the army they express a greater commitment to the state than she does. Indeed, other advantages of the military service surface in their talk more often than the national ideology: they are oriented towards maximal self-fulfillment, excellence in performance, utmost actualization of one's potential. They take pride in their participation in a selective, elite track, as if this were a sports arena and they are in the first league. This is in line with their biographies: whereas the alternative civilian national service offers tracks for all religious girls of all social classes and school records, the military tracks devised for religious girls are explicitly geared for "the stronger ones" religiously, who – surprise, surprise – are middle class, mostly Ashkenazi, and graduates of elite selective high schools. In other words, these are the religious counterparts of the secular Israeli middle class – socialized to succeed as individuals in a competitive liberal society, that puts an enormous value at the same time on collective, republican citizenship. This dual goal marks these girls more than their classmates, who opt for a clear hierarchy between these two contradictory directions – collective identity first, individual identity second.

The two roads that diverge for these 18-year-old religious Zionist females will make all the difference in the next few years of their lives. An Israeli woman who embraces the consensual "collective identity first" ends up with the gender perception delineated for her in Israeli society, that is – motherhood as her soldiering for the nation (Berkovitch 1997; see also Fishman 1994). Her entire life before biological motherhood is conceptualized so that it will flow smoothly into that role, and she does not wish her post-schooling preparatory years to be any different. The girls in the film face a less wholesome continuum.

Chana Urbach, in her library, with daughter Rachel Keren and granddaughter Tehilla Elitzur: "We need a critical mass of women, an army of women learning Torah." Cut. Long shot on a conference auditorium, mostly with heads covered, mostly women. Switch to stage. Behind the panel table there hangs a big sign, "The First International Conference, Woman and Her Judaism, Jerusalem 1999." Rivka Lubitch, a prominent young leader of Orthodox feminism in Israel, at the podium: "At the opening of the first grade in my children's school, the year my son entered, the principal – one of those I really respect – gave every boy a skullcap as they approached. I was wondering what he was going to give the girls, and saw that he gave each of them a hair-bow. I could not believe it. Later I asked him, 'How could you do this? In the past, when you gave both boys and girls a pencil box, your message was that you want them to study, now your message to the boys is that you want them to be religious, and your message to the girls is that you want them to decorate themselves?!' And what was his answer? 'What do you want me to give them, a

pan? An apron?'" The audience hisses, as if to say, 'what did
we expect, naturally...' Lubitch concludes emphatically:
"Women too need religious symbols."

Is the life flow of the religious woman of the more daring type as smooth as the scenes from Tehilla's life would have us believe? From early childhood on she "knows" that the only refuge from patriarchal limitations is the so-called gender-blind modernist philosophy, which is so fragile that it takes but one moment of negligence for it to collapse into an androcentrism that forces her, whether she likes it or not, to choose between submission and rebellion. And if submission means femininity, what does rebellion mean? Time and again we are confronted with the problematic tendency of women's resistance to submission to take on the form of imitating male behavior, role, dress, for male is the yardstick of everything that counts, and "equality" means stretching oneself to meet that standard (Shilo 1998; Almog 2000). It is problematic, because most women do not choose this: it is the unavoidable side-effect of their courageous choice. It is also problematic because most women are not aware that this is the trade-off imposed on them, and many even deny it when asked to confront the socially ascribed value of their practices.

Lubitch hints that there is "a third way," which can turn this dynamic in another direction: women need a "separate but equal" set of practices that will empower them as women, that will construct them neither as disinherited victims nor as usurpers of male power. She advocates the development of a new Jewish religious gender identity. In fact, she frames the Orthodox feminist movement as the alliance of women and men engaged in this endeavor. The audience is receptive: it is composed of the Ya'irs and the Tehillas of all ages. They know that this is what they are into, and they know that there is a long way ahead, not only in winning more hearts to this ideology, but also in protecting their children in a world which is largely unfriendly, to feminism in general, and to religious feminism in particular. They are here to recharge their batteries.

In the meantime, between school and adulthood, what do the religious girls do at 18, that is, those who choose to be part of this narrative? They undertake not one male role, but two, simultaneously, that of the Torah scholar as well as that of the soldier, and reinvent themselves on all levels – national identity, religious performance, social perception, and yes, gender too.

The radio is on, the girls clean their room in the kibbutz and sing along with Corinne Alal, a popular rock singer who is an out-of-the-closet lesbian: "We are a rare species, a strange bird" It stands to reason that this literal reading of the scene was not intended by the actors, but once it is included in the edited version of the film, I cannot resist the thought that Greitzer wanted them to be identified with this particular line. They know they are a rare species, and take pride in this idiosyncrasy. They enjoy this as role playing, almost a game, perhaps because they plan for this experience to be only a transition, an exciting youthful adventure into a new gender identity, before they settle down. The film basically argues that in order to arrive at an egalitarian marriage later in life, these females need to balance their overly feminine and secluded early socialization processes with a journey into male-land, so that they can enrich their gender repertoire and evolve into more interesting people, empowered, better skilled in an individuated life in a mixed-sex world which is diversified in other ways too (class, ethnicity), prepared to join their men on a "separate but equal" footing. Just like men, they need a rite of passage that will mark their coming of age, an act of culture production that will demarcate them as different from the docile girls they once were, and the docile girls they think their classmates prefer to grow into. In Josselson's (1991) terminology, these girls are of the "identity achievements" type: they take risks, and use them in a process of forging of their selves later on in life.

Another theoretical concept that may be useful in explaining the perception the girls have of their own situated, contextualized selves is androgyny. Shachar and Kaminer (2000) used the personality test developed by Bem (1986) in a group of senior year, high school Israeli girls, and Feldman (1999) unveiled the underpinnings of Israeli women's autobiographic fiction, following Virginia Woolf. Both research projects used feminist theories concerning the liberating potential of androgyny to explain practices attested in secular Israeli women. I for one would like to sum up this chapter with a quote from a story told by an American "revivalist" New Age rabbi, structured as a meeting he dreams up with the singular Chassidic nineteenth-century female leader Hannah Rochel, known as the Maid of Ludmir:

> Reb Zalman now replied, "The Sages once said not to 'make much talk with the women', and I understand now that they meant we should transcend gender. So we cannot really continue this conversation until you cease to see me as 'a man' and I cease to see you as 'a woman'."
>
> She agreed and said, "Since I am aware that I have in former lives been a man, and since no doubt you have lived before as a woman, let us both reach the balance of the Andro-gynos within ourselves, and converse as we might do between earth lives." (Schwartz 1988: 180)

In this story we are reminded that the androgynous myth served Plato, and then the Sages of the Talmud, as an image for the longing of the spirit for its passionate elevation towards the ultimate sense of goal attainment. It is interesting to note that in this dialogue, the male partner argues in favor of a gender-neutral, nirvana-type state of mind, as a prerequisite to a fruitful joint session of Torah study, whereas the female partner offers another view (without openly disagreeing with him!), namely, that they should both invoke their own androgyny in order to meet in that alternative reality which is so perfectly harmonious. At any rate, these two suggestions are equally planted in mystical fantasy. The girls and the women portrayed in the film are on Hanna Rochel's side rather than on Reb Zalman's, but they struggle for a more down-to-earth, practical, realistic type of a Jewish "gender liberation theology." And they do not want to remain "maids" while they are at it.

The visit in Tehilla's and Ya'ir's home was interrupted by a short visit from a friend, Yoni Yehuda, who came to interest them in joining a group of religious Zionist youth planning a meeting with Palestinians in the Gaza Strip (it was before the outbreak of the presently ongoing Intifada which put a stop to such activities). Greitzer left this sequence in her film, and even had Yoni explain the project directly to the camera. In another scene we see the couple's car drive to Jerusalem through the Tunnel Road that was dug underneath the town of Beit Jalla for the exclusive use of the settlers. These are unusual editorial decisions for a documentary which is otherwise an insiders' drama of the Jews in Israel: perhaps Greitzer intends to hint at the shortcomings of a feminist project that ignores the wider circumstances of its political niche. Speaking for myself, I definitely think that the achievements of these women are closely related to the decline of messianic Zionism, and that an explicit propagation of this link between gender and nationalism will result in overcoming militarism as the dynamo of Israeli society.

Acknowledgments

This chapter was first presented as a paper at the conference Militarism and Education, Hebrew University of Jerusalem, May 30 2001. A Hebrew version is included in *Gadish* (periodical on adult education) vol. 9, eds I. Bassok and P. Kirmayer, Ministry of Education, Jerusalem, fall 2004. I wish to thank Rachel Keren for weeding out a couple of inaccurate facts from the draft; the analysis offered, though, is mine along.

Notes

1. Torah means "teaching," literally. The term refers sometimes to the Pentateuch (the five books of Moses), but usually to the total bulk of Jewish religious learning, written and oral, and to one's commitment to it.

2. Throughout Zionist and Israeli history, until most recently, non-Orthodox denominations of Judaism, founded in Western Europe and then the United States, have not had a substantial presence, for reasons that go beyond the scope of this chapter. Terms used in this chapter follow therefore their popular use in Israel: "religious" means "Jewish Orthodox," solely. For characterization of Jewish Orthodoxy in its modernist context, see Katz (1986).

3. Brei Akiva means sons of Rabbi Akiva, a major Talmudist who in 130 CE supported the Jewish rebellion against the Romans and was tortured to death when that rebellion failed.

4. As this term was understood by Karl Mannheim in his paper "The Problem of Generations" (1927), a construct as powerful as social class in the shaping of group identity: see Murdock and McCron (1976).

5. The place where men meet to learn Torah has been called *beit midrash* (house of study) ever since the practice developed in conjunction with the *beit k'nesset* (house of gathering for prayer), in the last centuries BCE. As the culture of Torah study took root, it evolved sociologically, and a distinction arose a few centuries later between the common learners and the intellectual elite specializing in the highest level of Torah study; another term was coined for them, yeshiva (literally, "sitting," that is, those regulars allowed to sit up close before the rabbi, as opposed to the less learned, who stand behind them). Modern Orthodox Jews in the United States have no qualms referring to Torah institutions for women as "women's yeshivas," but in Israel the same circles are careful to name such a place Midrasha, even when the same curriculum is taught there by the same (male) rabbis. *Beit Midrash* is now used to indicate the central hall of study in either a yeshiva or a midrasha.

6. The issue of excluding or including women in the study of Torah is beyond the scope of this chapter: see for instance Zolty (1993); Rothenberg (2004).

7. Tehilla is Rachel's niece, not her daughter. Chana was one of the few female students allowed into the Rabbinical Institute in Breslau *c.* 1930, but not in the ordination track.

8. The Yiddish *rebetzn* means rabbi's wife, the equivalent of the German "Frau Doctor," a doctor's wife.

References

Admanit, Z. (1977), "In the Wake of the Rabbinate's Ban on the Conscription of Women," *Amudim* (Journal of the Religious Kibbutz Movement), (Hebrew).

Almog, O. (2000), "From Sabra to Yuppie: Changes in the Image and Social Status of the Israeli Woman," in T. Cohen (ed.), *The Israeli Woman: Roots, Reality and Images, Bikoret u'Farshanut* (Criticism and Interpretation, Journal for Interdisciplinary Studies in Literature and Culture) 34 (summer): 19–64.

Anderson, B. (1983), *Imagined Communities: Reflections on the Origins and Spread of Nationalism*, New York: Verso.

Bem, S. L. (1986), "Androgyny and Gender Schema Theory: A Conceptual and Empirical Integration," in T. B. Sonderreger (ed.), *Nebraska Symposium on Motivation 1984: Psychology and Gender*, Lincoln, NE: University of Nebraska Press.

Berkovitch, N. (1997), "Motherhood as a National Mission: The Construction of Womanhood in the Legal Discourse in Israel," T. Rapoport and T. El-Or (eds), *Cultures of Womanhood in Israel, Women's Studies International Forum*, 20(5–6): 605–19.

Boyarin, D. (1997), *Unheroic Conduct: The Rise of Heterosexuality and the Invention of the Jewish Man*, Beverley, CA: University of California Press.

Cohen, A. S. (1988), "Drafting Women for the Army," *Journal of Halacha and Contemporary Issues*, 16: 26–42.

Cohen, Y. (1979; additional sources 1982), *Conscription of Girls and Civilian National Service: Halachic Study*, Religious Kibbutz Movement and Ne'emanei Torah va'Avodah (a liberal Orthodox group).

Cohen-Amir, M. (1995), "Transition to Adulthood of Girls in a Complex Society: Modern Orthodox Girls in Israel Choose Between Military and Civilian National Service," unpublished master's thesis, Bar-Ilan University, Ramat Gan, Israel (Hebrew).

Elboim-Dror, R. (1992/1994), "Gender in Utopianism: The Zionist Case," *History Workshop Journal*, 37: 99–116.

El-Or, T. (2002), *Next Year I Will Know More: Literacy and Identity of Young Religious Zionist Women*, Detroit, MI: Wayne State University Press.

El-Or, T. and Aran, G. (1995), "Giving Birth to a Settlement: Maternal Thinking and Political Thinking of Jewish Women on the West Bank," *Gender and Society*, 9: 60–78.

Etzioni-Halevi, E. and Illy, A. (1993), "Women in Legislatures: Israel in a Comparative Perspective," in Y. Azmon and D. N. Izraeli (eds) *Women in Israel*, Studies in Israeli Society no. VI, New Brunswick, NJ: Transactions.

Feldman, Y. S. (1999), *No Room of their Own: Gender and Nation in Israeli Women's Fiction*, New York: Columbia University Press (esp. Chapter 4, "Who's Afraid of Androgyny? Virginia Woolf's 'Gender'," pp. 101–20.

Fishman, S. B. (1994), "Soldiers in an Army of Mothers: Reflections on Naomi and the Heroic Biblical Woman," in J. A. Kates and G. T. Reimer (eds), *Reading Ruth: Contemporary Women Reclaim a Sacred Story*, New York: Ballantine.

Golan, G. (1997), "Militarization and Gender: The Israeli Experience," in T. El-Or and T. Rapoport (eds), *Cultures of Womanhood in Israel*, special issue of *Women's Studies International Forum*, 20(5–6): 581–6.

Hazleton, L. (1977), *Israeli Women: The Reality behind the Myth*, New York: Simon and Schuster.

Helman, S. (1999), "Negotiating Obligations, Creating Rights: Conscientious Objection and the Redefinition of Citizenship in Israel," *Citizenship Studies*, 3(1): 45–70.

Horowitz, D. (1982), "The Israeli Defense Forces: A Civilianized Army in a Partially Militarized Society," in R. Kolkowitz and A. Korbonski (eds), *Soldiers, Peasants and Bureaucrats*, London: George Allen and Unwin.

Izraeli, N. D. (1997), "Gendering Military Service in the Israeli Defence Forces," *Israel Social Science Research*, 12(1): 129–66.

Josselson, R. (1991), *Finding Herself: Pathways to Identity Development in Women*, San Francisco, CA: Jossey-Bass.

Kaplan, D. (2000), "The Military as a Second Bar-Mitzvah: Combat Service as Initiation to Zionist Masculinity," in M. Ghoussoub and E. Sinclair-Webb (eds), *Imagined*

Masculinities: Male Identity and Culture in the Modern Middle East, London: Saqi Books.

Katz, J. (1986), "Orthodoxy in Historical Perspective," *Studies in Contemporary Jewry*, 2: 3–17.

Laqueur, W. (1972), *A History of Zionism*, London: Weidenfeld and Nicolson.

Levine, F. D. (1986), *Territory or Peace? Religious Zionism in Conflict*, New York: American Jewish Committee.

Lieblich, A. (1989), *Transition to Adulthood during Military Service: The Case of Israel*, New York: State University of New York Press.

Liebman, C. S. and Don-Yehiya, E. (1983), *Civil Religion in Israel: Traditional Judaism and Political Culture in the Jewish State*, Berkeley, CA: University of California Press.

Lubin, O. (2003), "'Gone to Soldiers': Feminism and the Military in Israel," in H. Naveh (ed.), *Israeli Family and Community: Women's Time*, London: Vallentine Mitchell.

Mayer, T. (ed.) (1999), *Gender Ironies of Nationalism*, London: Routledge.

Mazali, R. (2001), "Someone Makes a Killing off War": Militarization and Occupation in Israel–Palestine, keynote speech, Jewish Unity for a Just Peace Conference, New Profile Movement for the Civil-ization of Israeli Society, Chicago, May 5–7.

Murdock, G. and McCron, R. (1976), "Consciousness of Class and Consciousness of Generation," in S. Hall and T. Jefferson (eds), *Resistance through Rituals*, London: Hutchinson.

Rapoport, T., Penso, A. and Garb, Y. (1994), "Contribution to the Collective by Religious-Zionist Adolescent Girls," *British Journal of Sociology of Education*, 15(3): 375–88.

Rapoport, T., Garb, Y. and Penso, A. (1995), "Religious Socialization and Female Subjectivity: Religious-Zionist Adolescent Girls in Israel," *Sociology of Education*, 68(1): 48–61.

Rosenberg, L. (2002), "Women and Gender in Religious Zionism: Organization, Settlement and Defense 1918–1948," unpublished PhD thesis, Bar-Ilan University, Ramat Gan, Israel (Hebrew).

Rothenberg, N. (2004), "Written by men for Men: Feminist Revolution and Innovation in the Canonical Sources," in R. Elior (ed.), *Men and Women: Gender, Judaism and Democracy*, Jerusalem: Urim.

Schwartz, H. (1988) "Torah of the Menorah," in Schwartz, *The Dream Assembly: Tales of Rabbi Zalman Schachter-Shalomi, Collected and Retold, by Howard Schwartz*, Amity, NY: Amity House.

Shachar, R. and Kaminer, O. (2000), "Androgynous Traits: The Gap between their Approval and their Internalization by Female Students," in S. Shlasky (ed.), *Sexuality and Gender in Education*, Tel Aviv: Ramot Publishing House and Tel Aviv University.

Shaviv, Rabbi Y. (1983), "Women in Religiously-Sanctioned War" (national defense), *T'chumin*, 4: 79–89 (Hebrew).

Shilo, M. (1998), "The Double or Multiple Image of the New Hebrew Woman," *Nashim* (women), 1 (winter): 73–94.

Smooha, S. (1984), "Ethnicity and the Israeli Army," *Medina, Mimshal, veYehasim Beinle'umiyim* (State, Government and International Relations), 22: 5–32 (Hebrew).

Swirski, B. and Safir, M. P. (eds) (1991), *Calling the Equality Bluff: Women in Israel*, Oxford: Pergamon Press.

Welner, Rabbi M. D. (1952), "Women's Military Draft," *haTorah vehaM'dinah* (Journal of Rabbis of haPo'el haMizrahi Movement) 4 (September): 221–7 (Hebrew).

Zohar, Z. (1996), "Traditional Flexibility and Modern Strictness: Two Halakhic Positions on Women's Suffrage," in H. E. Goldberg (ed.) *Sephardi and Middle Eastern Jewries: History and Culture in the Modern Era*, Bloomington, IN: Indiana University Press.

Zolty, S. P. (1993), *"And All your Children Shall Be Learned": Women and the Study of Torah in Jewish Law and History*, Northvale, NJ: Jason Aronson.

10

Stones and Stories: Engaging with Gender and Complex Emergencies[1]

Nefissa Naguib

There is always an easy solution to every human problem:
neat, plausible, and wrong.

H. L. Mencken, *The Divine Afflatus*

Introduction

Towards the end of my visit to a village in the West Bank of Palestine, I was staying in the home of one of my informants, and enjoying the sounds and scenes which had become familiar to me. Then one morning we woke up to a raid on the village, and I stood watching, with other women and children, as the Israeli army uprooted olive trees and bulldozed part of the old spring, a couple of graves and the ruins of an old watch tower. A little girl came and held her arms around me, saying "Is this the first time you see this *yah khaliti* (auntie)?" It was not the first time I had seen this, and yet how shall we write about it? In gender studies we can use patriarchy and Islam as theories to describe cultural values. But how do we write theoretically about the wrecking of lives and link it to gender studies in the Middle East. This chapter is an attempt to create an interest in critical emergencies worthy of academic attention.

"Stones" and "stories" are metaphors which I borrow from the American anthropologist Nicholas Hopkins; they relate to my earlier research concerning Palestinian women's reflections about water, which I captured through their narratives. In choosing life histories during a time of immense human suffering in Palestine, there are several levels of abstractions and many issues which may be questioned. In this chapter, I want to take my experiences with life histories from Palestine further and engage more specifically with critical emergencies which impinge on the daily lives of many women in the Middle East.

The metaphor "stones" is used to imply deprivation and vulnerability which are the consequences of conflicts, while "stories" are the constructions of people's experiences. Stories create real lives for the people who tell them; stones revolve around issues that often seem to be lacking in the gender narratives from the Middle East. I do not discard the narratives; on the contrary there are several levels of discourses which inform gender in the Middle East. In my previous work I have been mostly concerned with the notions women have about testimonials and heritage. In this chapter I suggest that gender issues in the Middle East will need to contextualize more explicitly the lives of women as lived under conditions of emergencies such as war and occupation. Stones and stories frame my reflections on the ongoing tension between gender and complex emergencies in the Middle East.

We know that for more than half a century the United Nations (UN) has been involved in violent conflicts in the region. The rate of recurrence of wars has agonized the millions of individuals who happen to live where these conflicts develop. It was especially during my research in Palestine that I witnessed livelihoods being destroyed; I listened to women wondering whether they had enough food, milk and fuel, or worrying about getting a sick member of the family to a doctor or a hospital. My concern in this chapter rises from an issue closely related to both food and health. I will concentrate on what has been referred to as "complex emergencies"; of these, a village example from Palestine is only a small-scale example.

Complex Emergencies

During the time I have worked as an anthropologist in the Middle East, I have become increasingly surprised at the relative lack of anthropological contributions to the understanding of critical and urgent issues which upset and distress many lives in the region. To date, an extensive literature search on complex emergencies and anthropology has established that anthropologists have contributed little to the growing body of literature in the field of complex emergencies. We are always met with an assurance that research acknowledges the complexity of occupation and upheaval, while not losing sight of the local questions. Still, Barth (1994) has questioned the extent of anthropological concern for the developing world:

> A highly intellectual and internal critique has set priorities and focused interests so that we have lost much of our engagement in the real world and urgent issues ... Anthropology has had pitifully little to say on the phenomenon of poverty as it affects increasing hundreds of millions of people in all major cities of the world. We have not been able to articulate a position, or even a noticeable interest, in the fact that human activity seems to be destroying humanity's own global habitat. (Barth 1994: 350)

So far it seems that analyses of crises are based on prefabricated typologies that make all crises look much too much alike. Local contexts, variations between types of conflict and particular issues are seen as irrelevant or, if at all acknowledged, they are downplayed.

Warned against the pitfalls of emotional involvement, we are trained during our first years in anthropology to constantly attempt to reproduce a steady and well-adjusted account of "our people." Engaging with "lived emergencies" opens avenues which shed new light on theoretical approaches, from issues concerning gender and the development cycle, forms of gender negotiations during emergencies, to the everyday lives of women coping with multidimensional crises. As researchers and scholars engaged with gender we ought to probe critical transnational, global and local events. Furthermore, we must be more specific in our discussions on the impact of war-torn societies and complex emergencies on individuals as they live their lives on a day-to-day basis.

If we contemplate the amount of human suffering caused by conflicts in the Middle East and the scope of anthropological research in the region, it is remarkable that there are not more anthropological engagement and contributions to the understanding of critical issues of survival. We know that burning social issues are high on the agenda in governments, among local populations, the media, relief organizations and, not least, in the United Nations (2003) *Arab Human Development Report*. The global trade crisis, armed conflicts, occupation, dysfunctional governments and institutional breakdown are not gender neutral; these questions concern average households in the region.

Having been concerned with the importance of reflexivity in anthropological research and writings, we should go further, beyond the particular, and engage with the lived emergencies and crises which individuals face in the Middle East. My interest here is with women; according to the United Nations (2002) *Arab Human Development Report*, half of all Arab women are illiterate, and when it comes to health, the maternal mortality rate in the region is four times that of East Asia. The UN report points to the widespread neglect of the agency of women and their well-being. Theoretical and empirical contributions from scholars working on gender issues in the Middle East are essential to the understanding of the developmental cycle of complex emergencies; this is a task for which the grounded approach of reflexive gender research is particularly well suited.

Initially, the term "complex emergency" was first used in the late 1980s to refer to the civil wars in Mozambique and Sudan. The concept was later expanded by the UN to describe major crises, as when civil wars and the collapse of institutions that often follow are compounded by natural disasters, crop failure and famine (Naguib and Vaa 2003). At any rate "complex emergencies" was given a broader meaning and refers to situation where the international society shows concern (Berge 2000).

Rather than having been classified by academicians in an effort to restrict an area of growing social concern for analytical endeavors, the concept of complex emergencies was expanded and developed by practitioners. It developed with reference to circumstances that were reacted upon by particular actions from the international community. The fact that the term was used by practitioners, engaged in relating to some of the consequences of critical situations, has led to outlining heuristic approaches to capture some of the basic characteristics of the highly varying realties of emergencies. Definitions often emphasize that complex emergencies share the following characteristics:

1. multinational crises
2. profound human suffering
3. the roots of conflict are in part political, and may be complicated by natural disasters
4. the state is contested, weakened or collapsed (Goodhand and Hulme 1999: 73).

Obviously, different definitions tend to emphasize issues which are at hand; it is particularly the second and fourth points in the list that apply to the following example from Palestine.

Old Women in a Palestinian Village

Musharafah is a relatively small, rural Palestinian village that in many ways still conforms to the exterior images of a traditional village community. It is located in the Ramallah hills and overlooks other mountain tops on all sides. The village has a population of close to 250 inhabitants and is situated on the top of an elevated ridge approximately 720 meters above sea level. Ramallah is the closest large city, and it is the easiest route to take to the village.

The summers are hot and dry, with the seasonal hot winds coming during spring and early summer. This part of the West Bank has been under cultivation for several millennia, with the characteristic terracing that is still evident in the Ramallah hills. As in ancient times, olive trees and fruit trees are still grown on the terraces. Fruits such as figs, almonds, plums, peaches and apricots are picked in spring and summer. Chickpeas and lentils are gathered during the months of early summer; barley, tomatoes and cucumbers are harvested in summer. Yet it is the olive trees that dominate physically and emotionally the landscape. Olives are harvested from November to late January.

The general impression is of an arid and barren environment. The rocky hillsides are occasionally dotted with olive trees, virtually the only visible vegetation. Between the hills and in the valleys there are patches of green bushes. The closest village to Musharafah is the ancient village of Bir Zeit, located south-east of the village. To the south and on a higher ridge than Musharafah are two Israeli settlements.

Musharafah is a Muslim village and, resembling several other West Bank villages, it is also without sufficient local economic opportunities. The village does not have the expected bustling atmosphere, filled with events and people, which is supposed to be a characteristic of Middle Eastern villages. There is no market any more; the only meeting place for the women in the village is the shared stone oven.

There are no shops in the village; the nearest grocery store is closer to the village of Bir Zeit, and the store does not have as extensive a market as does Ramallah-Bireh. The Ramallah-Bireh district is in many ways a major locality in Musharafah life, and it is the administrative center for the whole district, which means it should serve most of the villagers' material and medical needs. In Ramallah and El-Bireh some women try to sell herbs or olives and crafts, such as embroidery. They also try to buy whatever they can afford, which is currently very little. Children must walk to Ramallah and El-Bireh to go to secondary school. However, during the last years of unrest, schools are closed and the road out of the village has been cut off from the surrounding towns by a deep and broad ditch.

The village of Musharafah is situated above the old ruins of what is generally called the old village. The physical arrangement of present-day Musharafah is remarkably different from the pattern of the old village. The homes are scattered in the landscape and are on top of the hill, which means that the village is now without a defined centre. In Palestine such villages are often referred to as newer types of villages – a street village with a main street that cuts through it.

Lack of household water has always been a major problem. Preceding the piped water system, water for the households was fetched from two springs. The closest source, referred to as the village spring, was in a field just below the village. During the summer months, water was scarce in the village spring and the women walked several hours to another source. Household water was not only used for human and animal consumption; women also had to make sure that some of that water was left for the small vegetable gardens in the backyard of each dwelling. Rain water was collected during the winter; this is described by the villagers as "winter water."

The village elders had made several attempts to solve the water problem, and finally in 1985 Musharafah got its much longed-for piped water. That year, the piped network from the Israeli water company Mekorot reached the village, and by the end of the 1980s all the homes had piped water. However, the villagers said that this water was not always available, and it was definitely not reliable during the summer months. Still, at the start of the village connection to in the water network, the women were delighted, happy not to have to walk in search of water. As a result of centralization of water they did not continue to maintain the old spring, and it did not take long before it was forgotten. The villagers depended only on cistern water and the "government's water." Piped water was partly financed by villagers who had families in Jordan, and it was largely a joint Palestinian–Jordanian committee that channelled funds for the extension of water networks to the village. Villagers in Musharafah, like most other Palestinians who were employed in Israel, also paid their taxes to the country, so a major source of capital was from the Israeli government through their development budget.

The initial reaction to piped water in the village was relief. Finally, after years of stagnation, the village market would grow; children would get an education, the men would find "good jobs," and life would be prosperous for all. The mothers and grandmothers in the village were tired of fetching water. They no longer got the help they needed from their daughters and daughters-in-law. The younger women sought to get higher education or to enter the job market, and they were not always available to help the older women. In short, people were waiting for "development" to reach their village. For the first couple of years, the advent of piped water was identified among the women and the men in the village as "a good." Water was going to be available for them to use – at any time and all the time. It was assumed that the resource would be evenly and fairly distributed. Piped water was not only for household chores, but also for the watering of small gardens and the irrigation of fields. The dry toilet sheds were locked up, and flush latrines were built inside the homes. Young mothers hoped that with modern sanitation their workloads would be lighter and that more infants would survive. With piped water, the older generation of women imagined that, finally, they might enjoy the blessings of old age: rest, respect and authority.

Piped water did not come alone. It was accompanied by connection to the electricity network, and in the two first years following the piped water and the installation of electrical services, televisions, refrigerators and washing machines were also introduced in Musharafah, brought home by sons, daughters and husbands working abroad. Everything seemed to go according to expectations: children went to school, men had jobs, and more young women joined the labor market. There was water inside the households, yet the washing machines were centrally placed outside the homes for all to see. The television set, outside or inside the house, was constantly switched on.

Following the first Intifada in 1987 the situation in Musharafah changed, and the services from Mekorot were no longer reliable. The Jewish settlements were given priority during the summer months and the village was left without tap water most of the summer. The springs were no longer accessible, because settlers roamed the area and threatened the women. Rain water cisterns remained the main source of drinking water for the villagers. Following the peace process that started with the Oslo Agreement in 1993, water was considered an interim issue, and the

Palestinian Water Authority assumed responsibility for local government. Again, Palestinians in the village looked forward to more reliable water supply, yet Israel continues to control the flow and volume of water used in the Palestinian areas, and villagers still rely basically on the storage of rain water.

Civil unrest which followed the first and the current Intifada brought about economic sanctions from Israel, resulting in an increase in migration among the younger generation. Day-to-day life demands more expenditure from the villagers, mainly because tap water is expensive. Water costs make the maintenance of a small vegetable garden difficult, so a growing number of villagers have become increasingly dependent on charity from religious institutions, NGOs, better-off neighbors or relative.

A significant characteristic feature of the village is that there is a majority of old women, either heading a household or living alone. Unlike the general representations of visibly manifested patriarchy in the Palestinian villages, Musharafah is now a village dominated by these older women, with some young women and children also living there. Most of the older women are widows, or have been abandoned by husbands who have been gone for most of their married lives. Some women "know" that the men will come back to their family, and they still receive the occasional money order; others "know" they are abandoned.

Sons, brothers and young husbands are abroad: some are studying, some are working (also in Israel) and some are serving time in Israeli prison cells. Several young families have moved to larger villages, to regional towns or abroad. People from Musharafah make up a large community in Amman, Jordan, and the village is also known for having close ties with the former Soviet Union. In Musharafah women talk about how in the past they were more in control of their lives. Now they have become more exposed and vulnerable to external economic and political market forces. The initial delight at the new water supply turned to anxiety, loneliness, poverty and deprivation.

Women in the village continue to say that piped water is a "good thing." They "know" about hygiene, the connections between dirt and sickness. They also know that piped water is what prosperous people have. They also "know" that, had the economic and political situation been different, perhaps piped water would have contributed to their well-being. However, life took an unexpected turn. The women's assessments and reflections on their living condition since the installation of piped water are that they are faced with more expenses. They are left alone to cope with the finances which are tied to running a household and paying for the water connection. Although women in the village express their concerns regarding the quality of water and the expenses attached to unreliable piped water, health workers from the Ramallah municipality and Palestinian NGOs continue their periodic rounds of villages and campaign for "public water awareness." The basic aim of the water campaigns is to encourage villagers to conserve and protect the resources, and to generate more awareness on the issue of the vulnerability of water. During the meeting with health personnel and NGOs from Ramallah, women agree that hygiene is "a good thing" and "running water" from the tap makes everyday life easier. Villagers also perceive tap water to be in the same group of "issues for progress" as education and health. Yet, on several encounters women remind officials from Ramallah that Palestine is still under occupation, that settlers roam their village and that life after the installation of piped water did not turn out as expected.

The main source of household water is now rain water collected in cisterns. Thus, although women agree that to have tap water would be easier, they consider the cistern water, or winter water, to be more reliable. It has also a couple of added values; it is good for tea, cooking and bathing. Essentially, cistern water is accessible and free of charge. More houses are going back to using dry toilets because of the lack of sanitary treatment of human waste. Basically, the sewerage system in the village consists of pipes that take the human waste away from the village and dump it into the nearby valleys without further treatment.

On a day-to-day level, I have observed old Palestinian women not only making contingency plans in case their home get hit or demolished, but also having to deal with the constant agony which accompanies human casualties and poverty (Naguib 2003).

Arab Women: The Cinderellas of Gender Studies

Palestine has several narratives, ranging from the political field to the area of development, to understanding women, to grasping Palestine itself. The complexities in Palestine involve occupation, environmental degradation, suicide-bombers, martyrs and bloodshed. The example from the village in the West Bank demonstrates that critical emergencies produce public and private poverty and challenge the narrative of the traditional Arab family. The case from Musharafah demands more engagement with the question of women's livelihoods during complex emergencies. We will now need to go beyond the particulars and also address women's lives within the larger story of conflicts.

What concerns me here is the trap of particularization, where the "woman" issue in the Middle East continues to involve a "special subject" approach regardless of the larger events which cause hardship on a growing number of women in the region. Tucker (1993) calls for a more scholarly involvement with, and reflection on, the total history of the Middle East in which women are also included without being reduced to something out of the ordinary (Tucker 1993). So far there have been the implicit comparisons with the "Western woman"; she is the "new," "modern," "aware," "Christian" and "benevolent" woman. And she is very different from the "traditional," "insignificant," "ignorant," "Muslim" and "wretched" woman in the Middle East. Still most studies fall short; they do not go further with the issues beyond patriarchy, Islam and feminist ethnographies "of the particular."

Without doubt, gender scholarship on the Middle East is far from static, and there are several path-breaking works. For example within the field of anthropology, a particular approach to women in Middle East has emerged, demonstrating that the social constituency of gender is fluctuating. The concern is to bring forth "real" individuals who have particular, complex and contradicting histories. This is an ethnography where the style of writing expresses the dynamism, variations and uniqueness of women's experiences. Present-day studies of gender issues are founded on taking women's stories seriously, and that is significant. Stories are based on individual perceptions of facts; they provide knowledge of women's lives and the gendered experiences of economic, social and political processes. Stories or narratives convey that, although lives are lived simultaneously, patterns of experiences show variations, contradictions and complexities.

Basically, the gender project in the Middle East is dedicated to observing, recording and figuring out the everyday happenings. In the quest for more authenticity, and in order to contest existing prototypical accounts of women in the region, it is crucial to include "native" stories or statements, including the marginal voices of women. Here we find path-breaking gender research. Several scholars have illustrated that narratives are valuable conveyers of information about the wealth in women's lives. They make the dynamism between creativity and agency more accessible for us. The complexity which surrounds the stories we are told demonstrates that, also among Middle Eastern women, there are no uncomplicated lives.

Contemporary academic texts promote liveliness and contradictions of everyday life and are concerned with women's agency and self-reflection. Thus, we have a gender research that includes more reflexive styles of writings, symbolic expressions and analysis of negotiated identities. Moreover, perhaps more frequently than in other localities in the gender project, these discussions are framed in the theory of patriarchy. It is reasoned that Islam is behind the emphasis on patriarchy in Middle Eastern gender studies. It is a patriarchal organizing factor in which options are created to control the social order, and therefore men's and women's social maps.

Even though Musharafah is no longer a village where men live, the esteem and significance of patriarchy remain. There is definitely still the ideal picture of a family with a male head, not only in the larger Palestine and Arab discourse, but also among the women when they speak about their "culture." Joseph and Slyomovics (2001) make the favored position of family a point very early on in their introduction to *Women and Power in the Middle East:* "This privileged position is enshrined in the constitutions of many Arab or Muslim states" (Joseph and Slymomovics 2001: 2) and they add that patriarchy is the foundation of every part of Arab society, that within the context of patriarchal rules we often define the role of women in the region.

Patriarchy is certainly the foundation of every part of Arab society, and within the context of patriarchal rules we often define the role of women in the region. For the purpose of this chapter I have simply defined patriarchy as the idea of the ideal "Arab family" – with a responsible adult male head. It is perhaps an "ideal" because, as Kandiyoti (1996) argues in her work on the role of patriarchy in Muslim society, the patriarchal ideals sought by the middle and upper classes of the region are, in all practical terms, unrealistic for the poorer women in the Middle East.

We find that recently there has been more emphasis on "gender" rather than "family." Still, as Hopkins (2003) reminds us, the "Arab family" is a recurrent and dynamic topic. Its image is all-embracing: a sheltered foundation within which men, women and children live and share whatever life brings along. The example from Musharafah demonstrates that while the impressions of patriarchal family structures which define the "Arab family" prevail: "The broad processes of social and cultural change in the Arab world guarantee that there is always something new to say on the subject" (Hopkins 2003: 1). Unrest in the region influences the increase in female-headed and solitary households and generates levels of human suffering which are often overlooked in Middle East research.

Events in Musharafah suggest that the gendering of the Middle East, until recently a European project, should be more aware of the pitfalls of secluding and isolating women in the region. Such studies create women as "subjects apart," frequently anchored in Western feminist studies, so much so that during the latter part of the twentieth century there were major economic changes in the region which were not addressed. The global trade economy, the expansion of the cities and the migration from the villages are matters that prove that economic policy is not gender neutral; these issues also affected the lives of rural women and their household activities.

In the economical reality of the village there is increasing unemployment among the children and grandchildren. Hunger is a growing, critical issue and a growing problem among older village women, because income shortage has created food shortages. The issue of hunger is sensitive and double edged: according to Palestinian traditional values the family is expected to stay together and support each other, yet occupation shatters such ideals.

Grasping the Stones

According to Amartya Sen (1999) the most basic condition of well-being is literally life itself. If we follow Sen it becomes clear that women's agency in the Middle

East is significant, because agency refers to the ability or disability of women to initiate action, engaging or resisting deprivation, a concern that is also clearly illustrated in both the United Nations *Arab Human Development Reports* from 2002 and 2003. Sen's capability approach is concerned with what persons are able to do and their inclusion in their specific society. The well-being of women, according to Sen (1993), is fundamentally dependent on the possibilities available for them to be active participants in society. To grasp and articulate women's well-being we need to explore the totality of women's lives which includes the tension between embedded cultural values and complex emergencies.

Gender writings that are concerned with the lives and experiences of women in the region have been concerned with bringing forth women's agency, which implies their capacity to take the initiative. Agency is, after all, about the ability to act, yet we must not ignore the fact that it hinges on the question of whether women in the Middle East can freely initiate an action. For instance, the agency of the village women in Musharafah living under complex emergencies is especially significant within the current political global discourse, because it refers to their ability to initiate action in engaging or resisting occupational powers and the stressful living conditions which are part of occupation. In Musharafah the women are positioned in a complex system inflicted by conflicts and occupation. The potentials for women to contest oppression and suffering are questions of contemporary importance to gender studies in the Middle East now. The civil unrest and deprivation in Palestine have effectively denied women's personhood by the continuous brutal system of repression and occupation. Still, we know that while many women perish, there are those who regained their agency – they assembled fragments and created beginnings.

The concept of "agency" is significant within gender and complex emergencies, because it refers to the ability of women to initiate action in engaging or resisting oppression. Consequently, attention to actual individuals is required. Women living under critical conditions are not packaged identities with common experiences. They have individual experiences and engagements with the local, regional and transnational world. Going back to the Palestinian village, we find that at a certain intersection in the life of the women in Musharafah, tap water, electricity and out-migration of their men were advantageous and signs of prosperity and autonomy on the path towards development. Still, at the changeover to modernization, unintended consequences interfered. The women are living on the margins of subsistence, and their everyday lives are transformed by events beyond their control – indeed outside their world.

Musharafah represents a typical Middle Eastern rural community which is ideally patriarchal; both Islamic traditions and society award the father, brother or husband with a significant sense of authority, power, security and decision-making. In Musharafah there are disruptions in the image of the Arab family.

Patriarchy is contested by the fact that the bigger story of politics and economy changes the family patterns, with the result that sometimes men are not able to support their families. Thus, we find that the relevance of urgent emergencies lies in its multidimensional characteristic. One such feature is the issue of an increasing number of women who are coping with all matters which were traditionally the domain and responsibility of the male patriarch.

It is in particular the local contexts, cultural constraints, ideals and individual responses to critical life situations that call for more engagement. There are general approaches to complex emergencies which have been defined, analysed and acted upon. These are expressions of international interest, international institutions, NGOs and all those who are engaged in complex emergencies on behalf of all the suffering in the world. Yet, as mentioned earlier, one of the main features of complex emergencies is that they are extensive and comprehensive, therefore the impact on the lives of women involves several layers of complexities and involvement.

Building on an already emerging body of scholarship on the "women issue" in the Muslim Arab Middle East, I am suggesting that we should take the women's narratives beyond the particular and articulate more convincingly the critical issues which cause daily sufferings. In a gender discourse on the Middle East there is room to examine women not only as guardians of the heritage of which they themselves so proudly speak (Naguib 2003) but also as people who have to daily cope with life at the edge of existence. We need to explore more pragmatically these tensions between stories and stones; both are approaches to multifaceted realities.

The case of the West Bank Palestinian village of Musharafah illustrates that the political turmoil and demographic changes redefine the living conditions and question women's well-being. Palestinian women are confronted with endless struggling under occupation and civil unrest. Women have to deal with dysfunctional institutions and the day-to-day degradation of having to rely on charities for basic life supplies. There are also more tricky contradictions in which old women labor with the image of the reverence that age demands in the Palestinian Muslim culture and which ideally should give them an effective role in the functioning of society.

Conclusion

There are too many conflicts that have been going on for too long in the Middle East. As conflicts go they involve human suffering, and academic interest and engagement with emergencies have been wanting. We find in the Palestinian village a breakdown of traditional values and social conditions. People are supposed to be cared for by the family and age demands respect. Women and children are supposed to be protected and supported by the patriarch. Instead, there is the problem of unreliable food supplies, lack of medicines and medical security – which are necessities in life. We find under-nourishment, especially among older women living alone or heading a household.

The matter of food vulnerability is an especially sensitive social condition and complicated: according to religious traditional values the family is expected to stay together and support each other, yet war and occupation shatter such ideals. I have argued for more concern with basic social issues, because the Arab/ Muslim woman continues to be enframed in theories which do not go beyond the traditionality of particularizing patriarchy and Islam. These are certainly essential themes, but they may also function as blinders, so that we neglect the importance of women's elementary needs and well-being.

Gendering the Middle East needs more involvement with the regional connections between emergencies, poverty and daily lives of people. Gender studies have provided important contributions to the study and understanding of the everyday lives of women and men in the Middle East. In contrast to local studies and fieldwork, these studies have a tradition for social critique. By using gender studies we can develop our theories further and use our field more in articulating issues people face when living under collapsing conditions.

As scholars skilled in gender studies we need to document, develop and suggest lines of thinking about the daily struggles of women living under complex emergencies. Perhaps one way to engage theoretically with gender and complex emergencies is to agree with Sen (1999) that tyranny, neglect of public services and armed conflicts are the main reasons behind poverty. Widespread complex emergencies and, for example, war, civil unrest and breakdown of institutions are an obstacle to women's well-being and therefore need to be taken into account and documented by scholars. References to the obvious connection between violation of basic freedoms and deprivations are rarely made in gender studies in the Middle East. We continue to be absorbed by the concepts of the Arab family, Islam, patriarchy and Arab women, overlooking the "stones" or the urgency of survival under critical conditions. The realization of how numerous complex emergencies are and how they impinge on the daily lives of women needs to be linked to our perception of development. Complex emergencies are widespread and armed conflicts are an obstacle to development; these must be taken into account and documented by scholars.

The prevailing obstacle to poverty reduction among women is probably armed conflict, yet references to this obvious connection are rarely made in the fora where poverty reduction strategies and meeting basic needs are discussed. Also on a day-to-day level, the multifaceted links between emergencies, water and health need more attention. The example from Musharafah shows clearly that during emergencies water becomes an issue of life and death.

As scholars engaged with gender issues, we also need to explore the connection between emergencies, poverty and daily lives of men and women and to develop theories, models, tools and practices that reflect the realities people face when living in such complex emergencies. Academic involvement with lived emergencies and crises does not alone define the risks people face, but documenting our findings can contribute to better understanding of the complexities of people's daily lives during emergencies, such as the seemingly mundane matter of having access to safe water.

I have suggested and argued for more concern with critical urgent issues which as mentioned earlier are given priority by the United Nations (2002, 2003) *Arab Development Reports*. I began with the importance of the narratives and stories, because they provide us with the "voice" of the women in the Middle East. We must listen and find a place for individuals and their actions, using narratives that bring out the voice that creates beginnings. Moreover, to capture agency, we also need to have those familiar cultural pegs, the foundational concepts, such as patriarchy, Arab family and Muslim women.

I drew on the metaphor of "stones" because the social fabrics of gender are intertwined with major events and transnational processes which cannot be understood in isolation. The skill and the challenge lie in ensuring a gender research that recognizes "stones" while not losing sight of the story. Ideally, we might want to develop an approach that expresses realist narratives that are much more accessible.

Note

1. This chapter is dedicated in fond memory to my mentor and friend Professor Mariken Vaa (1937–2004).

Bibliography

Barth, F. (1994), "A Personal View of Present Tasks and Priorities in Cultural and Social Anthropology,' in R. Borofsky (ed.), *Assessing Cultural Anthropology*, New York: McGraw-Hill.

Berge, G. (2000), "In Defence of Pastoralism," PhD dissertation, University of Oslo.

Goodhand, J. and Hulme, D. (1999), *NGOs and Peace Building in Complex Political Emergencies*, Manchester: Institute for Development Policy and Management.

Hopkins, N. (2003), "Introduction,' in N. Hopkins (ed.), *The New Arab Family*, Cairo: American University in Cairo Press.

Joseph, S. and Slyomovics, S. (2001), *Women and Power in the Middle East*, Philadelphia, PA: University of Pennsylvania Press.

Kandiyoti, D. (1996), *Gendering the Middle East*, Syracuse, NY: Syracuse University Press.

Naguib, N. (2003), *Knowing Water*, Oslo: Oslo University College Press.

Naguib, N. and Vaa, M. (2003), "Models and Realities in Domestic Water Supply," paper presented at the Third Conference of the International Water History Association, Alexandria, Egypt.

Sen, A. (1999), *Development as Freedom*, Oxford: Oxford University Press.

Tucker, J. (1993), *Gender and Islamic History*, Washington, DC: American Historical, Association.

UN (2002), *Arab Human Development Report*, New York: Oxford University Press.

UN (2003), *Arab Human Development Report*, New York: Oxford University Press.

11

Tradition and Change: Afghan Women in an Era of War and Displacement

Karin Ask

In the winter of 1980, several Pakistani newspapers reported on large-scale demonstrations among students in Kabul. In one of these accounts, we are told that hundreds of girls from Malalai School "jeer[ed] at the Afghan army and police officers, threw their *duppattas* at them, snatch[ed] their caps and told them to shut themselves in the four walls of their homes and let the girls defend their motherland."[1]

A *duppatta* is a veil draped by Afghan women over their hair. It operates as a tangible symbol of the emotionally powerful traditional ideas on the proper relation between women and men and also refers to a set of religious ideas on the significance of exemplary feminine behavior.[2] In this case, the gesticulation with the veil is also replete with allusion to the historical battle at Maiwand during the second Afghan–British war where the 17-year-old girl Malalai is said to have plucked a standard from the dying hands of its bearer, placed her veil aloft as a banner and led the faltering Afghan troops to victory. In a famous couplet attributed to her, she embraces the celebrated Afghan tradition of fierce national independence with these words: "I shall make a beauty spot out of my beloved's blood which will put to shame the roses in my garden. Young love, if you do not fall in the battle of Maiwand, by God, someone is saving you for a token of shame!"

This chapter is not the product of classic ethnographic fieldwork but reflects on topics raised by informants during applied research on gender-differentiated assistance in Afghanistan in 1993 and 1999 (Ask, Knudsen and Suhrke 1993; Strand, Harpviken and Ask 2002). Descriptions of episodes of the symbolic display of shame (*Sharm*) and honor (*Nang, namus*) reflect gender relations in the war and encompass noble modesty as well as shamelessness. In the narrow sense, *Nang* relates to the integrity, modesty and respectability of women and to the absolute duty of men to protect them. In its wider sense, it relates to the duty to protect the Afghan homeland. The measures used by the women to evoke deep-set habitual values of men's obligation to protect "their" women shares a prototypical resemblance to the processes of *bricolage*, where actors play with parallels and inversions of conventional signs to advance new interpretations in a social field. The complex dialectic between honor and its contrast, dishonor, is manifest in gender interaction in Afghan tradition on different levels and modalities.

During the Constitutional Grand Council (*Loya Jirga*) held in Kabul in December 2003 a young female delegate from Farah province, a modern-day Malalai,[3] defied the authorized collective story of jihad (holy war) when she took the floor and invoked the name of God and the "colored shrouded martyrs (*Shaheed*) of the path of freedom" before she accused several of the delegates for being jihadist.[4]

In a world that is increasingly marked in terms of global relations and migrating peoples, tradition is more fruitful to conceptualize "not as a discrete phenomenon that is bounded in time or space but as a phenomenon that spills into individual and collective histories" through acts manifested in social interaction (Hastrup 2004: 7–11). How were gendered forms of religious rituals and sentiment embedded in everyday life during the war? I explore the manifestation of a few elements of tradition in empirical networks that are not easily bounded in either time or space and where the importance of change lies in "the context of their interrelations, not in isolation or for their own sake" (Grønhaug 1978: 104).[5]

Places and People: The Fieldwork Settings

Refugees started fleeing from Afghanistan after the Saur revolution in 1978 and by the time of the Soviet invasion in December 1979, there was already a sizeable community of Afghan refugees living in Pakistan.[6] The refugees from Herat entered Iran during the regime of Khomein, while the groups of refugees from Kunar entered Pakistan during the military dictatorship of Zia-ul-Haq, which means that both groups entered neighboring countries at a time when Islamization with different political agendas also impinged on the refugees' life world of traditional behavior. In both countries, Islamization called attention to the religious norms to legitimize control of women and the female body, and in Pakistan the wearing of *duppatta* became mandatory for female staff on national television. Women's positions in the public eye developed, however, differently in the two major countries of refuge.

The first large exodus of refugees came from the rural areas of Afghanistan, from regions regarded as traditional (in the idiomatic sense of "backward" by their urban compatriots). Kunar is situated in the Nangrahar province adjacent to the federally administered tribal areas in Pakistan's Northwest Frontier Province, and belongs to the tribal periphery of Afghanistan. The refugees from this province formed the larger part of the first large influx after the mujahidin revolt began in 1978, and came from a region where free movement back and forth across the border was a traditional pre-war adaptation referred to as keeping of "two houses" (*Dwa Ghar*). The refugees, who were settled in the federally Pakistani tribal area, were also able to activate shared codes of traditions of hospitality (*melmastia*) and refuge (*nanawatai*) as a traditional norm in tribal customary law, Pakthunwali. The way local tradition interlinked with rules of transactions in the large-scale fields of refugee relief also created room for transforming depersonalized code of conduct in the large-scale bureaucratic relief administration into a personalized patron–client network. The scope to do this was created by rules stating that only individuals who could produce a certificate "duly signed and attested by a representative of one of the recognized political parties for Afghan Refugees," would be provided with a ration card (Fielden 1998: 471). Several of the single women interviewed in the refugee camps told us how they had attached themselves to these influential persons nicknamed "ration Maliks," to gain protection. These Maliks drew their reputation both from the field of jihad, from their gatekeeping role in dealing with camp authority, and from the protection given to women without male supporters. After the fall of Kabul to the mujahidin in 1992 and the Taliban takeover of Kabul in 1996, asylum seekers with an urban background arrived in Pakistan who settled outside the refugee camps (Damsleth 1993: 28).

In Iran less than 6 percent of the refugees lived in camps and most settled as casual laborers in large cities like Meshed and Teheran. The combination of the role as warrior and refugee among the male refugees was in principle the same as in Pakistan. The opportunity for female refugees to combine different roles and activities was wider in Iran. Female informants interviewed in Herat described how they had worked as casual labor in Iran in order to contribute to household expenses. Herat province is, in contrast to Kunar, an area of rich agricultural traditions dependent on cultivation by ancient irrigation techniques (underground canals or *karez*) that have supported urban civilization for more than a millennium. The larger ethnic groups in the province such as Tajik and Turkmen are not unlike the Pakthun of Kunar, organized in tribal corporate groups. Labor migration from the province to Iran was also a usual adaptation among males before the war, and among the households interviewed in Herat a third had organized the flight through professional networks (either through mujahidin leaders or through professional smugglers). Iranian authorities, like the Pakistani, received the Afghani refugees as fellow Muslims who fled the land of the infidel ruler, *dar-ul-harb*, to the land of the believers, *dar-ul-Islam*. In comparison to Pakistan, Iran received relatively less financial contribution to the relief and assistance provided to the Afghan refugees (Rajaee 2000). Afghans who escaped to Iran received until 1992 a document that recognized its holder as a *muhajir* and green cards that entitled the refugees to remain legally. This gave a refugee access to food at subsidized prices and free primary education, an opportunity several of the women I interviewed in 1999 had benefited from.

A minimal dictionary definition of tradition describes it as "the handing down of information, beliefs and customs by word of mouth or by example from one generation to the another." However, transmission and change in a tradition also depend on the social and demographic framework. In the case of Afghanistan, approximately half the refugee population were children under the age of 15 years (Christensen 1990: 108). UN sources estimate the population growth at approximately 4 percent, reflecting a total fertility rate of 6.9. The literacy rates among women, although being macro statistical estimates only, indicate a remarkable gap between the young and the elder generation of women in familiarity with inscribed tradition.[7] The translators who assisted me in 1992 and 1999 belonged to the generation of educated Afghan women who came of age during the war. They are competent in reflecting on and interpreting on tradition while working for international agencies and NGOs.

Memories of Flight

At the time of the invasion, Soviets directed the attacks against the resistance movement in the rural areas, using a "scorched earth" policy that inevitably caught civilians in the crossfire. The larger cities went relatively unscathed, an exception being the aerial bombardment of Herat in December 1979, which left approximately 24,000 killed in retaliation for the callous murder of Soviet advisors and their families in March of the same year (Adamec 1997: 384–5).

The women interviewed in Herat in 1999 recalled their personal memories of the massacres in graphic detail, crossed their arms and clasped their earlobes with the thumb and index finger and said "they were slaughtered like animals, God forbid! (*Tauba, Tauba!*)" Many of the villages visited had been caught in the fires between mujahidin and government troops during the 1980s, and some women articulated their memories like this: "Crying wailing in the street each day a new body was taken to the grave has made us throw up the milk our mothers gave us." The undigested bitter taste of despair is comparable to the feelings described by a grandfather, who is unable to make his deaf grandson understand the news about how death has struck their family (A. Rahimi 2001). The way women retold singular stories about death and misfortune was a "remembering behavior" which utilized traditional institutions to stitch together the gap between personal and collective memory.

The days of terror triggered the first flights towards Iran. Other escapes, however, were well thought out, like the one organized by the Cheshtiyya brotherhood. They organized what amounted to a localized *hijra* when "more than 300 families left the town of Chest-I Sharif (Herat) in a single day (April 11, 1981) only to return two years later" (Roy 1986: 166). Most escapes fall somewhere between these extremes, and flight as well as repatriation was often a result of coordinated movements by people belonging to the same tribe or village.

A comprehensive analysis of the way humanitarian assistance objectified ideas about Afghan gender tradition exceeds the scope of this chapter. However, the application of the concept of gender in the planning of humanitarian assistance often made women a target group in ways that disregarded the particular Afghan female–male relationship in intra-household and intergenerational settings, and "the woman question" acquired a taboo-like aura. In most societies, intervention in gendered traditions is hedged by moral restrictions. And in circumstances of violent threats to national integrity there is a universal tendency to close in upon traditional gender roles and family structures to protect against changes in what is represented as natural given, morally and historical immutable. Comparative studies on Muslim communities also emphasize the increased importance given to the safeguard of the private and personal piety and the collective struggles against moral disorder (*Fitna*) as important reactions to loss of political powers to infidels (see Kandiyoti 1991: 1–15.) When reflecting on personal experiences from two periods of fieldwork (the first during the mujahid period, the second during the Taliban), I agree with Cammack in that "the Taliban's social and gender policies are not that much different from those established by other mujahidin parties at home and in exile during the last fifteen years" (Cammack 1999: 94–5).

The "Refugee Warrior"

The refugee warriors drew on the global Muslim religious tradition of holy war (jihad), where believers are admonished to defend the faith with the sword. The struggle started within a decisive local tradition where call for revolt against modernizing changes introduced by the center, had used the idiom of jihad on several occasions before (compare F. Rahimi 1986 [1977]: 10; Olesen 1995: 137–9). This revolt was soon caught in the mesh of superpower rivalry on a global scale. When the Soviets invaded in December 1979, to support the faltering Afghan government, jihad became one among many local wars by proxy between the two superpowers. After the formal Geneva peace accords were signed in 1988, the ensuing civil war eventually interlinked with larger-scale Islamist networks, and the Taliban threw their card in with the terrorist network of Osama Bin Laden. The Wahhabist-inspired Deobandi tradition then encroached upon the frames set for Afghan women (Shalinsky 1993). The interrelations between local traditions of revolt, religious tradition of jihad, and global relations of the Cold War combined sets of codes and roles. In the first phase of the war, it projected the bearded male "refugee warrior" with the *pakuul* hat as an icon of Afghan tradition. In the last phase of the civil war, after the Taliban took control, Afghan women in burkha superseded the portrayal of the Afghan tradition, to the point of parading a woman in burkha before the US Senate Subcommittee on South Asian Affairs (*Dawn* (Pakistani newspaper), July 20, 2000).

Conflicting feelings to actions taken by the international community against the Taliban were conveyed to me in a meeting with Herati women. The women I met with talked about the need to resist the fear of the Taliban, and also how they might circumvent the restrictions imposed. They belonged to the small minority of literate Afghan women, and met in small groups where they read and exchanged news (compare Lamb 2002: 141ff.). One evening they brought up the issue about how to promote sanctions against Taliban without closing "the small windows of opportunity" they had been able to keep open. They referred to the example of the sanctions following Emma Bonino, Commissioner for Humanitarian Affairs. Her entourage (which included a male television crew) were briefly detained following their unauthorized entry into a female hospital in Kabul in the fall of 1996. The women voiced strong disagreement with the Taliban's religious interpretation of female segregation and code of dress. They were, however, also critical of institutions and agents that conveyed what they found a distorted picture of Afghan tradition.

Most Afghan parties and resistance groups active in the refugee camps at the time restricted direct foreign assistance to Afghan female refugees and the Afghan women who worked for national and international organizations that started projects of education. Training of girls was repeatedly intimidated, without meeting serious negative sanctions from the international community (compare Boesen 1990; Christensen 1990: 36). Intervention in this area acquired a taboo-like character, marked off as a high-risk zone within the assistance community, while in the refugee community a complex series of psychological, cultural and political factors aggravated the restrictions on the autonomy and mobility of Afghan women. Living in an environment where unrelated strangers were present also made anxious men control the visibility of "their" women, a crucial sign of the traditional values of self-respect and reputation for refugee men.

Observations made among female refugees, who were registered on a course of tailoring in one of the camps in Peshawar, illustrate the absurd conflicts engendered in this environment. Most of the women on the course were illiterate, and one of the participants was unable to learn to recognize and write down the numbers required to make a pattern to cut cloths according to a standard. Sewing courses for women had been closed in several camps because influential *maulwis* opposed the use of blackboards and chalk at sewing courses that involved women. The solution arrived at by the participants on the course was to let the woman bring her 12-year-old son to help his mother learn to write numbers up to sixty, which was considered sufficient for measuring to make the traditional baggy trousers (*shalwar*) and shirt (*kemiz*).

After Najibullah relinquished office, the international policy for assistance and relief to refugees sought to stimulate repatriation and international NGOs changed from mujahidin commanders cum warlords to channeled assistance to Afghan communities to liaise with traditional institutions like the local councils. International organizations at the time also tried to promote gender-sensitive projects through these traditional organizations like the *Shura* (Pakthoo) and *Jirga* (Dari). During a survey of needs assessment in a district where many refugees had recently been repatriated, an international NGO suggested that some of the projects should have widows and female-headed household as their main beneficiaries. The response came promptly; what the community needed was a new bridge, the needs of their women and their widows they would take care of themselves, thank you very much!

The field study in 1992 took place at a time where the deteriorating security situation in Kabul created a countermovement of new refugees. During fieldwork in Kunar, we met some of them: five young girls who had been sent by their parents for protection among *mahram* (close male relatives) in rural villages. In some of the houses visited, the tradition of jihad was also reflected in the display of a martyred *Shaheed* in the family. Questions about this picture would open the way to the personal story behind. In one of the houses, my attention was drawn to a different type of picture, a colourful poster of a group of mujahidin brandishing Kalashnikov rifles. On my inquiry, the translator read the text on the poster: "The person who wants to stop jihad is like a *Shurawi* (Soviet) in this situation. If the believers follow the Koran, then both the *Shurawi* and the American ideas will be destroyed."[8] The widow who lived in the house had lost her husband in the fight between different factions of the mujahidin. Her refusal to accept our condolences, asking instead for congratulations for her sacrifice in the way of God, was an echo of the message on the poster that might be intended for the ears of influential people in the village rather than for inquisitive outsiders.

The episode reflects the paradoxical situation where the large-scale international assistance to repatriation occurred at the same time as the transfer of power to a variety of mujahidin-controlled areas, produced new streams of refugees. Our host was able to help his relatives who escaped the mujahidin in Kabul only because he was himself protected by the local mujahidin.

Shifting Priorities

The discussion on assistance to Afghan women reached the top of the agenda in the international assistance community only after the Taliban movement consolidated its control over Afghanistan in the years between 1995 and 2001. When they first emerged as a political force, they enjoyed considerable support for the way they disarmed warlords and re-established a basic sense of security after the factional war and lawlessness under the Rabbani government. In the founding myth of the Taliban movement, Mullah Omar is said to have acted against a mujahidin commander who had reportedly abducted, raped and killed three women in Kandahar in mid-1994. However, when they entered the cities of Herat in 1995 and Kabul in 1996, whatever popular support they had acquired after disarming warlords vanished with their callous rule, an assortment of Sharia edicts heavily influenced by tribal Pakthun traditions comparable to the processes Gingrich refers to as Haramization (Gingrich 1997: 159–60).

The concept of *haram* is a term with many references. It denotes both that which is set aside and forbidden, and by extension the sacrosanct and protected domains where women are supposed to lead a protected pious life. The way the Taliban made guarding of religious "correct" practice in the domain of personal relations between the two sexes a state concern represented a new ideological twist to the way gender tradition was appropriated by Afghan rulers. The "justice" promoted by the Taliban and their religious police criminalized a range of acts and behavior of the individual by moving them from the realm of private morals into acts punishable under Sharia law. A particular local brand of veil (burkha), which was prescribed as mandatory for Afghan women to wear by referring to religious sayings about the proper use of *hijab*, illustrates a characteristic trait by several decrees by the Taliban where rural tradition (*riwaj*) was imbued with the appearance of religious authority. A comparable example is the way strict gender segregation (*purdah*) and chaperoning of women in the public sphere by close male relatives (*mahram*) became a matter of public jurisdiction.

Atmar (2001) argues that the vacillating reaction by the international assistance community to the gender discriminatory policies and practices of the Taliban in effect used change in local tradition as a criterion to gender-equality and development, while Dupree (1998: 151) makes a case of the fact that the sanctions from the international organizations were not coordinated and that these decrees from the Taliban side were administered in a haphazard manner as Afghan women continued to benefit from both UN and NGO assistance. Below I give examples of the way Afghan women reversed *mahram* regulation to develop the possibility of investment in gender assistance.

A Case of Mahram Regulations

Islamic normative tradition Sharia classifies cross-sex relationships within two categories: lawful (*mahram*) and unlawful (*na-mahram*) and has developed rules for how men and women may associate in everyday life. A *mahram* relationship is formed by either birth or marriage and will include an individual's immediate family, spouse(s), spouses of children and their children. The Taliban's interpretation of Sharia when they gave the infamous *Mahram* decree was contested by most other Muslim nations, as demonstrated by the critique from the Organization of the Islamic Congress against the Taliban in 1997. The decree obliged all Muslim women who moved about in public to be chaperoned by a male relative. This edict caused an outrage both because of its violation of basic human rights and because of the difficulty it created for foreign organizations to employ female Afghan staff.

In 1999 I employed as interpreter an unmarried woman who was the *de facto* main breadwinner in a household of four adults and three children. The way she broke the expected traditional gender division of supporting a family is perhaps atypical but by no means extraordinary. She had worked as a translator on health projects, the only type of work excluded from the Taliban ban on paid work for females at the time. However, the health project had to be closed down pending renewal of their certificate from Taliban authorities in Kabul, so she was (like many other educated women) looking for waged employment to support her family

Returning from a field visit together with my translator after darkness, but well within curfew hours, I had just left the car when a Taliban (who turned out to be the officer in charge of liaison with foreigners in the city) tapped on the front windscreen. The three male passengers, two Afghans and one Norwegian, were asked what they were doing in the company of an Afghan woman. Not waiting for the explanation offered by the males, my female interpreter volunteered that she was the *mahram* of her younger brother. This statement caused displeasure and consternation, and in the exchange that followed, the female interpreter, her *mahram* brother and I were summoned to explain ourselves at the Taliban ministry of interior the next morning. When we arrived at the ministry, I was given a lecture about the tradition of *mahram* while my translator was warned by her interrogators that Shia interpretations were blasphemous (*shirk*) and she was advised to mend her irreligious ways.

The timing and setting in which my interpreter presented herself as her brother's *mahram* was not only an incongruous interpretation of traditional *mahram* rules, but also constituted an unacceptable challenge to the Taliban authorities' administrative controls. The identification of herself as *mahram* for her younger brother was most probably a slip of the tongue, but echoed, nevertheless, the veracity of many *mahram* couples where women inverted traditional roles and expectations in the *mahram* code to protect the well-being and honor of the family.

Religious Aspects of Coping

After we were released, the mother of my translator travelled to a shrine (*ziarat*) to offer prayers and a vow to return regularly with ritual food (*nazr*) to protect her daughter from future harm and punishment by the Taliban. She revisited the shrine in order to honor her vows. When women continue to visit the shrine with yearly offerings of *nazr*, they create a recurrent pattern of a pilgrimage that in Doubleday's (1988: 50) words "charter family crisis." The strength of this tradition is also indicated by studies from the refugee setting where we learn about female refugees who travel from Peshawar to Kabul to help a female relative cope with damaged nerves by a visit to a shrine (Damsleth 1993: 92). The faith in healing powers of visits to shrines is recognized among urban and rural Afghans, and to be cut off from the spiritual force and blessing (*barakat*) of the *ziarat* is reported by female refugees overseas to be a major sorrow; Kamalkhani (2001: 103–6) describes how a renewed investment in religious gatherings accompany the adaptation to new surroundings.

The large-scale migration during the years of war no doubt undermined the range and possibility for Afghan women to routinely follow the traditional itineraries of female pilgrimages. On the other hand, the networks of exchange established during migration seem also to have bolstered the religious practice as a shared tradition among Afghan communities on the transnational level.

Most of the information about how women kept the rituals of seeking religious blessing (*barakat*) and religious merit (*sawab*) alive emerged as explanations that women gave of observations on acts initiated by women to contribute to honorable survival strategies of the household. In *dari* the term for vulnerability (*asi-pasir*) signifies he or she "who deserve more," a category recognized to have religious and moral claims upon the community. Orphans (*Yateem*) and widows (*Bewa*) are two categories that are specially recognized as worthy receivers of *zakat*.

Images of disrupted domesticity were a persistent topic in the narratives of women about the changes that had effected their traditional in the sense of recurrent daily life. In one village where the extended family had to disband after a large flood had destroyed the compound (*kala*), the women referred to the experience as their *hijra*, the point of reference towards which all subsequent events was related and measured. The flood disturbed the traditional routines of female cooperation, for example cooking bread in the large oven (*tandoori*) by dispersing the women around several hearths in smaller compounds. This village had escaped relatively unscathed from the fights between the mujahidin and government forces because they were located close to the military barracks. At the start of the new war of terror, Operation Enduring Freedom, what had once been their good fortune became their tragedy when the village came under heavy bombardment that killed twelve and displaced more than forty-two families after their homes were shattered on October 21, 2001.

Badal

The term *badal* carries multiple semantic references in Pakthunwali, with revenge, retribution and exchange being the main ones. Revenge is often given as men's immediate explanation of the term, while women's usage of the term in daily parlance habitually incorporates a wider array of positive exchange in different social fields (Grima 1993: 71). The importance of women's investment in traditional forms of *badal* were exemplified in my fieldwork both by observation of their daily investment in reciprocity and by answers to questions about borrowing and lending (delayed exchange). Women's customary usage of *badal* also depended on the strong lattice between secular and religious tradition, made evident in the informants' answers to our technical questions about needs assessment. Reflecting on the question, women would use the criteria of those who deserve more (*asi pasir*) as defining the category. This was the potential recipient of *zakat* like widows, orphans and infirm and elderly people.

The old woman who came to ask for food and shelter for the night blessed the women in the household, who made a bed for her and served her food. These occasions exemplify the positive aspect of *badal* as an element in the chain of tradition that grants refuge (*nanawatai*) and voluntary hand-outs (*sadaka*) to the deserving. The spiritual return for this transactions is religious merit (*sawab*) and in the tribal tradition, personal dignity and familial honor (*geheirat*). The young boy who was used to circumventing the restrictions on formal teaching of women, together with numerous other young boys who served as *mahram*, also provided a defence to the jihadist tradition developed in the all-male madrasas of the Taliban.

The example of adolescent daughters who helped their parents to deal with the bureaucracy of international assistance also reflects the change witnessed in the field of female education by the war generations. The factual details about the narrow pre-war base of formal education and minimal female literacy rates is spelled out by Rahimi (1986), who underlines the unparalleled changes that have been made to change the framework for transmission of tradition to new generations of girls both in refugee setting and in the underground schools inside Afghanistan.

The rituals of women seeking God's blessing (*barakat*) and gathering *sawab* on behalf of themselves and their near ones are of a type that has often been categorized as belonging to popular Islam. This distinction relegates an important field of female ritual religious activity to a residual category, in a way that obfuscates the ethnographic reality in a field where women's religious work actually "may carry a religious load of greater transcendental importance to the community than that borne by men" (Tapper and Tapper 1987: 92).

The religious activity of Afghan women contributes to bringing together the gaps between personal distressing loss and the fissures in communal networks in the midst of the displacement. Women who are active in religious work incorporate a range of practices and rites that stretch from the prayers (*dua*) offered outside the prescribed five daily payers (*namaz*), cooking of ritual food for blessing (*nazr*) and serving of votive meals and visits to martyrs and saints' graves (*ziarat*). The organizing of rituals in domestic settings includes the condolences and reciprocal visits to ask for good health among the family members (*tapos*), and religious rituals like the complete reading of the Koran (*Khatam Koran*) and the celebration of the Prophet's birthday (*Mevluds*) for example. Through these activities the women are agents of distribution for material goods through gestures of public giving that incurs *sawab*. The women also take responsibility to search for protective amulets (*tawiz*) made by religious specialists like a mullah, who writes verses from the holy Koran on paper concealed in the charm – attached to the person they are meant to protect.

The women also continued to economise resources in order to fund the traditional obligations like marriages and funerals and reinforce the social capital that cements communities (Tapper 1991; Grima 1993), even if expenditure in connection with such ceremonies was on a reduced scale. Women complained that resources available for spending on marriage payments and ceremonial outlays at weddings and funerals were inadequate; nevertheless, the priority given to fulfill expectations at these life cycle ceremonies was strong. Women interviewed on income-generating projects both in Kunar and Herat provinces gave these as among the most important categories of expenditure

To give an example, the widow who was responsible for organizing the sewing courses as income-generating courses in Kunar reported that the top priority for the widows in the program was to earn money for a proper ceremony of memorial (*Urs*). The outlay varies according to both the social importance of the deceased and the social ambition of the bereaved. Mourning properly conducted helped the bereaved to publicly conclude the relationship with the person who had died, at the same time as funerary ceremonies contributed to reproductive exchanges that prevent the room left empty by the deceased to sever social relationship in the network of social relations of the household. The body was never retrieved for a religious burial ceremony and remained a haunting memory of the dead manifested by means of shifting lights on the side of the canal. Two widows narrated how they had to take the responsibility to perform the *fathea* and burial of their husbands when they were killed. The details of the stories were told in front of neighbors, who interjected the narratives with statements on circumstances of their personal sorrows (*Gham*) and misfortunes. The traditional style of narration used by women when they meet to inquire about and partake in each other's sorrows in the informal forum of the *tapos* parallel and evokes a shared ethos of honor (Grima 1993).

Continuity and Change

The martyrs (*Shaheed*) of the jihad are mentioned in the preamble to the Bonn agreement as "having brought the highest national and religious sacrifice" and in the new Constitution they are given homage, while the young female delegate who challenged the jihadist contested the image of tradition by rising the spectres of the traumatic collective memory of numerous female victims of official jihad.

I have concentrated my argument about gender, religion and change in Afghanistan around those segments of tradition and religious practice that emerged as recurrent points in the information given by female refugees about their investment in the traditional institutions of *mahram*, *tapos* and *badal*.

This Afghan tradition of "symbolic shelter" supposed to protect the *purdah* keeping women has been challenged by the contradiction between moral reinforcement of norms to protect the sanctity of the realm of *haram* and the social reality of its increasingly violent destruction (Gingrich 1997: 171).

At the time of writing, the Afghan Assistance Authority has just finished the Constitutional Loya Jirga and registration of the electorate is underway in preparation for the first free election in Afghanistan in forty years. Those who have access to institutional channels inscribe their version of the immediate past to mold social habits and the authorized version of the national tradition. In local community shrines (*ziarat*) have been raised to a few of the female victims of the violation of the values of *haram*.

Notes

1. The story appeared in the English daily newspaper *Muslim* in Islamabad, June 8, 1980. The same year more than seventy schoolchildren were reported to have died in demonstrations against the government and the Soviet invasion, among them the 12-year-old schoolgirl Naheed.
2. The religious tradition for wearing of *hijab* is based on reference to the Koran, Sura 24: verses 31–2 where women are told to "guard their private parts and throw a scarf over their bosom" and Sura 33: verse 54 which states "when you ask any of the wives of the Prophet for something, ask from behind a curtain" (*hijab*).
3. Malalai is one of the few nationally acknowledged Afghan heroines. The symbolic act of shaming men who shirk or betray their traditional role as protectors of women has been used on several public occasions during the war, for example by women who prevented former President Rabbani from entering the Loya Jirga tent in June 2002.
4. The paradigmatic model for the refugees is the Prophet's flight to defend the faith and seek alliance in Medina. This momentous event, the *Hijra*, is described in the Koran (Sura 6: verses 41–2) and is the reference year for the Islamic calendar. A common term for refugees fleeing persecution of this type is *muhajir*. Jihads literally "struggle" in the way of God. Islamic theology distinguishes between the "great" jihad, an internal (personal) moral and spiritual struggle which involves changes of personal mores, and

the "lesser" struggle of holy war for the defence or expansion of Islam. The pejorative shorthand jihadist attacks and belittles the mujahidin.

5. The ethnographic data are based on interviews and observations made during field visits to refugee camps in Pakistan's Northwest Frontier Province and to returned refugees in Kunar in November and December 1992, and two months of anthropological fieldwork in Herat province from March to May 1999. The focal point for both field studies was to collect data to expand gender-sensitive assistance to Afghan women.

6. As the war continued, the numbers of refugees in Pakistan swelled to around 3.5 million while more than 2.3 million found refuge in Iran.

7. The national literacy rate for women over 15 years was given as 4 percent in 1978. Kabul University opened to women only in 1950/51 and the first provincial high school for girls was established in Herat in 1957, followed by the other provincial capitals in the 1960s. The World Bank set female literacy rates at 14 percent in 2001. Latest estimates by US sources in 2004 are 20 percent literacy (http://www.odci.gov7cia/publications/factbook/geos/af.html).

8. The wealth of information about amount spent on ceremonies of burial and ceremonial commemoration no doubt reflects the overrepresentation of widows in the sample of informants.

Bibliography

Adamec, L. W. (1997), *Historical Dictionary of Afghanistan*, London: Scarecrow Press.

Ask, K., Knudsen, A. and Suhrke, A. (1993), *Socioeconomic Effects of Training Programs for Refugees: An Evaluation of Norwegian Refugee Council's and Norwegian Church Aid's Income Generating Programs in Pakistan and Afghanistan*, report no. 4, Oslo: Norwegian Refugee Council (NRC).

Atmar, H. (2001), "Politicisation of Humanitarian Aid and its Consequences for Afghans," *Disasters*, 25(4): 321–30.

Boesen, I. W. (1990), "Honour in Exile: Continuity and Change among Afghan Refugees," in E. Anderson and N. H. Dupree (eds), *The Cultural Basis of Afghan Nationalism*, London: Pinter.

Cammack, D. (1999), "Gender Relief during the Afghan war," in D. Indra (ed.), *Engendering Forced Migration: Theory and Practice*, New York and Oxford: Berghahn.

Christensen, H. (1990), *The Reconstruction of Afghanistan: A Chance for Rural Afghan Women*, Geneva: UNRISID.

Damsleth, B. (1993), "Coping with Disrupted Lives: a Study of Afghan Girls and their Family Networks," unpublished MA thesis, University of Oslo.

Doubleday, V. (1988), *Three Women of Herat*, London: Jonathan Cape.

Dupree, N. H. (1998), "Afghan women under the Taliban," in W. Maley (ed.), *Fundamentalism Reborn?*, London: C. Hurst.

Fielden, M. B. (1998), "The Geopolitics of Aid: the Provision and Termination of Aid to Afghan refugees in North West Frontier Province, Pakistan," *Political Geography*, 17(4): 459–87.

Gingrich, A. (1997), "Inside an Exhausted Community: An Essay on Case Reconstructive Research on Peripheral Moralities," in S. Howell (ed.), *The Ethnography of Moralities*, London: Routledge.

Grima, B. (1993), *The Performance of Emotion among Paxtun Women*, Karachi: Oxford University Press.

Grønhaug, R. (1978), "Scale as a Variable in the Analysis: Fields of Social Organization in Herat, Northwest Afghanistan," in F. Barth (ed.), *Scale and Social Organization*, Oslo: Universitetsforlaget.

Hastrup, K. (2004), *Action: Anthropology in the Company of Shakespeare*, Copenhagen: Museum Tusculanum Press, University of Copenhagen.

Kamalkhani, Z. (2001), "Recently Arrived Muslim Refugee Women Coping with Settlement," in A. Shahram and A. Saeed (eds), *Muslim Communities in Australia*, Perth: University of New South Wales Press.

Kandiyoti, D. (1991), *Women, Islam and the State*, London: Macmillan.

Lamb, C. (2002), *The Sewing Circles of Herat*, London: HarperCollins.

Olesen, A. (1995), *Islam and Politics in Afghanistan*, London: Curzon Press.

Rahimi, A. (2001), *Aske og Jord* (Khākestar-o-khāk), trans. H. Salih and I. Østenstad, Oslo: Aschehoug.

Rahimi, F. (1986 [1977]), (with a 1985 update by N. H. Dupree), *Women in Afghanistan, Frauen in Afghanistan*, Liestal: Stiftung Bibliotheca Afghanica.

Rajaee, B. (2000), "The Politics of Refugee Policy in Post-revolutionary Iran," *Middle East Journal*, 54(1): 44–63.

Roy, O. (1986), *Islam and Resistance in Afghanistan*, Cambridge: Cambridge University Press.

Shalinsky, A. C. (1993), "Women's roles in the Afghanistan Jihad," *International Journal of Middle East Studies*, 25: 661–75.

Strand, A., Harpviken, K. B. and Ask, K. (2002), *Afghanistan and Civil Society*, Oslo: Norwegian Ministry of Foreign Affairs.

Tapper, N. (1991), *Bartered Brides: Politics, Gender and Marriage in an Afghan Tribal Society*, Cambridge: Cambridge University Press.

Tapper, N. and Tapper, R. (1987), "The Birth of the Prophet: Ritual and Gender in Turkish Islam," *Man*, 22(1): 69–92.

12

Vows, Mediumship and Gender: Women's Votive Neals in Iran

Azam Torab

Introduction

Middle Eastern scholarship is familiar with the debates about the artificial distinction between so-called formal Islam and popular belief.[1] This distinction is current within Islamic societies themselves. For instance, the religious authorities in Iran distinguish between so-called true religion (*rast dini, eslam-e rastin*) and its supposed deviations, which are often used to assess the beliefs and practices of different classes of population. Formal Islam is treated as normative and is generally associated with the learned scholars (*'ulama*) of Islamic texts, who are predominantly men. Popular Islam suggests an "informal" or "local" Islam and is often associated with women, the illiterate and the rural. To follow Asad (1986), such distinctions are historically situated, authoritative discourses, defined by those in positions of authority. In Iran, discriminatory dichotomies such as these are particularly salient for ceremonial votive meals, called literally "votive meal cloth" (*sofreh-e nazri* or simply *sofreh*). These ceremonies are dedicated to Shia saints or supernatural spirits, who act as intercessors with God for requests and favors. *Sofreh* are all-female activities and popular, though highly controversial, as several other authors have noted.[2] The religious authorities recognize vows to the established saints, but do not approve of the many *sofreh* varieties that exist, treating them as products of ignorance (*jahl*), superstition (*khorafat*) or "innovations" (*bid'a*), hence un-Islamic. Women themselves, however, regard their activities as perfectly compatible with Islamic belief and practice.

The question that arises is why are the votive meals so popular with women and why should they be disparaged or at best tolerated by the religious establishment. I will argue against the notion that the denigration of women's votive ceremonial meals by men of learning suggests the denigration of women, gender antagonism or domination. Such an idea would imply acceptance of earlier gender models that suggest either alternative male and female worldviews, or complementary genders within a single worldview.[3] These models are based on a coexisting, dualistic and mutually exclusive model of gender, rather than the current understanding of gender as inherently flexible and unstable (Moore 1988; Strathern 1988; Butler 1990a, 1990b, 1993; Moore 1994). Yet, it seems that the idea of separate, unitary genders needs to be upheld, as attested by the pervasive separation of the sexes in many domains of life in Iran, as elsewhere in the Muslim Middle East. The issue is complicated by the fact that although *sofreh* is an all-female activity, men may ask women to act on their behalf in activities that they themselves ostensibly condemn as spurious.[4] This means, paradoxically, that women acquire sacred authority because of their inferior status.[5] In other words, women appear both weak and powerful, and men seem both to dominate women and delude themselves.[6] To resolve such dilemmas, a fresh approach to women's ceremonial votive meals in Iran is required.

The theoretical relevance and premise of this chapter is in the field of social anthropology. My argument follows current understandings of gender as context-ually specific constructions encompassing many aspects of life, beyond simply gender identity, roles and relations. In other words, even though the votive meals are all-female activities, they are not simply about "women" or their relation to men, but about much wider social and cultural values, which nonetheless come to be expressed in terms of a symbolic male/female contrast. But the issue is further complicated because the symbolic and the social do not necessarily correspond (Moore 1999a: 26ff., 1999b: 152). Women or men may be represented as powerful symbolically, but discriminated against socially. In other words, sociological differences, such as class, intersect with gender symbols and values in complex ways. Feminist scholarship has long argued that gender is one strand among others like class, race, ethnicity, age, sexuality and so on. Such classifications are of course problematic. They are not intended to inscribe identities, but to indicate how people themselves understand their relations to others. Certainly, in Iran, gender is not the only salient marker of difference. Class differences are an important factor in people's conceptualizations of social life. Haraway (1990: 197) writes, there is nothing that "naturally" binds women divided by forced consciousness of class, race or other such categories. Similarly, it can be argued that "patriarchy" makes no sense when a man's position in the household is not confirmed by his experiences of race or class in the wider society outside his own household. So, the question is, if categories like gender and class are artificial constructs, how do they come about, when do they intersect and why.

It is an established premise in social anthropology that serving and sharing food is a means of constructing and redefining identities such as gender, class, religion and ethnicity.[7] My focus is on how gender is understood and produced through actions of a specific kind. I argue that small face-to-face units formed around ritual activities are particularly effective for creating unitary identities as a sphere of social and political agency. I suggest that through their votive ceremonial meals, women create a collective, unitary identity as "women" by drawing on the powers and capacities that are definable as female. They thereby create a sphere of political agency that accommodates their claims in a context where discourses of morality vie with those of politics and self-interest.[8] In the process, they paradoxically highlight the contingent nature of gender and blur the gendered boundaries, extending their range.

The Concept of Saints as Intercessors with God

Vowing to the saints is a regular feature of everyday life among practising Shia Muslims.[9] The established Shia saints are the twelve Imams, who are the male successors of the Prophet, as well as some female saints, in particular Fatemeh and Zeynab, all of whom are looked upon as primary role models for morality and ethics. The male Imams, in particular Imam Husseyn (the third Shia Imam and grandson of the Prophet), are also linked to ideas of leadership of the Shia community (*'ummat*), and thus play an important political role. There are also many less prominent saints and a host of unidentified supernatural spirits. The religious establishment regards the latter spirits as suspect, even though ordinary individuals may favor them as intercessors with God. The saints thus have multiple roles. They serve both individual interests as personal intercessors with God, as well as serving the interests of the community at large in matters of morality, ethics and politics. Much like Turner's (1961, 1967) notion of the "multivocal symbol" with a "fan of meanings," the roles played by the saints in people's everyday lives coexist sometimes in harmony, but also in tension with each other.

The choice of a saint as a spiritual intercessor with God is personal, depending on the saint's perceived accessibility, empathy with the problem at hand and their responsiveness to the requests made to them by the supplicants. The more accessible among them are popularly designated as "gateway to favors" (*Bab-ol-Hava'ej*).[10] Notably, Imam Husseyn is not among them, despite his more general significance. People often refer to their favorite saints as friends or relatives who are expected to help in times of need. The saints are felt to be more likely to reach God than individuals appealing directly. As one woman told me jestingly, "To reach God, we need to pull strings as we do to reach an important person in our daily lives." The perception of a distant God who can be reached more effectively through the saints is comparable to the common practice of lobbying (*parti-bazi*) in daily life, whereby the disempowered find powerful persons to help resolve their problems.[11]

As powerful benevolent figures, the saints are believed to work miracles, granting all kinds of favors. I heard remarkable stories of cures from terminal illness and infertility, of the resolution of marital disputes, of help with children's welfare and education, of relief from financial burdens or debts and housing problems. These were all items on an endless list to be resolved by the intercession of the saints with God. Vowing is therefore considered very efficacious and propitious (*mojjarrab*) for obtaining results. However, when problems are resolved, the agency of the individual making the vow is nonetheless dissolved into a general idiom of divine providence.[12] The slippage between human agency and the miraculous is central to the votive practices. It legitimizes social or political claims of supplicants in religious terms.

The Votive Meals

The practice of vowing is a conditional agreement. A person vows to a saint or a supernatural spirit to intercede with God for a favor (*morad, hajat, plural hava'ej*) in return for an offering (*nazri*) specified in advance. Offerings vary from the simplest to the most elaborate, requiring various degrees of money and effort. An offering may, for example, consist simply of giving alms, or making a charitable gesture, or the recitation (*zikr*) of a short verse from the Koran. It might include fasting for a specified length of time, proffering respect to a saint by visiting their shrine, or simply distributing a mixture of so-called "problem-solving nut-mixture" (*ajil-e moshgel-gosha*) during a ceremony. Particularly popular are offerings of food cooked by women. Specific votive dishes are cooked for religious anniversaries for door-to-door distribution to friends, neighbours and relatives, or to the public, for instance at shrines, in mosques or at gravesites, where the votive food is distributed to the poor as a charitable deed for the benefit of the deceased spirits. These votive dishes are eagerly sought and eaten because they are considered imbued with divine grace (*barakat*). Especially popular among women are the sharing of votive meals and dishes in the home with invited guests around the meal cloth (*sofreh*) – from which the ceremony derives its name – traditionally spread on the floor. *Sofreh* are convivial, social affairs. They allow for displays of pious virtue, social competence or competitive displays as the case may be. The occasion may be a more or less subdued one, with recitations from the Koran or chanting of dirges, or it may be joyous, involving dancing and merry-making. Very often, the serious and the joyful are combined. A cantor of religious songs may be invited to provide the ambience and mood appropriate to a religious ceremony, but female preachers who preside over religious meetings called *jalaseh* are less likely to be asked to preside over the ceremony.[13] The more orthodox disapprove in any case of some of the more creative *sofreh*, which they consider as a perversion of religious ceremonies, in particular if they are dedicated to unrecognized supernatural spirits or involve dancing and merry making.

There are many *sofreh* varieties, each one associated with a particular saint.[14] The display of meals ranges from the simplest to the most elaborate, often corresponding to the perceived significance and stature of the saint in question for the Shia community. The simplest meals, which are common among the marginalized sections of society – the urban and rural poor – consist often of bread, fresh herbs, cheese or dates only. These are dedicated to the minor saints, such as Imam Husseyn's infant girl *Hazrat-e* Roqiyeh, or to unidentified supernatural spirits, whose ambiguous, hence peripheral status corresponds to the marginalized status of the supplicants themselves. The most lavish meals are dedicated to the prominent saints, such as Imam Husseyn or his half-brother *Hazrat-e* 'Abbas, who it is said sacrificed his life at the battle of Karbala fetching water for Husseyn's thirsting infants. They are held in high esteem for their exceptional bravery and their perceived role in ensuring the survival of the Shia community. The meals dedicated to these saints often reach levels of conspicuous display, becoming a means of validating and legitimizing relative prosperity or wealth in religious terms. Votive meals offer, therefore, a wide spectrum of possibilities and the differences are a function of social, economic and political factors that are expressed through religious practice.

Creating a Unitary Gender Identity

I would now like to present an example of a votive *sofreh* that I attended in 1993 in a working-class area of south Tehran in order to demonstrate how it is an effective means for the construction of imagined affinities based on things female as a sphere of political agency.[15] The ceremony is similar to one identified by Shokurzadeh (1967), an Iranian scholar of folklore, as having rural origins and which Jamzadeh and Mills (1986: 44–9) have analysed in terms of the themes of female power, solidarity, humility, generosity and dependency on divine providence. The one that I attended was a small ceremony of about twelve women neighbors. The meal was dedicated to two female supernatural spirits called Lady Hoori and Lady Light (*Bi-bi Hoor* and *Bi-bi Nur*). They are not among the established saints, although the women themselves identified them as the daughters of the seventh Imam. It is particularly interesting that the sponsor of this ceremony was the son of the hostess. During the Iran–Iraq war (1980–8), he had asked his mother to vow to the two female supernatural spirits for his safe return from the front, where he was sent as a medical assistant with the Red Crescent (the Iranian version of the Red Cross).

The procedure for this ceremony was to offer three meals, two before the granting of the favor and the third held in abeyance (*gerow*) until some time after the favor is granted (the time may, but need not be specified when making the vow). An orthodox female preacher warned me that this was a particularly superstitious kind of ceremony. The women however treated it like a religious event. They inaugurated the meal in the name of God and consecrated the food with recitations of prayers and intercessionary supplications (*du'a-ye tavassol*) in the name of the Shia saints. These preliminaries were followed by ritual greetings (*salavat*) dedicated to the ill, the debtors, the deceased spirits and the prisoners of war. The votive dish consisted of a simple sweet pudding called *kachi*, made with flour tossed in oil and rosewater. Before its consumption, we sat in silence in a darkened room listening to a story.

This was a Cinderella-type story.[16] It concerned a peasant girl who ends up marrying a prince after eating *kachi* cooked by the two supernatural female spirits, Lady Hoori and Lady Light. She encounters these spirits in the wilderness, where she had been sent by a jealous stepmother to perform arduous tasks (spinning wool, tending sheep and cows). After her marriage with the prince, the girl sets out to fulfill her vow to cook the votive *kachi*. Her mother-in-law denounces her for acting below their station and the prince, influenced by his mother, kicks the cooking pot in anger. The girl casts a curse on the prince and he is sent to gaol, allegedly for murder. When he repents and agrees to let his bride fulfill her vow to cook the votive dish, she secures his release with the help of the supernatural female spirits.

Folk or so-called fairy tales are similar to myths. They may be fictitious, but they are often allegories of social values and relations deeply rooted in the lived world of the people themselves. The story of the two supernatural ladies revolves around powerful, resolute female figures. There is a stepmother who controls the father, a mother-in-law who controls and influences her son and two supernatural spirits who act as surrogate mothers, who guide, protect and above all nurture with a votive pudding, the power of which makes it possible, in theory, to transcend social barriers like class. That which is possible, but not reality, is a relation of power that only superhuman effort can confront. But this story does not portray women as weak, or as passive prizes for daring princes, with obedience, submission and beauty as feminine values, which are themes familiar from classical collections of fairy tales edited by men.[17] Instead, the story focuses on powerful women who strive resolutely to control their lives. They may not question the justice of gender hierarchy, but neither do they let abuse of authority by men go unchallenged.

The prince represents men's failure to rise to the standards they set themselves and their weakness and dependence on women's special access to the supernatural. Significantly, the sponsor of this ceremony was the son of the hostess. This dependence by men on women's access to the supernatural when problems arise in their daily lives replicates one of the themes in the story, namely the prince's dependence on his wife for his release from prison. It demonstrates that even if men do regard women as superficial, they also recognize their worth in specific contexts. Women on their part uphold the religious laws as defined by men, yet choose to interpret them in ways that address their own concerns. By helping men to resolve their problems, women strengthen their own positions when negotiating their relations with men, transforming thereby "domestic" activity into political agency. But, rather than compete with men, the story demonstrates that the women compete with each other as wives, mothers and daughters over the control of men, displaying thereby variant female capacities for plotting, matchmaking and above all nurture.

Votive Dishes as a Channel for Divine Grace

Central to the story and the votive meal are the rewards to be gained by women by keeping cooking and nurture under their sole jurisdiction. A key premise of nurture is the possibility of influencing and controlling others, for those who are "fed" become dependants, like infants (Carsten 1995, 1997). This power is not based on domination, although women manipulate it to their advantage. In terms of a gender symbolism, the emphasis on nurture in the women's ceremonial activities is the key to the creation of an identity as female and a means of expressing a collective agency as women. This female agency is underlined by the extraordinary power and potency attributed to the votive dishes.

Votive meals are widely regarded as channels for *barakat*, with women as recognized agents. Guests are encouraged to take a portion home to share with other members of their household, so that they too may partake of the *barakat*. People identify *barakat* empirically as bounty, prosperity, good fortune, well-being and so on, corresponding broadly to the notion of divine grace or blessing. Votive meals are widely considered to be imbued with *barakat* (*tabarrok shodan*). *Barakat* can be somatized through ingestion and has the power to transform.[18] In effect, people become possessors of *barakat* by being treated as such and through the actions they themselves undertake.[19] *Barakat* is thus linked to ideas about agency and power. All food, for example, is said to be God's *barakat*, but only ritual food is talked about as being imbued with *barakat* by being treated as such.[20] It thereby comes to be distinguished conceptually from similar food outside the ritual context, even if cognitively they are virtually indistinguishable.

The markedly regenerative associations of traditional votive dishes (such as *kachi*, *halva*, *shol-e zard* and *samanu*) are underlined by the fact that they are cooked for key moments of renewal and transition like birth, death, the procurement of health and worship. In addition, rosewater and saffron, which are key ingredients of these dishes, have themselves regenerative associations and are highly recommended by religious source books (such as Majlesi 1991). One of the votive dishes called *samanu*, which is associated with the craving of Fatemeh (the Prophet's daughter) during pregnancy, is made from germinating wheat, using a particularly laborious process. An obvious analogy can be made between germinating grain and the swelling of the womb (Bourdieu 1992 [1972]: 116). Votive dishes are thus strongly suggestive of the female principle of fertility. In terms of a gender symbolism, they express a collective agency in terms of women's experience of their bodies, through which they lay claims to the reproduction of the human, natural and cosmological worlds (compare Moore 1999a: 28). The practice of vowing is thus a means of negotiating the relationship between self, society and the transcendent. Representations of these practices as selfish obscure both the strong underlying sense of renewal associated with women's fecund dishes and female power to nurture and create life.

The Prescriptive Texts: Self-interest Versus Morality

The religious authorities call for restraint in women's votive practices. Vowing is approved only as a means of approaching God and honoring the saints that are recognized by the religious establishment. But vowing for selfish ends or this-worldly concerns (*donyavi*), rather than with other-worldly ones (*okhravi*), is denounced as self-indulgence, materialistic and as giving free rein to envy or desire, which according to the religious authorities must be deferred and channeled to the world to come. This is based on a salvationist ideology of worldly restraint and reward in the afterlife. This ideology promotes an imaginary ideal and ethos of equality. It denies the reality of social and material exclusion, serving the interests of those in positions of authority who fail to provide the material necessities of life and equality for those members of society that are marginalized on account of their gender, class, race and so on. Women's votive *sofreh* implicitly reject and challenge the ideology that calls for restraint. Among the poor, vows clearly voice a desire for things denied, but to which they feel they have a right. But votive practices are not simply a function of economic deprivation. The ceremonial meals are popular among the prosperous middle classes. As indicated, they provide possibilities for competitive, status enhancing displays as well as for legitimizing relative prosperity in religious terms. In this sense, women, though divided by class, reveal themselves as self-determining agents who work against the prevailing authoritative discourses that tell them not to vow for selfish ends. In the process, the women also blur the boundaries that underly the dominant discourses on gender.

Prominent Islamic gender discourses oppose reason and morality to self-interest, which are defined in terms of a male/female contrast of '*aql* and *nafs*.[21] Reason and morality are constructed as male and associated primarily with men, while self-interest, desire or envy are constructed as female and associated primarily with women, reminiscent of the familiar Cartesian mind/body opposition in some gender discourses in the West.[22] Based on the construct that men are more rational than women, and women more susceptible to desire, envy and excess, the religious rules stipulate that women must obtain the permission of their husbands for vows. The controversy over women's votive ceremonies is therefore an expression of wider social and moral values, even though they come to be expressed in gendered terms. This is not about the denigration of women, but what they symbolically represent.

Women themselves do not see their votive practices in terms of either self-interest or disinterested morality, and insist on the primacy of intent (*niyyat*). Their actions are not intended to be monopolistic. Anyone attending a *sofreh* can call on a saint for requests. The ceremonies demonstrate a concern for others through the supplications for the health and vitality of the community, including the spirit of the deceased. The women indicate thereby that they have the interests of others in mind beside their own. Moreover, *sofreh* may be held weekly on an open-house basis, or shared with passers-by, for example at gravesites or at shrines. Food sharing is itself a key symbol of equality and a means of striving for harmony (R. Tapper and N. Tapper 1986: 67). The intention is often to maintain and extend social linkages and supportive networks. Unlike contractual agreements in the market, where social relations end when the contract ends, and where reward is assured rather than merely expected as in the realm of gift exchange, the ceremonial votive exchanges create moral obligations for reciprocity. Consistent with Mauss (1954), who asserts that a gift always implies (though it does not assure) a return, *sofreh* are a prime example of the way in which humans enter into relational debts with each other and with the saints through canons of hospitality, food and respect. Successful vows generate further vows and more *sofreh*, which in turn generate further social exchanges that continue even after the fulfillment of a vow.

To compare women's votive practices with any economic activity is, therefore, pointless. The crude economic model of maximizing self-interest and rational choice presupposes the existence of equal choice for all. Nor can the moral discourse based on disinterested piety or "pure gift" serve those with limited options. Individuals shape their aspirations according to what seems accessible and possible.[23] Yet, despite the spirit of equality and harmony and the communal ethos of the votive meals, there is nonetheless tension of a kind. Status imbalance arises from competitive display. The desire to surpass and dazzle others with conspicuous display is exemplified by, for example, the *sofreh* dedicated to Imam Husseyn's brave half-brother (*Hazrat-e 'Abbas*). Sponsors inevitably derive spiritual reward (*'ajr*) and merit (*savab*) for their generosity, even in the simpler *sofreh* variety. Such generosity is "a sacrifice designed to win in return the blessing of prosperity" (Bourdieu 1992: 180). Those who are able are expected to make ceremonial expenditures appropriate to their wealth, or else be deemed niggardly and selfish. But this benefits them, in that their wealth is purged from taints of selfishness and thus legitimized. The rich are therefore doubly rewarded. Their wealth is transformed into generosity, which reaps spiritual reward ('*ajr*) and prestige. They thereby gain a competitive edge, which alters their relationship to others. Even among the poorer sections of society, the involvement of others in the celebration of the positive outcome of a vow enhances a person's reputation for piety. It makes their special relation with the saint "appear" publicly to a wider circle, thus providing the possibility of bolstering their stock of "symbolic capital" (Bourdieu 1992: 171–83), through which they can define and redefine themselves within their social group. These votive meals are therefore sites where women mask and reshuffle the gendered values of self-interest and morality in a social space they can control. They thereby accommodate their claims to the reproduction and regeneration of the social and cosmological world.

Conclusion

It has been argued that women are different from men because of their bodies; that nature or biology determines the difference.[24] This implies that the body genderizes the acts, and that even if women do the same things as men, they are still different. But, what I have tried to demonstrate, following Strathern (1988: 129–30), is that women's particularity in relation to men is precisely because they "do" things differently. Identification is what one does and thus becomes rather than what one is and therefore does. What is essential is to examine those contexts where gender difference is insisted upon, and where certain gender discourses become more appropriate or powerful than others, depending on the interests and voices of those concerned. The argument underlying this chapter is that gender is not the cause of ritual activity, but an effect. The votive ceremonial meals provide women with the possibility of creating an agency as "women" in order to lay claims of a social, political and cosmological kind. A unitary gender becomes so only through specific acts in given contexts. I have also demonstrated that *sofreh* are a prime example of how women transform the gendered values of self-interest into morality, or following Kopytoff (1992), how rules are broken, masked and reshuffled by moving between the spheres of "gift" and "commodity."[25] This talent is particularly enabling in the contest over religious meaning and control, through which women express their agency. Specific definitions of intentions and persons, including relations to the saints as extensions of self, are involved.

Notes

1. For helpful discussions and overviews on the distinction between so-called formal and informal Islam see Jansen (1987: 86–91), N. Tapper and R. Tapper (1987: 69–71), Lambek (1990) and Eickelman (1998: 249 ff.).

2. See Jamzadeh and Mills (1986: 35, 50–5), Betteridge (1989 [1980]: 104, 108–9), Adelkhah (1991: 147–8). For descriptions of various *sofreh*, see also Hedayat (1963), Shokurzadeh (1967), Braswell (1975: 160–7), Torab (1998: 178–88, 424–31), Kalinock (2003).

3. On gender-specific ritual activities compare N. Tapper and R. Tapper (1987: 72): "We do not suggest that women and men necessarily have discrete systems of belief and practice ... but that different aspects of a religious system may be the province of one sex or the other, and an understanding of any particular Islamic tradition depends on examining both; Boddy (1989: 279): "The *zar* and orthodox Islam are not competing religious ideologies, but different facets of a single conceptual system"; Lewis (1986: 106): "Thus if there is a dual spiritual economy [male and female], its two branches are interdependent and complementary." Compare also Abu-Lughod's (1986) complementary model of genders within a shared moral universe with Kapchan's (1996) study of feminine speech genres in the Moroccan market, which parts with a dualistic model by placing gender "within a context of heterogeneity, where discourses of religion, morality, and kinship vie with those of self-interest, capitalism, and commodification" (Kapchan 1996: 5–6).

4. Lewis, who says that women's *zar* in the Sudan offers men "the privilege of vicarious participation in what they ostensibly condemn as superstition and heresy." (Lewis 1986: 106, cited also in Boddy 1989: 144–5). Boddy (1989: 6) states that "It is important to realize that if women are constrained by their gender from full participation in Islam, men are constrained by theirs from full participation in *zar*."

5. N. Tapper and R. Tapper (1987: 86) argue that women's religious practices in Turkey are paradoxically also vehicles for religious sentiments that men cannot express in the state-established religious orthodoxy, so that women acquire sacred authority because of their inferior status.

6. Strathern (1988: 98–9) makes this point regarding some of the feminist assumptions about gender relations in Melanesia.

7. See, for example, N. Tapper (1983), R. Tapper and N. Tapper (1986), Jansen (1987), Varisco (1986), Yamani (1987), N. Tapper (1990), R. Tapper (1994), R. Tapper and Zubaida (1994) and many earlier contributions in the *Anthropological Quarterly* (47(1), 1974).

8. On creating a unitary identity for making political claims see Butler (1993: 227–30). See also Strathern (1988: 158–9) on creating collective identities in Melanesian ceremonial exchanges as spheres of political agency.

9. The term "saint" has different connotations in Christianity and in Islam (see Eickelman 1998: 278). I use the term here merely as a pointer. On the problems of translation of notions that are neither universal nor necessarily homogeneous within the same society, Needham (1975) suggests viewing these as "polythetic" (with sporadic resemblances) rather than "monothetic" (with definite features) that risks exclusion of significant features in comparative studies.

10. The five are Fatemeh, Husseyn's half-brother (Hazrat-e 'Abbas, also known as 'Abol Fazl), two of Husseyn's infant children (Hazrat-e Roqiyeh and Hazrat-e Ali 'Asghar) and the seventh Imam Musa ibn-e Ja'far (or Musa Kazem). Zeynab, Husseyn's sister, is also popular, as are a host of other, unidentified spiritual spirits.

11. On the pervasive lobbying in Iran, see also Beeman (1986: 48). See also Eickelman (1998: 283), who notes that in Morocco, relations with the supernatural are similar to those between people.

12. Compare Christian (1989), who argues that for the Spanish community of his study, the underlying assumption in communications with God is a theory of action by God as a result of actions by humans.

13. For descriptions of *jalaseh* see Adelkhah (1991), Kamalkhani (1993) and Torab (1996, 1998, 2002).

14. See note 2 for references to various descriptions.

15. For a detailed description of the ceremony, see Torab (1998: 424–31).

16. Mills (1982) identifies a similar story widespread in eastern Iran and western Afghanistan as a combination of 510A "Cinderella" and 480 "The kind and the unkind girls," which she examines for its role in an all-Ismaili Muslim ceremony called *ash-e bibi murad*, with food offering as a petition to a saint called "The Lady of Wishes" (*Bi-bi Murad*). See also Mills (1985) and Jamzadeh and Mills (1986: 48–9).

17. On feminist critiques of fairy tales, see Carter (1998[1992]) and Zipes (1989).

18. The ingestion of food imbued with *barakat* is similar to the bread in Holy Communion officiated by the Church and hence also unlike it, in that *barakat* is in theory accessible without an intermediary.

19. See Gellner (1962), to whom Douglas (1966: 112) refers with a quote.

20. Hubert and Mauss (1964[1898]) demonstrated long ago that ritual activity sacrilizes things, people or events, rather than ritual merely reflecting ideas already present. See Bell (1992: 15).

21. The words '*aql* and *nafs* are themselves polysemic, with many implicit meanings, and have been discussed more or less explicitly with regard to their gender implications by a number of authors in a variety of Islamic contexts. See, for example, Anderson (1982: 405–9), Rosen (1984: 31–47), Abu-Lughod (1986: 90–1, 283–4 note 6), N. Tapper and R. Tapper (1988), R. Tapper and N. Tapper (*c*. 1990), N. Tapper (1991: 15ff.), Kapchan (1996: 104, 107, 116), Torab (1996), Eickelman (1998: 197–8).

22. See Lloyd (1984).

23. Gell (1996: ch. 27) favors the use of the economic concept of "opportunity costs" for maximizing self-interest in social theory, in the sense of evaluating given possibilities in relation to each other.

24. See Moore (1994) for a discussion of the so-called school of *écriture féminine* comprising of writers such as Irigaray, Cioux and Kristeva.

25. Compare Kapchan's (1996: 176–7) argument that the talent for turning "commodity" into "gift" permits women to accommodate their claims in the commodity realm and to find a social space they can control, where tradition is being redefined.

References

Abu-Lughod, L. (1986), *Veiled Sentiments: Honor and Poetry in a Bedouin Society*, Berkeley, CA and London: University of California Press.

Adelkhah, F. (1991), *La Révolution sous le voile: femmes islamiques d'Iran*, Paris: Karthala.

Anderson, J. W. (1982) "Social Structure and the Veil: Comportment and the Composition of Interaction in Afghanistan," *Anthropos*, 3(4): 397–420.

Asad, T. (1986), *The Idea of an Anthropology of Islam*, Occasional papers series, Washington, DC: Center for Contemporary Arab Studies, Georgetown University.

Beeman, W. O. (1986), *Language, Status, and Power in Iran*, Bloomington, IN: Indiana University Press.

Bell, C. (1992), *Ritual Theory, Ritual Practice*, New York and Oxford: Oxford University Press.

Betteridge, A. (1989[1980]), "The Controversial Vows of Urban Muslim Women in Iran," in N. A. Falk and R. M. Gross (eds), *Unspoken Worlds: Women's Religious Lives*, Belmont, CA: Wadsworth.

Boddy, J. (1989) *Wombs and Alien Spirits: Women, Men and the Zār Cult in Northern Sudan*, Madison, WI and London: University of Wisconsin Press.

Bourdieu, P. (1992[1972]), *Outline of a Theory of Practice*, Cambridge: Cambridge University Press.

Braswell, G. W. (1975) "A Mosaic of Mullahs and Mosques: Religion and Politics in Iranian Shi'ah Islam," PhD dissertation, University of North Carolina at Chapel Hill.

Butler, J. (1990a), "Gender Trouble, Feminist Theory, and Psychoanalytic Discourse," in L. J. Nicholson (ed.), *Feminism/Postmodernism*, New York and London: Routledge.

—— (1990b), *Gender Trouble: Feminism and the Subversion of Identity*, London and New York: Routledge.

—— (1993), *Bodies that Matter: On the Discursive Limits of "Sex"*, London and New York: Routledge.

Carsten, J. (1995), "The Substance of Kinship and the Heat of the Hearth: Feeding, Personhood and Relatedness among Malays of Pulau Langkawi," *American Ethnologist*, 22: 223–41.

—— (1997), *The Heat of the Hearth: The Process of Kinship in a Malay Fishing Community*, Oxford: Clarendon Press.

Carter, A. (ed.) (1998[1992]), *The Second Virago Book of Fairy Tales*, London: Virago.

Christian, W. (1989) *Person and God in a Spanish Valley*, new revised edn, Princeton, NJ: Princeton University Press.

Douglas, M. (1966), *Purity and Danger: An Analysis of Concepts of Pollution and Taboo*, London: Routledge and Kegan Paul.

Eickelman, D. F. (ed.) (1998), *The Middle East and Central Asia: An Anthropological Approach*, 3rd edn, Englewood Cliffs, NJ: Prentice Hall.

Gell, A. (1996), *The Anthropology of Time: Cultural Constructions of Temporal Maps and Images*, Oxford and Washington, DC: Berg.

Gellner, E. (1962), "Concepts and Society," in International Sociological Association (ISA), *Transactions of the Fifth World Congress of Sociology*, vol. 1, Washington, DC: ISA.

Haraway D. (1990), "A Manifesto for Cyborgs: Science, Technology and Socialist Feminism in the 1980s," in L. J. Nicholson (ed.), *Feminism and Postmodernism*, London and New York: Routledge.

Hedayat, S. (1963[1342]), *Neyrangestan* (Land of Deception/trickery), 3rd edn, Tehran: Amir Kabir.

Hubert, H. and Mauss, M. (1964[1898]), *Sacrifice: Its Nature and Functions*, Chicago: University of Chicago Press.

Jamzadeh, L. and Mills, M. (1986), "Iranian 'sofreh': From Collective to Female Ritual," in C. W. Bynum, S. Harrell and P. Richman (eds), *Gender and Religion: On the Complexity of Symbols*, Boston, MA: Beacon Press.

Jansen, W. (1987), *Women without Men: Gender and Marginality in an Algerian Town*, Leiden: Brill.

Kalinock, S. (2003), "Supernatural Intercession to Earthly Problems: Sofreh Rituals among Shiite Muslims and Zoroastrians in Iran," in M. Stansberg (ed.), *Zoroastrian Rituals in Context: Studies in the History of Religions*, Leiden: Brill.

Kamalkhani, Z. (1993), "Women's Everyday Religious Discourse in Iran," in H. Afshar (ed.), *Women in the Middle East: Perceptions, Realities and Struggles for Liberation*, London: Macmillan.

Kapchan, D. (1996), *Gender on the Market: Moroccan Women and Revoicing of Tradition*, Philadelphia, PA: University of Pennsylvania Press.

Kopytoff, I. (1992), "The Cultural Biography of Things: Commoditization as Process," in A. Appadurai (ed.), *The Social Life of Things: Commodities in Cultural Perspective*, Cambridge: Cambridge University Press.

Lambek, M. (1990), "Certain Knowledge, Contestable Authority: Power and Practice on the Islamic Periphery," *American Ethnologist*, 17(1): 23–40.

Lewis, I. M. (1986) *Religion in Context: Cults and Charisma*, Cambridge: Cambridge University Press.

Lloyd, G. (1984), *The Man of Reason. "Male" and "Female" in Western Philosophy*, Minneapolis, MN: University of Minnesota Press.

Majlesi, M. B. (1991[1370]), *Helliyat-ol-mottaqin: Dar adab va sonan-e Eslami va akhlaq va dasturat-e Shar'e Motahhar-e Nabavi* (Adornment of the pious: Islamic conduct, custom and ethics and Sharia Prophetic injunctions), Tehran: Ahmadi.

Mauss, M. (1954), *The Gift*, transl. I. Cunnison, London: Cohen and West.

Mills, M. A. (1982), "A Cinderella Variant in the Context of a Muslim Women's Ritual," in A. Dundes (ed.), *Cinderella: A Folklore Casebook*, New York: Garland.

—— (1985), "Sex role reversals..." in R. Jordan and S. Kalcik (eds), *Women's Folklore, Women's Culture*, Philadelphia, PA: University of Pennsylvania Press.

Moore, H. L. (1988), *Feminism and Anthropology*, Cambridge: Polity Press.

—— (1994), *A Passion for Difference: Essays in Anthropology and Gender*, Cambridge: Polity Press.

—— (1999a), "Gender, Symbolism and Praxis: Theoretical Approaches," in H. L. Moore, T. Sanders and B. Kaare (eds), *Those Who Play with Fire: Gender, Fertility and Transformation in East and Southern Africa*, London and New Brunswick, NJ: Athlone Press.

—— (1999b), "Whatever Happened to Women and Men? Gender and Other Crises in Anthropology," in H. Moore (ed.), *Anthropological Theory Today*, Cambridge: Polity Press.

Needham, R. (1975), "Polythetic Classification: Convergence and Consequences," *Journal of the Royal Anthropological Institute*, 10(3): 349–69.

Rosen, L. (1984), *Bargaining for Reality: The Construction of Social Relations in a Muslim Community*, Chicago and London: University of Chicago Press.

Shokurzadeh, I. (1967[1346]), *Aqa'ed va rosum-e 'ameh-ye mardom-e Khorasan* (Popular beliefs and customs of the people of Khorasan), Tehran: Cultural Foundation of Iran.

Strathern, M. (1988), *The Gender of the Gift*, Berkeley, CA: University of California Press.

Tapper, N. (1983), "Gender and Religion in a Turkish Town: A Comparison of Two Types of Formal Women's Gatherings," in P. Holden (ed.), *Women's Religious Experience*, London and Canberra: Croom Helm.

—— (1990), "Ziyaret: Gender, movement and exchange in Turkish Islam," in D. F. Eickelman and J. Piscatori (eds), *Muslim Travellers: Pilgrimage, Migration and the Religious Imagination*, London: Routledge.

—— (1991), *Bartered Brides. Politics, Gender and Marriage in an Afghan Tribal Society*, Cambridge: Cambridge University Press.

—— and Tapper, R. (1987), "The Birth of the Prophet: Ritual and Gender in Turkish Islam," *Journal of the Royal Anthroplogical Institute*, 22: 69–92.

—— and Tapper, R. (1988), "Concepts of Personal, Moral and Social Disorder among the Pashtuns in Northern Afghanistan," in B. Huldt and E. Johnson (eds), *The Tragedy of Afghanistan*, London: Croom Helm.

Tapper, R. (1994), "Blood, Wine and Water: Social and Symbolic Aspects of Drinks and Drinking in Islamic Middle East," in R. Tapper and S. Zubaida (eds), *Culinary Cultures of the Middle East*, London and New York: I. B. Tauris.

—— and Tapper, N. (1986), "'Eat This, it'll Do you a Power of Good': Food and Commensality among Durrani Pashtuns," *American Ethnologist*, 13(1): 62–79.

—— and Tapper, N. (c.1990), "Possession, Insanity, Responsibility and the Self among Durrani Pashtuns in Northern Afghanistan," unpublished manuscript.

—— and Zubaida, S. (1994), "Introduction," in R. Tapper and S. Zubaida (eds), *Culinary Cultures of the Middle East*, London and New York: I. B. Tauris.

Torab, A. (1996), "Piety as Gendered Agency: A Study of *jalaseh* Ritual Discourse in an Urban Neighbourhood in Iran," *Journal of the Royal Anthropological Institute*, 2(2): 235–52.

—— (1998), "Neighbourhoods of Piety: Gender and Ritual in South Tehran," unpublished PhD thesis, University of London.

—— (2002), "The Politicization of Women's Religious Circles in Post-revolutionary Iran," in S. Ansari and V. Martin (eds), *Women, Religion and Culture in Iran*, Richmond, Surrey: Curzon.

Turner, V. (1961), *Ndembu Divination: Its Symbolism and Techniques*, Manchester: Manchester University Press.

—— (1967), *The Forest of Symbols*, Ithaca, NY: Cornell University Press.

Varisco, D. M. (1986), "On the Meaning of Chewing: the Significance of Qat in the Yemen Arab Republic," *International Journal of Middle East Studies*, 18: 1–13.

Yamani, M. (1987), "Fasting and Feasting: Social Aspects of the Observance of Ramadan in Saudi Arabia," in A. Al-Shahi (ed.), *The Diversity of the Muslim Community: Anthropological Essays in Memory of Peter Lienhardt*, London: Ithaca Press.

Zipes, J. (1989), *Don't Bet on the Prince: Contemporary Feminist Fairy Tales in North America and England*, New York: Routledge.

Index